The history of the United States is in crucial respects the history of a developing country, not only in its transition from agricultural and commercial colonies to an industrial nation, but in modern times and the foreseeable future as well. The seven studies are primarily concerned with the United States as a developing country in the early twentieth century, evolving from a competitive stage of capitalism to a corporate stage, and from an industrial to a "postindustrial" society.

The chapters treat the emergence and early phases of corporate capitalism and their implications for domestic affairs and foreign relations, the origins and character of corporate liberalism, the pivotal role of Woodrow Wilson in these areas, and the emergence of postindustrial trends. They also explore some critical linkages among economic, political, and cultural developments, in tracing parallels among Henry Adams in the Progressive Era, the "Young Intellectuals" of the twenties, and the New Left in the sixties.

The studies also address broader interpretive and philosophical questions such as theory and factuality, periodization and historiography, mode of production and social change, as well as the interplay in human affairs of the transhistorical and the historical, the artistic and the political, contingency and determinism, freedom and necessity, and the intermixture of capitalism, socialism, and liberalism in the making of modern U.S. society.

The United States
as a Developing Country

Also by Martin J. Sklar

The Corporate Reconstruction of American Capitalism, 1890–1916: The Market, the Law, and Politics (1988)

The United States
as a Developing Country

Studies in U.S. History
in the Progressive Era and the 1920s

MARTIN J. SKLAR

CAMBRIDGE
UNIVERSITY PRESS

Published by the Press Syndicate of the University of Cambridge
The Pitt Building, Trumpington Street, Cambridge CB2 1RP
40 West 20th Street, New York, NY 10011-4211, USA
10 Stamford Road, Oakleigh, Victoria 3166, Australia

First published 1992

Printed in the United States of America

Library of Congress Cataloging-in-Publication Data
Sklar, Martin J., 1935–
The United States as a developing country : studies in U.S.
history in the progressive era and the 1920s / Martin J. Sklar.
p.   cm.
Includes index.
ISBN 0-521-40060-0. – ISBN 0-521-40922-5 (pbk.)
1. United States – History – 1865–1921.   2. United States –
History – 20th century.   3. Capitalism – United States – History.
4. United States – Economic conditions – 1865–1918.   I. Title.
E741.S55   1992
973.8–dc20   91–31519
                                         CIP

A catalog record for this book is available from the British Library.

ISBN 0-521-40060-0 hardback
ISBN 0-521-40922-5 paperback

To the Memory of
SOPHIE LAUB SKLAR and KALMAN SKLAR
Children of Immigrants
Parents of Teachers

Contents

Preface

The seven essays in this book include three previously published, one written long ago but hitherto lying unpublished, and three written in recent years and now published here.

Of the three previously published, the essay on Woodrow Wilson (Chapter IV) I worked on and wrote over a period stretching from 1957 to 1960 and published in 1960 in *Studies on the Left;* subsequently, it was republished in various anthologies and in the Bobbs-Merrill reprint series. The essay on political and cultural consequences of the disaccumulation of capital (Chapter V) I worked on during the 1960s and published in 1969 in *Radical America.* The essay on Henry Adams and the 1960's "New Left" (Chapter VI) I prepared as a presentation to the Socialist Scholars Conference of 1966 in New York City, and published much later, on invitation, in the *Maryland Historian,* in 1982, as something of a document of one aspect of leftist thinking in the 1960s.

The unpublished older essay, on Dollar Diplomacy (Chapter III), I wrote as a chapter of my University of Wisconsin Master's Thesis, completed in 1962, "Woodrow Wilson, the Six-Power Consortium, and Dollar Diplomacy: Essays in the Ideology of Modern United States Liberalism in Its Period of Emergence."

Of the three essays written in recent years, the essay on the United States considered as a developing country (Chapter I) I wrote specifically for this volume; it represents my thought in its latest phase. The essay on U.S. political development in the Progressive Era (Chapter II) is one I had been working on since 1979 or so; parts of it made their way into my book, *The Corporate Reconstruction of American Capitalism, 1890–1916* (1988); I had delivered an earlier version of it before a panel of the Organization of American Historians in 1984; the latest version appears here and, with some differences, in the journal *Studies in American Political Development* (Fall 1991) along with commentary by Steven Hahn and a brief response by me. Finally, the essay on the capitalism–socialism mix (Chapter VII) I first prepared as a presentation for a panel of the Center for Social Theory and Comparative History at the University of California, Los Angeles, in February 1989; the version published here is substantially the same as the original, with some minor editorial revisions.

When it was first suggested to me that there was interest in having some of my older essays brought together in one volume with some of my more recent work, I was skeptical of the prospect of their making a coherent package. Aside from their dealing with some aspects of a critical period in the history of the United States, the 1890s to 1920s, it turns out that the essays collected here embody a theme that has been a long-term interest of mine, namely, studying the United States as a developing country, an interest that began as early as 1955 when I wrote an undergraduate paper for Merrill Jensen at the University of Wisconsin analyzing Hamilton's *Report on Manufactures* and his funding program as a pro-British, antimanufacturing strategy for early national development as against the Jeffersonian Republican (Madisonian) anti-British, pro-manufacturing strategy for development, a theme picked up two decades later by a student of mine at Northern Illinois University, John R. Nelson, who ably worked it and other study and themes of his own into a prize-winning essay (*Journal of American History,* LXV, 1979) and part of his book *Liberty and Property* (1987). As perhaps adumbrated in this early interest, my subsequent work, including the examples in this volume, led me to a continuing consideration of the interrelation of the nation's internal development and its international affairs. Insofar as an enduring interest of mine has been understanding the United States as a developing country, it may be said that I am a "Turnerian," or perhaps a true student of the "Wisconsin School." As this may suggest to the not altogether uninitiated, on the interrelated international plane, I am a student also of Mills and Marx. I will, however, resist the very strong temptation to turn a preface into a review of my own book, leaving that to reviewers and critics if these essays should prove worthy of their attention, and perhaps to some future retrospective self-commentary in a more appropriate time and place.

Suffice it to say here that the subject matter of these essays ranges over a period of time, roughly the 1890s to the 1920s, or something over three decades in the nations' history, and their writing ranged over a similar period of time in the life of the author. They treat historical change in a past time, while affording a view of a historian's changing thinking in a more recent time.

As to the nature of my changing thinking, I have some perspectives and ideas, but again, I leave that for now to readers and critics, whose responses would surely further inform and modify my own. I would only observe here that the essays in this book, with and without my own conscious intent, display some common thematic threads of the broader cloth of my mind, such as (simply to list without commentary): (1) the transhistorical and the historical in human affairs; (2) the interplay of freedom and necessity, contingency and determinism, in shaping human history; (3) mode of production and periodization in historical interpretation; (4) the interrelations of scientific method, quests for self-determination, and human history; (5) the interrelations of consciousness, social movements, and changing social relations; (6) the nature and interrelations of capitalism, socialism, and liberalism; and (7) the meaning of "development." As to the last, my own most recent understanding is succinctly conveyed in the definition attempted in the last chapter of this book, and explored at greater length in chapter I.

For their valuable critical thought, suggestions, and exchange of views, directly and indirectly, over an extended period, relating to the subject matter of these essays, I wish to acknowledge Loren Baritz, Eugene D. Genovese, the late Herbert G. Gutman, Fred Harvey Harrington, Nao Hauser, Ellis W. Hawley, James Willard Hurst, Stephen Kern, Gerd Korman, the late Olga Brody Oller, Carl P. Parrini, Arlene Sklar Pullara, Trent Schroyer, Richard L. Sklar, the late Warren I. Susman, Hayden V. White, and the late William A. Williams. I am also grateful, for critical exchange of views in more recent times, to Scott Bowman, William Burr, Robert D. Cuff, Steven Hahn, Stanley N. Katz, James Livingston, James P. May, Karen Orren, Richard Schneirov, Stephen Skowronek, and Paul Wolman.

For their painstaking and expert editorial care and work in preparing the manuscript for typesetting, I am grateful to Cynthia Insolio Benn, copy editor, and Louise Calabro Gruendel, production editor, at Cambridge University Press, and for the index, to Glorieux Dougherty.

For their encouragement, specifically, in bringing these essays together here, I wish to thank Nao Hauser and Stanley N. Katz, as well as my principal editor at Cambridge University Press, Frank Smith.

Harrisburg, Pennsylvania
March, 1991

I

Periodization and historiography: The United States considered as a developing country

Society . . . is the ultimate thing disclosed by an analysis of human relations.

Henry Carter Adams (1887)

I

It is by now a familiar mark of sophistication to acknowledge that there can be no purely "objective" study of history, in the sense of its being entirely value-free: Objectivity is best served when the historian explicitly discloses the interpretive framework and underlying assumptions guiding the research and its outcome. Taken no further, however, this axiom can become a justification of subjective license, if not incoherence. The question remains whether, above and beyond rules of evidence and technical competence, there is a common standard of objectivity, which may be adopted by historians in forming comprehensive conceptions of an historical period and in guiding specialized inquiry as well, but which nevertheless leaves them free, even while maintaining the most rigorous criteria of logic and empirical method, to differ not only on normative matters, but also on the particular interpretations and conclusions they may draw from inquiry based on that common standard.

This essay, completed in January 1991, is published here for the first time, except that Section 1 appears also as part of Section 1 of the essay, "Periodization and Historiography: Studying American Political Development in the Progressive Era, 1890s–1916," *Studies in American Political Development*, Fall 1991. It originated in a presentation prepared, on invitation, for the panel on periodization of the Conference on American Politics in Historical Perspective, held at the University of California, Los Angeles, 12–13 May 1990, convened by Karen Orren of the Department of Political Science and Joyce Appleby of the Department of History, of UCLA. The panel consisted of Walter Dean Burnham (Chair) of the University of Texas, Austin, Eldon Eisenach of the University of Tulsa, Stephen Skowronek of Yale University, and myself. The conference brought together historians and political scientists for an interdisciplinarian exchange of views.

The principle of periodization itself offers a common standard satisfying these conditions. What general and special theories are to the meaning and indeed the very designation of facts in the physical sciences, so periodization may be to their meaning and designation in history. As referred to in this way, periodization means not the familiar device usefully invoked for narrative or connotative convenience, such as the Age of Jackson, the Gilded Age, the Progressive Era, Prosperity Decade, the New Deal, and the like. It means, rather, a constructive or a postulated definition of the society-type in question, the system of its social relations, with its historically evolving requirements, capacities, patterns of authority, and structures or relations of power, in its general historical formation and in its more historically specific circumstances and stage of evolution.

The requirements and capacities of a society include not only their manifestations in geophysical, technoeconomic, and other "material" conditions, but also their manifestations in social consciousness, both secular and religious, including theories, ideologies, and outlooks or world-views, of those who exercise authority or power, whether governmental or nongovernmental, as well as of those in subordinate positions in society. As this implies, there is some causal connection between a society's requirements and capacities as a social system, and its pattern of authority and structure or relations of power.

As theory that postulates society-type and its state of evolution in this way, periodization establishes not only the ground of permissible deductive reasoning about a society's prevalent modes of behavior and thought and how they interrelate, but also the essential foundation for fashioning the inductive framework of inquiry into them and their interrelations, into their genesis, their development, and their transformations. Periodization also thereby informs the range and limits of reflective generalization respecting the society's actualities and potentialities in the political, economic, social, and cultural spheres. As a method of study, or theory of history (and all theories, in whatever field, are at bottom methods of study), periodization imposes a discipline upon inquiry that acts as a control against the presuppositions, the fashionable interpretations, as well as the appealingly irreverent ones, the personal intuitions, the current political persuasions, or the professional infighting, of the inquirers and their critical audience.

Understood in this way, periodization fosters vigilance against the arbitrary adoption of a tight interpretive grid, on the one hand, or the loose invocation of dissociated concepts, principles, sentiments, or axioms, on the other, not well founded in evidence, context, logic, or reason. Made explicit, periodization invites constant testing of interpretation, by both deductive and inductive reasoning, against rules of coherence and empirical inquiry. Periodization also subjects to such critical assessment the range and limits of its own efforts at reflective generalization. Periodization, or theory, in this sense, yields historical knowledge whose meaning is subject to objective verification, or more precisely to falsification, and establishes at the same time the ground of its own validation, alteration, or discard. As and when its set of premises, or its range, falls short of comprehending pertinent materials in a manner consistent with its discipline, it signals the limits beyond which it is unable to proceed, and therefore its impending modification or demise and displacement by a theory, or periodization, more sufficient. In this sense, periodization, or theory, in history is no different in general principle from theory in the physical sciences.[1]

Without the discipline of periodization, history tends to be written and perceived on the run, skimming surface appearances without reference to their essential sources in the matrix of social relations. On the

1. The difference lies in the forms of reasoning and the character of empirical evidence, not in the role of theory and its relation to the discovery and definition of empirical evidence (or facts). On theory and scientific method in the social realm, analogous to that in the physical realm, see, e.g., Arnold Brecht, *Political Theory: The Foundations of Twentieth Century Political Thought* (Princeton, N.J.: Princeton University Press, 1959; Third Princeton Paperback Printing, 1970), chs. I and II, pp. 27–72 and 73–116. Cf. Charles S. Peirce: "Induction consists in starting from a theory, deducing from it predictions of phenomena in order to see how nearly they agree with the theory. . . . by steadily pursuing that method [i.e., experiential theory subjected to testing over time] we must in the long run find out how the matter really stands. . . . Thus the validity of induction depends upon the necessary relation between the general and the singular. It is precisely this which is the support of Pragmatism." In this connection, Peirce designated laws as essential to reasoning in both the physical and social sciences, precisely because the sciences of either type have as their fields of inquiry matters that are not predetermined and are in principle open-ended: "The principle of the demonstration is that whatever has no end can have no mode of being other than that of a law, and therefore whatever general character it may have must be describable, but the only way of describing an endless series is by stating explicitly or implicitly the law of succession of one term upon another. . . . " Peirce, 1903 Lectures on Pragmatism, quoted and discussed by Manley Thompson, *The Pragmatic Philosophy of C. S. Peirce* (Chicago: University of Chicago Press, 1963), pp. 174–175. Peirce's view stands in partial contrast to that of Karl R. Popper, who in positing the necessity of theory in the study of history no less than in the physical sciences, drew conclusions warranting a large degree of discretionary license: "For undoubtedly there can be no history without a point of view; like the natural sciences, history must be selective unless it is to be choked by a flood of poor and unrelated material. . . . The only way out of this difficulty is . . . consciously to introduce a *preconceived selective point of view* into one's history; that is, to write *that history which interests us*. This does not mean that we may twist the facts . . . , or that we may neglect the facts that do not fit. . . . But it means that we need not worry about all those facts and aspects which have no bearing upon our point of view and which therefore do not interest us." Popper, *The Poverty of Historicism* (New York: Harper Torchbooks, 1961), p. 150 (Popper's italics). For a critical discussion of Popper's *fallibilist* view of science, and its contrast with Peirce's "contrite fallibilism," see Ernest Nagel, *Teleology Revisited and Other Essays in the Philosophy and History of Science* (New York: Columbia University Press, 1979), pp. 64–77. Nagel (p. 76) nevertheless considers Popper "correct . . . in pointing out the indispensable role of theories in the conduct of research and the growth of science."

surface, when "facts speak for themselves," they may preempt meaning other than that to which the historian or audience may be predisposed. A particular fact can not yield a verifiable meaning apart from the context within which it belongs to, and derives from, a larger whole. It is the interrelations among those items or events designated as facts, the relation of each to the others and to the whole, and the way that each fact represents a particular manifestation of the whole, that imposes a cognitive discipline upon historian and audience. A fact speaking for itself, in short, is no fact at all, if a fact signifies information having an objectively verifiable, or more precisely, falsifiable, meaning. By itself, it becomes a plaything of convention or indulgence, or a manipulative ploy upon the undiscerning. Put another way, the meaning of a fact, indeed its very discovery, lies in its context, and historical context is in essence established by periodization.[2]

2.   On context as essentially constitutive of meaning, and on the corollary role of theory, or the hypothetico-deductive method, in science, rooted in constructive postulation subject to falsification, see Heinz R. Pagels, *The Dreams of Reason: The Computer and the Rise of the Sciences of Complexity* (New York: Bantam Books, 1989), pp. 94–95, 126–127, 241–269. Pagels notes that meaning is necessarily context-dependent (in his words), and I would add that in history, periodization critically defines context. See also, A. Brecht, *Political Theory*, pp. 28–34, on the role of ideas, "creative imagination," genius, selective relevance, and hypotheses, in the construction of theory and its relation to the very designation and discovery of facts, and note Brecht's statement (p. 34): "Strictly speaking, there is no scientific observation, however direct, that does not contain . . . some sort of hypothesis." For similar perspectives on meaning, see also, Hanna Fenichel Pitkin, *Wittgenstein and Justice: On the Significance of Ludwig Wittgenstein for Social and Political Thought* (Berkeley: University of California Press, 1972), especially chs. III–V, pp. 50–115, and ch. IX, pp. 193–218. While warning against a priori static, absolute laws as the basis for historical interpretation, especially those of a statistical or quantitative kind from the field of economics, Frederick Jackson Turner nevertheless also had this to say about a Rankean faith in facts: "Those who insist that history is simply the effort to tell the thing exactly as it was, to state the facts, are confronted with the difficulty that the fact which they would represent is not planted on the solid ground of fixed conditions; it is in the midst and is itself a part of the changing currents, the complex and interacting influences of the time, deriving its significance as a fact from its relations to the deeper-seated movements of the age. . . ." Turner, "Social Forces in American History," *American Historical Review*, XVI (January 1911), pp. 217–233, in *Frontier and Section: Selected Essays of Frederick Jackson Turner*, ed. Ray Allen Billington (Englewood Cliffs, N.J.: Prentice-Hall, 1961), p. 179. To similar effect, see Alfred Marshall, "The Old Generation of Economists and the New," *Quarterly Journal of Economics*, XI (January 1897), p. 119: "As the nineteenth century has worn on, there has been a growing readiness among economists, as among students of physical sciences, to recognize that . . . every inference from one set of facts to another . . . involves a passage upwards from particulars to general propositions and ideas; and a passage downwards from them to other particulars. We can seldom infer particulars from other particulars without passing through generals, however simple be the subject-matter of our study; and we can never do so in the complex problems of social life." The essay (pp. 115–135) originated as an address to the Cambridge Economic Club's first meeting, delivered at Cambridge, England, 29 October 1896. In the same vein, cf. Gunnar Myrdal, *The Political Element in the Development of Economic Theory* (Cambridge, Mass.: Harvard University Press, 1955),

The need for periodization as the ground of coherence and objective inquiry may not be universally accepted, but it is not necessary for the present purposes to assume that it is especially controversial. The earnest controversy begins beyond this point, with the criteria and substance of periodization. The increasing and currently well-praised resort by historians to social-science disciplines testifies to their acknowledgment that facts neither speak for nor define themselves, and that adequate periodizations, or interpretive frameworks (or theories), beyond the implementation of innovative research technique narrowly taken, are necessary to historical inquiry.[3]

It may be that historians have made greater strides toward recognizing the importance of theory than social scientists have made toward understanding the nature of, and in practice engaging in, historical research in primary sources. It may be, too, that the evergrowing vogue of interdisciplinary study among historians represents further testimony in this direction. But in the absence of making the theoretical dimension integral to historical study, and to the training of historians, this "external" resort to the social sciences by historians lends credibility to a view of the historical discipline as being inferior to the social sciences for inquiry into and grasping social reality. The engagement in the quantitative rigors of

"Preface to the English Edition," p. vii: "Facts do not organize themselves into concepts and theories just by being looked at; indeed, except within the framework of concepts and theories, there are no scientific facts but only chaos. There is an inescapable *a priori* element in all scientific work. Questions must be asked before answers can be given. The questions are an expression of our interest in the world; they are at bottom valuations. Valuations are thus necessarily involved already at the stage when we observe facts and carry on theoretical analysis. . . . " In this sense, Myrdal rejected as "naive empiricism" the idea that value-free facts speak for themselves.

3. Research technique is undoubtedly a basic matter of concern as integral to theory in historical inquiry, but that is different from acquiescing in a tendency to reduce the question of theory to that of information-gathering technique, which properly takes its direction from the broader conceptual framework. See, e.g., Abraham Kaplan, *The Conduct of Inquiry* (San Francisco: Chandler, 1964), pp. 24–27, where in discussing "The Myth of Methodology," Kaplan referred to the strongly entrenched belief among American intellectuals that equated scientific method with technique. Insofar as a resort to quantitative technique implies an effort at making history more an "exact science," like the physical sciences, by the discovery of indissoluble facts (data), from which incontestable theory may be derived, it misconceives both the nature of the physical sciences and the relation between fact and theory (notes 1 and 2, and related text, above). Sigmund Freud's characterization of scientific method is relevant here: "It is a mistake to believe that a science consists in nothing but conclusively proved propositions, and it is unjust to demand that it should. It is a demand only made by those who feel a craving for authority in some form and a need to replace the religious catechism by something else, even if it be a scientific one. Science in its catechism has but few apodictic percepts; it consists mainly of statements which it has developed to varying degrees of probability. The capacity to be content with these approximations to certainty and the ability to carry on constructive work despite the lack of final confirmation are actually a mark of the scientific habit of mind." Freud, *A General Introduction to Psycho-Analysis*, tr. Joan Riviere (New York: Liveright, 1935), p. 47.

cliometrics by many historians has been to some extent a response to this view. In any case, the external resort has far from constructively overcome the division between social theory and historical study that set in and has developed since the late nineteenth and early twentieth century, with the rise of academic specialization in the historical and social science disciplines.

The division may be observed in the tendency of social scientists, in constructing their theories, seldom to engage in sustained and systematic historical research in primary sources, and too often to regard quantitative data as coterminous with primary sources, while historians, in pursuing primary research, seldom seek or find training, as historians, in social theory. Historians and social scientists (including social theorists) tend, accordingly, to borrow across disciplines from one another in naive or "user-friendly" ways that mutually reinforce each others' predispositions, if not their weaknesses, more than their scientific objectivity or their investigatory strengths. In general, the resort to other disciplines by historians for an interpretive framework, or in terms used here, for guidance in periodization, suggests an implied criticism not only of the current shape of academic specialization, but of the deficiencies of current prevalent historiographical method and training.

2

The concept, periodization, presupposes an assumption of change. As related to society or social relations, it designates a subject characterized by its being historical, that is, a subject the essence of which is change, whether cyclical or cumulative, or a blend of the two, although at times decumulative. Like other subjects in the natural universe, it is a subject that in the long run, at least, and taking humanity as a whole in its many societies, preserves itself, or realizes its potentialities, through change – a kind of change that is evolutionary from relatively more simple to relatively more complex modes of being: a kind of change that, however cyclical in many respects, or however slow the pace, is cumulative in significant characteristics, involving an evolution of social formation and mind interacting with the rest of nature, and yielding a growing and deepening knowledge and willful use, modification, or reshaping, of both the physical and social orders.

The subject, human society – society, or sociality, being essential to human being as we commonly use the latter term – therefore exhibits characteristics that are both transhistorical and historical. The transhistorical refers to those characteristics that are preservative, generative or potential, cyclical or relatively persistent, variously rooted in or involving geophysics, biology, thought, culture, art, habit, custom; the historical refers to those in flux through time, a flux that however random or subject to contingency, also exhibits systemically causal characteristics, whereby what happens in the present has its causes in what happened in the past and serves as causes of what will happen in the future, although these causal relations may be neither precisely predetermined nor predictable – something like the weather as it stands to the climate. The transhistorical includes transepochal and transsocietal characteristics, as well as shorter-term characteristics of eras or stages within epochs or within specific societies or society-types.[4]

Periods, or efforts at periodization, track change on a field of permanence – the historical on the field of the transhistorical – as well as the transhistorical proceeding through the historical. If this sounds Hegelian, well Hegel knew a thing or two. If nothing else, he contributed greatly to our understanding of evolutionary process, particularly to our ability to think complexly in evolutionary terms.

The subject, being human, in sum, involves social relations *and* consciousness, matter *and* mind, institutions *and* ideas, custom *and* reason, fact *and* value, intersecting with, or manifested in, regularity *and* contingency, permanence *and* variability, necessity *and* freedom, all sharing in both transhistorical and historical dimensions. Whatever else it is, the subject, human society, is complex, and therefore so is periodization.

In this respect, the theoretical situation corresponds with that in the physical sciences; that is, the relations of the transhistorical and the historical may be considered analogous to (but not identical with) those of general relativity and quantum physics. General relativity, in applying to the macrouniverse, views nature as a deterministic, predictable continuum: given a set of conditions, for a particular physical situation, it yields precise predictions about the outcome. By analogy, the transhistorical, while it does not apply only to macrohistory, views human history as a long-term continuum involving a significant degree of determined and predictable development in the relations of mind, social organization, and physical nature. Quantum physics, in applying to the microuniverse, views nature as composed of discrete particles (quanta), involving an inherent element of chance, and makes its predictions in terms of probabilities. By analogy, the historical, while not applying only to microhistory, deals with specific societies at specific times and with their specific characteristics, and views human history as composed of

4. Examples of transepochal and transsocietal characteristics are philosophical and theological ideas, some scientific and mathematical thought, tools and production methods, foods, motherhood, fatherhood, monarchy, aristocracy, tyranny, conscience, sexual relations, music, architecture, literature, other works of art; examples of shorter-term transhistorical characteristics include those just listed and also: aspects of the U.S. Constitution, racism, sectionalism, class formations, political principles, morals and manners.

diverse components involving inherent elements of chance, unpredictability, and probability.

Just as in the physical sciences, general relativity and quantum physics may be considered to contradict each other philosophically, so with determinism and contingency in the transhistorical and the historical; and just as a unified theory in the physical sciences would reconcile general relativity and quantum physics, so a unified periodization theory would integrate the transhistorical and the historical in some rigorous set of conceptions. Similarly, just as the continuing absence of a unified theory in the physical sciences neither invalidates general relativity or quantum physics separately, nor suspends research and thought in either field and thinking about their interrelation, so the absence of a unified periodization theory, and even the absence of the broad agreement on macro- and micro- theory that exists among physical scientists, need not invalidate the transhistorical-historical method. Rather, the analogy suggests that history involves the play of chance on the field of necessity, or the interrelation of freedom and determinism, characterized by complexity, or, the complex interrelations of relatively more simple components (individuals, families, groups, interests, classes, ideas, values). Following Heinz R. Pagels's formulation, as he derived it from his own and others' work, we may take complexity to denote conditions characterized as somewhere between a completely ordered and a completely random system: a self-organizing system, in the sense of not having been predesigned or at least not having a predesign that can be known; a system involving a hierarchy of interacting, operating constituent systems, and networks among them or their components, and more, involving a diversity or variability in interactions among the components and systems, some of which may be predictable and some unpredictable. This diversity or variability of interaction constitutes the essential feature of complex behavior characteristic of systems composed nevertheless of elementary parts. As with the physical sciences so with history, or the study of humanity, what is involved is the study of intermixing systems demanding sciences of complexity based as much upon the principle of uncertainty as upon that of certainty.[5]

3

In the task of formulating a constructive or postulated hypothesis as the ground of inquiry, the following may be considered as ranking among the essential questions of periodization:

5. Pagels, *Dreams of Reason*, pp. 64–67, et passim.

What general type of society is it? What criteria are best suited to determining or defining the society-type?

If an observably evolving society, what kind of evolution characterizes it,
and in what historically specific phase of its evolution is it?

What are the currently prevalent, declining, and emergent social relations and modes of consciousness, their requirements, capacities,
patterns of authority, and structure or relations of power?

What are the prevalent, or critical, causes and agencies, ranges and limits, of change, or failures to change, or obstructions to change?

Which aspects of the society are transhistorical, and which historically
transient or specific to current or very recent periods, and how do
they interact?

How are transhistorical aspects modified, if at all, over time, in adaptation to, or in shaping, historically transient or more specific aspects?

Which historically more specific aspects are changing or evolving at
more rapid, or less rapid, rates than others? What are the causes and
consequences of such differential rates of change and their interaction?

To what extent are such differentials in rates of change critical to the
ways in which a society changes, or evolves, or fails to?

There are many other questions, of course, as these few suggest. These
are sufficient for indicating the framework of inquiry, from which we
may turn to American society in particular and pose a postulated hypothesis with respect to type of society, and draw out some of its implications.

Suppose we begin by saying that through all or most of its history,
from colonial times forward, the society we associate with the United
States of America has been a political society (or group of political societies). This assumes a society in which politics is critically important
to, perhaps constitutive of, the society in its essence. In the case of the
United States, it is observable that continuing change, or history, characterizes this politics, and that indeed politics is the activity or system
through which people have engaged in formulating, promoting, and
managing (or resisting) change – that is, history.[6]

As a political society in this sense, it has been one in which people have
been engaged in consciously, or intentionally, seeking to shape or make
change, that is, their history, – or, in words of human drama, define or

6. Among the major strategies of managing history seized upon by Americans, a prominent one is the idea – some would say, the conceit – of having "escaped from history"
   (from the Old World) and therefore being "born free" to shape their own fate: the
   self-made people.

embrace and fulfill what they conceive to be their society's "destiny" –
or future, as well as their own as individuals. Periodization itself, then,
concerned as it is with defining the course of change, with its unavoid-
able implications for the present and the future, becomes infused with
intentionality and therefore with controversy. In sum, the society that we
are assuming is in some critical sense a political society undergoing continuous change, and in the case of the United States, open to a range of
dialogue, conflict, consensus, and division concerning the character and
rate of change. Our efforts at periodization, and the circumstance that
they can not escape differences of opinion and controversy (in a way not
common among physical scientists), may be taken to signify that we are
indeed members of a political society, and a political society undergoing
continuous change, or evolution, or *history*. The "end of history" is not
yet upon us; no such relief is in sight – or if it is, then it would signify
that the United States was no longer, or was becoming something other
than, a political society.[7]

In some greater detail, by political society I mean one in which associative activity, centered upon defining issues and formulating and implementing measures or programs through public discourse, lawmaking,
election of governmental officeholders, electioneering and campaigning,
litigation and judicial process, involving in all of these spheres large
numbers of the people, and in general becoming more inclusive of people
and issues as time goes on, rather than being confined to religious institutions and leaders, prescriptive elites, or dynastic or closed or closely
restricted circles, becomes increasingly, as the society evolves, essentially
constitutive of authority and power in the society, and of the society's
pattern and pace of change or evolution. It follows from this that a political society is one whose pattern and pace of change or evolution is
inexplicable apart from its politics in this sense. It also follows that the
evolution of United States society, in particular, can not be studied or
taught without reference to the centrality of its *political* history. Here is
an example, to begin with, of the way periodization designates the facts
to be discovered, analyzed, studied, and reasoned with.

Not all societies are political in this sense. Most societies in world history have not been. But the United States is, and has been, as also has
been the case, more or less, with those societies of the Western world
identified with the passage from a *Gemeinschaft* (communality) to a *Gesellschaft* (association) type in the modern epoch since about the six-

7. To set political scientists at ease, let me say that I would agree that all societies are
    political in some important, even constitutive, sense. Here, *political society* is a term
    meant to convey a more particular meaning.

teenth century, and typically involving an ascending and then regnant bourgeoisie – an ultimately dominant property-owning class that made work-in-the-world, both productive labor in the physical world and social labor in the shaping and reshaping of society, central to its own identity, morality, and fulfillment, or, freedom. Not all societies undergo continuous, rapid change. There are degrees of a society's being "political," degrees of changeability. For example, the Soviet Union, Eastern European countries, China, to name no others, are having a quite difficult time trying to become political in this sense. Not all change is internally generated. Much of it comes from intersociety relations, as anthropologists have long held. In some societies, change may be fatal; in some, sustained change or changeability may become to some large degree the function of external intervention: as with Indian societies in the New World in the sixteenth through nineteenth centuries and beyond, or with those of Germany and Japan after World War II, or with those of Eastern Europe and the Soviet Union currently, not to mention the more familiar examples associated with imperialism, modern capitalist or otherwise. Also, there are differences in rates of change, and in the kind of change, transpiring within a society at different times, and from society to society, as implied in such words as "progressive," "conservative" "liberal," "radical," "reactionary" that, whether we care to acknowledge it or not, we do use (and think) not alone in our politics as citizens but also in our scholarly work.

In general, the more "political" a society, the more strongly it tends, or can be expected, to undergo continuous change, variation, or evolution. It may well be that the more political, the more rapid the change. Soviet society, for example, may be becoming political more rapidly and more pandemically than its leaders, people, and institutions can manage. In an essential sense, twentieth-century Communism that came to power there and elsewhere represented the limitation and ultimately the retardation of politicalization, even the depoliticalization of society; although professing to be revolutionary, and in some ways it was, Communism represented at the same time deeply conservative, antidevelopmental (antimodernizing) trends.

Recent events in the Soviet Union, Eastern Europe, and China are significant to the historian and social scientist interested in the causes and conditions of social evolution, and hence to the question of periodization. It may be kept in mind that these are societies that had not been considered "Third World" by "Third-World theorists" and had not been considered as ranking among those societies regarded as currently and directly stifled by capitalist imperialism. On the contrary, they had been regarded as societies peculiarly committed to progressive development, insofar as they had succeeded in keeping themselves free or insulated from capitalist imperialism or from the capitalist "world system." These recent events suggest that

a. A society's evolution, or development, is not automatic, nor is it certified or assured by "self-determination" or national independence, on the one hand, or by "internationalism" or international cooperation, on the other.
b. Some forms of social organization are conducive to, and some obstructive of, continuing evolution, or development, along particular lines, or altogether.
c. Evolution or development, along whatever lines, requires adequate human agency, and that means modes of consciousness and their translation into behavior and institutions, that is, in the spheres of social movements and social relations, including politics and economics, government and law, thought and culture.
d. Production and exchange – modes of production or property-production systems – are essential elements of human evolution, and they involve "politics" and "culture" as well as "economics."
e. Production and exchange are natural to human beings, but *no particular mode* of production and exchange is natural to human beings, or inherent in human nature. Rather, each mode of production and exchange – including, and perhaps the most complex mode of all, the money-market system – is a social-cultural construct, involving the whole range of human characteristics from social psychology, personality and character, values and emulative morality, to law, politics, and government. The same may be said of the constituent elements of a system of production and exchange: Technology or technique is not simply scientific knowledge, or machinery, or inanimate force, but in the first place, "know-how," that is, modes of consciousness manifested in social relations; similarly with such components as the corporation or firm, the bank, the trade union, the cooperative, the credit union, the courts, the legal system, the political party, the interest group, the family, the church, the laboratory, the consulting firm, the university, the elementary school – each and every one is a complex of consciousness or know-how, manifested in social relations that at one and the same time serve as constituent components of the system of production and exchange, and of the system's broader context or milieu. Together they form a complex system of complex systems embodying determinism and contingency, certainty and uncertainty, durability and variability.

4

Returning to a consideration of the United States in particular, we may say that it has been (whether from colonial beginnings or sometime soon thereafter) a political society (or group of political societies) undergoing continuous evolutionary change, relatively more rapid with time, in which there has been a close and necessary relation between politics and change, or, in which politics and change have been, to some critical degree, reciprocally the function of one another, if not one and the same thing: In different words, the United States has exemplified a society devoted to change, or unable to avoid it – one might say, addicted to change – and a society in which politics is an essential process or set of processes that not only registers, but to a large degree defines, initiates, implements, and manages change, as well as resistance to it.

What kind of society, more specifically, is this U.S. political society? Through most of its history, it has been a market society, or more accurately, a complex of different types of market society, one (or some) of which eventually dominated or dissolved another or the others.

In earlier times, to the Civil War, the United States encompassed both a self-employed and wage-labor market society, or a mix of "free-labor" modes of production (with some "feudal" or, more accurately, nonfree-labor characteristics involving indenture, master-apprentice, master-servant, and guild relations, traditions, and law, which receded with time and in proportion as market relations spread and developed); and a self-employed and slave-labor market society. These were characteristic of the market systems and property-production relations that had emerged and developed with the rise of the bourgeoisie in Western Europe and the British Isles, and then extended to the New World. As the "free-labor" market society developed in agriculture, transportation, communications, and industry in the United States, it became increasingly diversified along dynamic self-employed and wage-labor lines; as the slave-labor market society developed in the United States, although not without some diversity, it became strongly monocultural along slave-labor agricultural lines, with minimal, stunted, or arrested development along self-employed, wage-labor, and nonagricultural commercial and industrial lines. The more each society developed, the less strongly its vital components intermeshed (or bonded) with the other, the less like each other and, more important, the less complementary, they became as constituents of one nation-state, and the more each constricted, or sought to constrict, or seemed to leaders of each to constrict, the development of the other. Each denied or interfered with the "equal liberty" of the other. The U.S. Constitution of 1787 had represented, inter alia, a political framework for the coexistence and codevelopment of the free- and slave-labor modes of production – or two types of market society – within one (federal) governmental system. The crisis of the Union and the Civil War represented the breakdown and the violent end of the codevelopment.

The post–Civil War Constitution, or Second Constitution, signified a U.S. society encompassing a new complex, consisting of a rapidly developing industrializing capitalist society intertwined with a vigorously growing self-employed market society, and, in place of the slave-labor market society, an agropeonage market society that dominated the southern states until, compared with the Civil War and the end of slavery, its relatively more gradual and peaceful dissolution in the mid–twentieth century (roughly from the 1930s to the 1960s). In general, U.S. history well into the twentieth century has displayed a record of a developing market society of the predominantly capitalist type codeveloping and coexisting with, and then dominating and dissolving or displacing, slave-labor and peonage-labor market societies.

The term "market society" is meant to designate a society where market relations constitute the prevalent mode of social organization and control of the allocation of labor and resources, as well as of their distribution and redistribution, of organizing and reorganizing production and reproduction, and of effecting and proportioning consumption, saving, and investment. Government intervention in these spheres generally has proceeded through measures inducing, modifying, limiting, undertaking, or regulating market activity and relations. In broader terms, a market society in the sense meant here is a society in which money-market relations, involving the production of goods and services for money-exchange rather than for immediate subsistence, use, or consumption, constitute the prevalent network of social organization and control in the society as a whole.[8] Or, to draw upon Woodrow Wilson's

8. So that, those not in the market are widely considered to be dependent, asocial, deviant, criminal, disabled, altruistic, matriculating, retired, or insane, that is, something connoting interim, exceptional, or abnormal status. Alternatively, upwardly mobile or striving persons may enter market relations via illegal activity – referred to by analysts as part of the "unofficial economy." In a slave-labor market society, the laborer's person and offspring (not labor-power alone) are commodities bought and sold among slaveowners, in accordance with money prices determined by market relations of cost, supply, and demand. In a "free-labor" market system associated with capitalism, labor-power (not the laborer) is a commodity sold for a term, and in principle, the laborer is the owner and seller of the labor-power, the employer the buyer, who may resell the labor-power only with the laborer's consent. Indenture and contract-labor systems retain strong slave-labor characteristics. In an agropeonage market society, the laborer as such is not a commodity but is tied to employment by debt and rent obligations measured by market-determined money prices (often destorted by coercion and fraud). In either case, slave-labor or agropeonage, the laborer is accorded a status short, or entirely denuded, of the full humanity and citizenship accorded to those contracting about and exploiting labor and other property. Civil Rights, antidiscrimina-

astute phrasing, it is a society in which "the world of business" changes "and therefore the world of society and the world of politics," a society in which, when "our economic conditions from top to bottom" change, so therefore does "the organization of our life," a society in which "the life of the nation running upon normal lines" grows "infinitely varied" and yet centers upon "economic questions," and these are also "questions of the very structure and operation of society itself."[9]

A market society, more precisely, is one increasingly permeated by associative activity based upon contract, and therefore public law and a highly articulated legal order, accountable to those engaging in associative activity and contractual relations, that is, to the broad range of those regarded as the people or the citizenry. By corollary, government as maker, enforcer, and administrator of public law, comes under steadily mounting pressure to become accountable to the people, the servant of the people, subordinate to the sovereignty of the people, who elect the government and attend to it and change it with relentless scrutiny, suspicion, and interest. Limited government is the transhistorical watchword: constitutional government – a government of law not persons. In sum, the crowning principle of the sovereignty of the people in a market society means the supremacy of society over the state, the "free" society, of which, again in Wilson's words, "government is only the instrument."

The market society is, therefore, one than which there is no other kind of society more political. Hence, for example, insofar as people in the Soviet Union, Eastern European countries, and China wish their societies to become more political, that is, more development- or change-oriented, the more they find themselves being driven to market – and markets. The more they wish their societies to become market societies, the more they must, as they have found, be rid of political monopolization or the restriction of political activity to narrow elites ("vanguard parties"), and open themselves to massive and diversified politicalization among the people at large; they find, also, that they must establish systems of public law, shaped by and accountable to the people. It is no accident that Soviet President Mikhail S. Gorbachev and his advisers, for example, at least in their reform phases, have spoken of making over the Soviet Union into both a "regulated market economy" and a "rule-of-law state,"[10]

tion, and affirmative action measures are designed, in principle, to offer universal access to market relations and citizenship in a free-labor market society.

9. For discussion of this aspect of Wilson's thought, and these quotations, see M. J. Sklar, *The Corporate Reconstruction of American Capitalism, 1890–1916: The Market, the Law, and Politics* (Cambridge: Cambridge University Press, 1988), pp. 390–391.

10. See, e.g., "Party's Agenda: Liberty and Justice" (Soviet Communist Party Platform), tr. Tass press agency, as reprinted in *New York Times*, 14 February 1990; "Excerpts from Gorbachev Speech on Presidency," tr. Tass press agency, *New York Times*, 16

and that at length the Soviet Communist party, "the Great Party of Lenin," has had to surrender its "vanguard" political monopoly, or in the
contradiction of terms, its constitutionally guaranteed "leading role" –
in the end, most likely, if *perestroika* is to endure, its very existence,
whether literally or by transformation into a normal parliamentary political party.

The United States, as a market society in the sense just indicated, has
been a society of, and permeated by, law and legislation and legal process, shaped by and accountable to those included among the people in
their unequal exercise of liberty and their contests among themselves to
aggrandize, ameliorate, or nullify their inequalities. It is a society, then,
to the functioning of which the role of government in making, promulgating, enforcing, and administering the law, is essential, and therefore
a society that can not be understood apart from public politics and
government, precisely because it is so much a "market" or "economic"
society.

5

To say that the United States has been a market society, and what is the
same thing, a political society, in the sense described, is also to say that
it is a society whose essence has resided in its mode or modes of production and exchange, or, in its property-production system (or systems). If
market relations have constituted the paramount social relations of the
society, the principal network of social organization and control, then, as
market relations have changed or not changed, so with society: In U.S.
history, market development has correlated strongly with societal development. The history of the United States has centered upon the stages of
development of a market society, or of market societies codeveloping and
interacting within the framework of one governmental system. The history of U.S. politics has been in essential respects a function of these
stages of development, codevelopment, and interaction, as an itemization
of the major issues in the nation's political history will attest. Frederick
Jackson Turner's lasting historiographical importance is only superficially grasped as his having been a "frontier" theorist of U.S. history, and
more substantially understood as a stages-of-development theorist of
U.S. history (for whom "the West" was not so much a place as a stage of
development), stages of development drawn in terms applicable, in prin-

March 1990; *New York Times*, 10 April 1990, front page story by Craig R. Whitney:
"Kremilin Hesitates as Deadline Falls for Economic Plan"; "Gorbachev Interview,"
Time, 4 June 1990, pp. 27–34.

ciple, to all societies, namely, land–people ratios, property and market relations, class formation and conflict, and the relation of all these to individualism, nationalism, equalitarian or inequalitarian mores, principles, and conditions.

In U.S. history, each stage of national development has involved a developmental complex, or a mixed development, involving the interacting, intersecting, and overlapping of modes of production, in phases of complementarity and conflict, and growing out of or giving rise to or suppressing one another. In this sense, the United States may be understood as the quintessential developing nation, its history as the history of a developing nation, and the history of its politics as a function of the stages of development of a market society, and in its fuller complexity, the stages of codevelopment and interacting of complementary and conflicting market societies.

Adding to the complexity of development and the politics of development through most or all of its history, the United States has been a nation of intersecting regions of differing prevalent modes of production and differing stages of development, as well as more or less diversified development *within* each region, underlying interregional conflicts *and* alignments. The history of the U.S. political system has been in essential respects a history of its representing and blending the intra- and cross-regional, and the corresponding intra- and cross-class, conflicts and alignments, and transacting their continuous evolving – and sometimes abrupt passage – from stage to stage of development: from one set of class conflicts and alignments to another, and from one interregional system to another. Hence, James Madison remains the great American political theorist, with his formulations concerning an extended republic, federalism, checks and balances, and policymaking filtration, in managing or reconciling the conflicts of the demands for liberty, equality, and development (progress, improvement) incessantly pressed by a market-immersed citizenry representing differing kinds and stages of market development as well as the factions and classes pertaining to each of them.

To put it another way, U.S. politics has been to some large and essential degree, the art of reconciling different modes of production and transacting the passage through differing stages and mixtures of market development. The astute members of the Constitutional Convention of 1787, for example, understood with Madison that the key question before them was not that of small states versus large states, but of the free-labor mode of production versus the slave-labor, and how to reconcile them, or provide for their codevelopment, within one frame of government. Subsequent U.S. political history may be understood in a similar way.

Federalism, Republicanism, National Republicanism, Jacksonian laissez-faire, nullification and state's rights, concurrent majority doctrine, the Compromises over the control of the vast western territories, all centered upon managing the coexistence and codevelopment of the nation's two great modes of production, until its breakdown in the Civil War and the vanquishment of the slave-labor mode, and slavery's replacement by an agropeonage mode more suited to codevelopment with an industrializing capitalist mode, within one national framework. After the Civil War, the politics of capitalist continentalism (protection, national banking and currency, fiscal and monetary policies, disposal of public lands, veterans' benefits, railway subsidies, land grant state colleges, rivers and harbors projects, etc.) and extralegal "state's rights" (Hayes–Tilden arrangements, racist terror) reinforced by judicial rulings restricting civil rights, centered upon managing the codevelopment of industrializing capitalism and agropeonage, from the 1870s to the 1890s. The politics of antitrust, regulatory Progressivism, institutional racial segregation and disfranchisement, Open Door and imperialist expansion abroad, centered upon the codevelopment of corporate capitalism in its early phases and agropeonage in its later phases, from the 1890s to the 1930s. The politics of the New Deal system of social security, collective bargaining, subsidized agriculture, public finance, public works, Atlantic Alliance (including World War II) and Cold War, and the civil rights revolution, presided over the codevelopment of corporate capitalism and socialism and the dismantling of the agro-peonage mode of production, from the 1930s to the 1960s. The politics of Great Society programs, civil rights legislation, affirmative action, feminism, African-American empowerment, "supply-side" deficit budgeting, and the end of the Cold War has represented the management of a new stage of capitalist-socialist development, dissolving transhistorical patriarchal and racial social relations, a stage both national and transnational and still in search of a name, and in need of clear delineation of its mode or modes of production – something more evocative than postindustrial or service or information economy – a "social market society," for want of a better term, representing the "synthesis" or outcome of the capitalist-socialist mix.

6

Each stage in the succession of modes of production and their intermixtures has involved an evolving set of class relations characterized by both complementarity and conflict. Where the passage from one stage to another has proceeded through a relatively sudden displacement of one set of class relations by another, the politics of what we may reasonably identify as those of violent revolution ensued, as for example, in the time of the American Revolution and that of the Civil War. Where the passage has proceeded through a relatively more gradual transformation of one into another, or a gradual accommodation of one with another, the politics of what we might reasonably identify as those of peaceful evolution – or peaceful revolution if the change be judged as sufficiently deep or profound – ensued, as for example, in the time of Jacksonian Democracy, the Progressive Era, or the New Deal. As a quintessentially developing society, the market society of the United States has undergone incessant change, continuous "progress" or evolution, and at times revolution as a condition of continuing evolution.

In this connection, U.S. history brings into focus an understanding of the nature of revolution (or of those changes we may identify as revolutionary with respect to society as a whole) that may be applicable to other societies as well as that of the United States: A revolution need not be, if it ever is, the simple "overthrow" of one class by another, but the passage from one set of class relations to another set, or the rise of one set to dominance over another set. To put it from a different angle, class conflicts and changing class relations, corresponding with developing modes of production, *generate* conditions and pressures for changes of profound effect, but emergent cross-class alignments *transact* them.

In seeing the United States as a developing nation, and its politics as a function of the stages of development of a market society, it comes more clearly into focus that by and large for Americans, politics has been "about" government's developmental responsibility and people's participation – their rights and privileges, duties and disabilities – in the work and processes of development; this has shaped the principal "mainstream" content of party politics, the "serious" substance of it, whatever other issues might temporarily intrude upon or perturb it. The principal content of legislative work and governmental functions, at the local and state as well as the national levels, has been providing for developmental rights and responsibilities of people and government. What is more, whatever other issues Americans brought into their politics, they constantly brought the belief, through all the stages of development, that with government resided the responsibility, first and foremost among any of its others, to assure development within the framework of reconciling market activity with social goals and human rights as currently understood. In sum, to Americans, party politics and government are to be concerned above all with defining and redefining, shaping and reshaping the interaction of government and market, and hence of state and society, but always (transhistorically) within the broader framework of the supremacy of society over the state. To return to a previous formulation, there is no society more political than the market society.

In studying classes, associations, interest groups, with the corresponding enterprises, social movements, leadership personalities, and politics that are characteristic of the evolving market society and its modes of production and exchange, we are also encountering and therefore studying modes of consciousness in their genesis, development, change, decay, and interaction. They give rise to, and manifest themselves in, what we may refer to as *critical discourses* that display transhistorical trends and also define an age (or the particular historical period). Periodization guides the identification, study, and comprehension of a society's critical discourses, and these in turn will serve to validate, modify, or replace the periodization in use. Significant changes in style and content of critical discourses, their rise, decay, displacements, or transformations, signal the passage from one historical period, or stage of development, or mode of production, to another. It is in the critical discourses of a people (including those of popular culture) that their history becomes intelligible, that the interplay of the transhistorical and the historical is revealed, and nowhere more so than in the market society, the political society, that is and has been the United States.

7

The market society is both historical and transhistorical. With respect to past human history, its origins and early development as an enduring society-type were historical, as were its successive stages of development. With respect to its own stages of development, the market society has contained transhistorical elements from prior history, and has been itself transhistorical as it traversed its own stages of historical development. Historians have identified those stages, broadly, with such terms as mercantilism, laissez-faire, corporate capitalism, the welfare state, and the mixed economy, and complementarily or alternatively, with such terms as agrocommercial, preindustrial, industrializing, and postindustrial. Slavery and peonage as modes of production with essential roles in the historical development of market societies have often been treated by historians as anomalies, or as superannuated vestiges of prior history, and where present, especially in the New World, they have been often dealt with by historians as evidence of "unfinished revolutions." My own view is that to treat modern slavery and peonage in that way is somewhat narrowly teleological, that each comprised both transhistorical and historical components or modes of the development of market society, and that it was only at a rather late or mature stage of the market society's historical development in the United States, that slavery and peonage, as major market-based modes of production, passed away (slavery in the 1860s, peonage in the 1930s–1960s).

In any case, the emergence of the market society scarcely five centuries ago inaugurated the developing society as such. It marked the great departure from prior human history, rooted in *replacement* modes of production, to modern human history based on *reproductive,* transformative, endlessly changing modes of production and ever-expanding human powers over physical nature, and ever-growing human self-governance in social relations, both associative and individualistic. It is a mistake, commonly made, and especially pronounced in current public discourse and among ideological currents running the gamut from left to right, to equate market society exclusively with capitalism, and socialism exclusively with nonmarket society. Historical and transhistorical, in its emergence and development through its various stages, capitalism represents one mode of market society (or set of modes); similarly with the self-employed mode of production and exchange of the smaller merchant, the shopkeeper, the artisan, the farmer; similarly with modern slavery and peonage; and, although not often thought about in this way, similarly with socialism. At any given historical stage of development of the market society, two or more of these modes of production and exchange, and perhaps subordinate nonmarket modes as well, may be found intermixed and interacting.

In this connection, particularly in its bearing upon capitalism and socialism, and without unduly repeating what I have written elsewhere, in Chapters II, V, and VII of this volume, and in my book, *The Corporate Reconstruction of American Capitalism,* I wish here to take up some implications of points made there, and to introduce some new considerations that have since arisen or taken firmer shape in my own thinking, about the nature of corporate capitalism, or the corporate capitalist mode of production or property-production system.

The passage of industrializing capitalism from its proprietary-competitive stage to its corporate-administered stage in its early phases of development, from the 1890s through the 1920s, marked a deep-going change in the capitalist mode of production and exchange. The corporate reconstruction of capitalism, however, did not mean the disappearance of small or medium-sized enterprise, any more than it meant the immediate demise of agropeonage; nor did it mean the end of competition among enterprises; nor the end of markets or the market society. It represented a new stage in the development of market society, and the emergence of new kinds of markets corresponding with the reorganization of the property-production system in major sectors of the economy.

It meant new relationships between smaller and bigger business, as well as new ways of organizing enterprises and markets within and between bigger and smaller business. Smaller enterprise in agriculture, industry, finance and banking, trade, transportation, and communications, continued to operate, often thriving and playing innovative roles, but now in a new environment significantly reorganized by the rise of large corporations along with related new arrangements in the organization of capital markets, banking, currency, and credit.

It is also important not to make the mistake of equating administered markets exclusively with large corporations as such, or even with capital-intensive, as against labor-intensive, industries. In some industries inhabited by large corporations, as in textiles, administered markets were for long not achievable; in other industries, populated largely by small enterprise, as in farming (increasingly capital-intensive) and construction (relatively labor-intensive, even in more recent times), administered markets have been achieved to a greater or lesser degree, greater as the years passed. Administered markets have involved regulation by private or public parties, more usually some mix of private and public regulation. Apart from "public utilities," like railroads or providers of energy, where public regulation and indeed public direction came to dominate, the general tendency has been (a) for private regulation to predominate – subject to a secondary public regulation by judicial and administrative means – in industries of high concentration of production and market share, and (b) for public regulation to play an essential role – in the form of banking and credit arrangements, government contracts, government-arranged production agreements, price-supports, or subsidies – in the less concentrated industries, such as agriculture and construction, although private arrangements such as cooperatives, employers' or trades councils, and trade unions have played important complementary roles. (All this is not to mention the strong government role in maintaining or developing industries considered vital to the national interest, but to which private market incentives alone were too weak to allocate sufficient capital, as with postal service, shipbuilding and merchant marine, and the early phases of the aircraft, airline, space, and nuclear energy industries.) In most cases, administered markets have been effected, fashioned, and refashioned over time, seldom all at once, by some mix of private and public authority. They are better understood, moreover, as the result or work, not simply of "objective economics," but of associative activity involving social movements and thus modes of consciousness – in short, intentional human agency, or a "Visible Hand," however much intent and consequence may have diverged. Property and market relations, their maintenance as well as their modification, reorganization, or abolition, involve social movements and modes of consciousness no less than what are thought of as reform (or "radical" or "revolutionary") efforts "outside" the market proper: all the more so, indeed, because property and market relations are basic social relations.

In some further detail, what do we mean by the idea of administered markets, and by the correlated idea of the passage from the proprietary-competitive to the corporate-administered stage of capitalism? Here let us proceed, if still somewhat sketchily, under two subheadings, first, the "organizational" or "structural" aspect, and second, the "flow" or "process" aspect, although in essence, and hence in the discussion, the two are intertwined.

First, the ideas in their organizational aspect refer to a growing tendency of enterprise and property ownership engaged in production and exchange activity to become less and less individualized (or proprietor-owned and managed) in form, and more and more associative (or corporate-owned and managed) in form, and hence to undergo a transformation in substance, or kind, as well. In the corporate stage, furthermore, even individualized enterprise tends toward a growing engagement in franchise or distributive systems of large corporate networks, or in business units (including, and especially, farms) heavily dependent upon highly articulated associative arrangements, both private and public.

In replacing individualistic ownership of private property with associational ownership of private property, corporate enterprise came to be considered as "publicly" held. Indeed, while individuals owned stock, no individual as such owned the physical property or any part of it. Accordingly, corporate capitalism accelerated the transformation of productive and other enterprise relations from an individual and personal to an associational and impersonal basis.

Corporate capitalism intensified the division and specialization of labor, but on the basis of their horizontal and vertical reintegration under more centralized or coordinated control. In socializing ownership as well as liability and risk, the corporate form of enterprise separated the investor and ownership roles from the managerial roles, thereby indicating the distinction between the enterprise in its technoeconomic function as such, and the enterprise in its specific property form. These changes correlate with what theorists have referred to as "bureaucratization" of enterprise, but I am trying here to avoid charged – and in some quarters pejorative – terms.

The corporation brought into cooperative association managerial, professional, and technical labor of all kinds, as well as manual labor of all kinds – skilled, semi-skilled, unskilled. The more so as it developed in the United States, corporate enterprise brought into cooperative association office and shop floor, Northerners and Southerners, Euro-Americans and African-Americans, men and women, metropolitans and provincials, and so on. By sheer size and complexity of its associational activity, by widespread ownership among the public, and by its many-sided and large-scale socioeconomic impact, the large corporation, regardless of its field of enterprise, could no longer be considered to be purely and simply private property as a matter of policy, but property both affected with and embodying a public interest, or property in which the public had no choice but to take an interest.

In all these ways, among others, corporate capitalism represented an advanced state of socialization, not only of productive and market relations and enterprise activity, but also of social, political, educational, and cultural relations of the broadest sort. This was all the more so in combination with the necessarily concomitant and related quickening of urbanizing and proletarianizing trends among the American people that required, invited, or induced the provision of essential services, which increasingly became *public* services (although far from exclusively) – beyond the capacity of individuals, families, or the private investment system to provide.

In addition, the public character and market power with which large corporate organization vested capitalist enterprise and capitalist property-ownership called forth growing government intervention in market and property relations, of a regulatory, distributive, and countercyclical nature, on behalf of the national interest and the general welfare as defined in the political arenas. Moreover the global dimension inherent in the large corporate economy stimulated new kinds of international relations and perspectives among capitalists, workers, reformers, intellectuals, professionals, and political leaders, in a context favorable to growing government involvement in international investment management, development planning, and sociopolitical reform.

Corporate capitalism, in other words, represented a new stage in the organization and development of capitalist property relations, a stage pushing beyond capitalism, and hence at the same time, the emergence of an early stage of a modern, highly industrialized, public economy with strong associational and integrative, or socialized, characteristics, permeating not only enterprise relations but also broader sociopolitical relations, on a national and transnational plane.

Second, the terms administered markets and corporate-administered stage of capitalism refer, in their flow or process aspect, to a growing capacity to manage, regulate, or modulate investment and supply, and to influence, shape, or modify demand, and thereby to adjust supply and demand and to some large degree *make,* rather than simply *take,* prices.[11] Under the competitive regime, enterprises with large fixed investment produced to full capacity; investment entry remained relatively wide open, continuously augmenting capacity and supply actually brought to market; production and distribution functions were more segmented in separate firms than integrated within one large organization; and firms took prices that, as a result, tended relentlessly toward the level of costs of the most efficient, in a process that capitalists came increasingly to designate as "ruinous" or "destructive" competition. The competitive market system registered rising productive efficiency in declining prices, but at the expense of "social efficiency," because its boom–bust cycle of dynamic development (for example, in the 1870s, 1880s, and 1890s in the United States) periodically left large sectors of the economy with bankrupt firms and unemployed plant and labor, with their deleterious social effects, and this in turn reacted negatively upon productive efficiency itself with recurrent interruptions of high or full capacity utilization. Administered markets put an end neither to markets nor to competition, but introduced new rules, conditions, and kinds of markets and competition, in the process – or at least the effort – of bringing production-distribution efficiency and "social efficiency" back into some better balance, that is, softening the business cycle by more closely matching supply and demand.

11. Cf., e.g., the following succinct and authoritative descriptions of prevalent characteristics of the new market system associated with corporate capitalism: (a) Alfred D. Chandler, Jr. and Herman Daems, "Administrative Coordination, Allocation and Monitoring: Concepts and Comparisons," in Thomas K. McCraw, ed., *The Essential Alfred Chandler: Essays toward a Historical Theory of Big Business* (Boston: Harvard Business School Press, 1988), pp. 398–424, at p. 399: "In modern advanced market economies, markets, firms, and interagency arrangements are used jointly and alternatively as instruments for coordinating, monitoring, or allocating." "In the latter part of the nineteenth century, as the economies of the United States and Western Europe became technologically complex, and particularly as the new technologies vastly expanded the output of the individual units of production, interagency [cartel] agreements and administrations increasingly replaced market mechanisms in carrying out these basic functions. In the United States interagency agreements were short-lived. Instead, in many sectors of the economy the giant multiunit business enterprise came to coordinate, monitor, and allocate. As these firms began to substitute for the market and price system, their owners and managers devised organizational structures and control systems to permit them to carry out these functions efficiently, that is, at lower costs than if they had been carried out through market mechanisms." (b) Chandler, "Scale, Scope, and Organizational Capabilities," in ibid., pp. 472–504, at pp. 493–494: "that is, they [large firms] no longer competed primarily on price as firms had done previously, and as firms continued to do in the more fragmented labor-intensive industries. The largest firm . . . became the price leader, basing prices on estimates of demand in relation to its own plant capacities and those of its competitors."

From this perspective, once again, it may be seen that globalization of the national system of investment and trade, as well as the raising of effective demand at home, inhered in the corporate reconstruction of American capitalism. This was because, unless demand was extended and deepened, especially given the rising productivity derived from new machinery and processes, from economies of scale (size) and scope (integration or diversification), and from new managerial technique and organization, the economy would proceed at high levels of unemployment of capacity and labor, and this would negate the advantages of the new economies of scale and scope, and, no less important, provoke sociopolitical instability and disorder. Without global extension and domestic deepening of demand for capital and labor, as well as for finished goods, both productive efficiency and social efficiency would be lost, and along with them, continuing or progressive national development.

To continue with our second aspect, the administered-market system of price making meant, in effect, replacing the old tie between cost and price with a new one, or to put it more precisely, it meant that although continuing to decline in real terms over the long run, price no longer tended toward the level of sheer operating and overhead costs of the most efficient enterprise, but instead diverged above it. Administered prices returned revenues exceeding not only sheer costs, but also exceeding what was needed or feasible for reinvestment in expansion or improvement of capacities in the given marketing line or lines – at least to the firms of average or above-average efficiency, as well as to those with some temporary monopolistic advantage (including that from patents). Consequently, many of the larger corporations, and many of the better-run medium-sized and smaller ones too, became vehicles for the allocation of income, investment funds, and ultimately, of resources and labor outside their own immediate spheres of enterprise – through allocation above and beyond the customary dividend and interest payouts, such as through portfolio investment, direct investment (e.g., in integration or diversification), spending on advertising and public relations, pension programs and other benefits or amenities, donations to institutions of higher education, culture, and philanthropy, research and development funding, tax payments, and the like, all of which were carried in the price of the corporations' products.

To put the matter another, and a most significant, way, funds for social investment or spending that under the old competitive regime would have come from savings withheld from, and drawn out of, the consumption stream, now found increasing sources in the consumption stream itself; this began to be true as well, on a growing scale, of funds for productive investment. The corporate reorganization of capitalism represented another passage: that from the stage of human history in which consumption and investment were "contradictory," to a stage in which they became increasingly complementary. The passage was registered, for example, in the observation that began to surface among economists in the United States by the last years of the nineteenth century, that Mill's "Fourth Law" no longer held – that contrary to that law consumer revenue streams did feed operating-capital and labor-employment streams, and in a companion observation then also surfacing and that later became associated with Keynesianism, the observation, namely, that savings had come chronically to exceed investment demand, making disequilibrium rather than equilibrium the economic norm.[12] The surplus, therefore, of savings, capital, and capacities needed to be applied to developing the "underdeveloped" countries; it might also be applied to the development of new products and services; and it might also be ploughed back directly into consumption, whether in the form of rising real wages and benefits, or of social and cultural consumption and display, or, as it subsequently emerged strongly in the United States beginning in the 1920s, in the form of "investment" in consumer credit and in government debt to finance public works and activities (not to mention war spending and financing of international war debt, beginning massively before the 1920s). Unlike the old competitive price system, the administered price system registered the new circumstances in *rising* nominal prices, or secular "inflation" from the turn of the century forward, in the midst of strongly rising productivity and impressively declining real unit costs and real unit prices in the goods-production spheres.

The price system, in other words, came to carry the responsibility not simply for meeting operating and overhead costs of business enterprise, but also, to a degree and of a character not true under the competitive regime, for "social overhead costs," or for social planning – however well or badly, justly or unjustly, the planning may be judged to have been carried out. This gave business enterprise a social and political significance it had never had before. It placed large and critical powers of broad public concern in corporate managerial hands. Aside from the ways in which corporations, through their size or impact in the market proper, became affected with a public interest, and aside from the ways in which their powers of market administration and price making called forth countervailing governmental regulatory powers, not only to assure

12. Sklar, *Corporate Reconstruction*, ch. 2; Carl P. Parrini and M. J. Sklar, "New Thinking about the Market, 1896–1904: Some American Economists on Investment and the Theory of Surplus Capital," *Journal of Economic History*, 43:3 (September 1983), pp. 559–578.

fair practices, but also to reinforce or sustain a discipline in favor of innovation and rising efficiency, a discipline that the old competitive regime had once but no longer sufficiently supplied, corporations and
corporate managers now assumed vital roles in society at large, calling
for social accountability and therefore political check, balance, and regulation. Political theory soon began to designate the corporation not
merely as an economic entity but also as a complex social organization,
even (if somewhat erroneously) as a quasistate.

Viewing the same process from a somewhat different angle, the transformation of the old tie between cost and price meant that a large degree
of compensatory social discretion, in ways already indicated, but in other
ways as well, needed to be, or could be, brought into play to supplement
or modify the results of the administered price system in allocating labor
and resources not only to productively or economically, but also to socially or culturally, necessary, convenient, and desirable spheres. In part,
that social discretion came to be exercised in the private sector by officers and directors of corporations themselves, in their coordinating,
monitoring, and allocating functions, to draw upon Alfred D. Chandler's
analytic terms. In part also, as "collective bargaining" became more effective in agriculture (cooperatives, Federal Farm Land Banks, other
such associational credit arrangements, and later the production-
agreement and price-support system of the Agricultural Adjustment Administration (AAA) and subsequent government programs), and in
capital–labor relations (to some extent in 1900–1935, but more so after
the Wagner Act of 1935), farmers and workers, too began to participate
in the exercise of such social discretion. In part, the new social discretion
also came to be exercised by a growing "nonbusiness" sector of society –
cultural, civic, educational, political, charitable associations – making
claims upon, or appeals to, the allocation of corporate revenues, in addition to individual and government revenues. In part, the new social discretion also came to be exercised in growing quantity and scope, and in
qualitative departures from the past, by government, that is, by public
policy and law at all levels (local, state, and national), increasingly engaged in defining social goals, requirements, and conveniences, and in
the process, redefining and reorienting them, as well as inventing or discovering new ones. Human intentionality, not appealing for legitimacy
to divine guidance or to hallowed precedent, but rooted in utilitarian
and rationalistic conceptions of economic or social efficiency, amenity,
or convenience, or of social justice or national interest, came to play a
larger and larger role in the shaping and reshaping of society. The scope
of freedom and contingency, as against determinism, necessity, or fate,

expanded, and the substance of human freedom changed, developed, and deepened in what may be considered a qualitative break with the past.

With respect to the government role, the national government began to play a major part, in the first place, chronologically, by cooperating with corporations and banks in the globalization of the system of investment and trade, or, the globalization of the market society and the developmental imperative, involving foreign relations ranging from imperialism to multilateral diplomatic initiatives and rising engagement in world politics, both peaceful and martial. In domestic affairs, short of outright ownership or dictation, as with public utilities, government at the various levels, but increasingly at the national level, began to exercise the new social discretion through taxation and spending, banking, monetary, and credit measures, public works, subsidies, and production and marketing agreements, as well as by regulatory law and administration.

In sum, the corporate reconstruction of American capitalism brought into play a mix of "public" and "private" associational authority – more accurately, governmental and nongovernmental associational or, social, authority – acting within and upon market relations in allocating revenues, income, supply and demand, resources and labor, thereby subjecting market relations to social and political accountability: a mix in which social discretion, exercised as deliberate decision making by associated individuals, grew and developed as never before, and in which that exercised by public authority subject to political process – in the United States subject to its species of democratic and electoral politics – took on new functions, scale, and scope. In all these ways, human self-governance in both nongovernmental and governmental spheres grew, spread, and deepened.

From this perspective, the passage of the U.S. market society from its proprietary-competitive to its corporate-administered stage of capitalism also brought with it an ongoing enlargement of the sphere of associative human self-determination, in correlation with an ongoing enlargement of the degree of socialization of the market society. Indeed, the more corporate capitalism developed, the stronger the socializing tendencies. I specifically mean here socialization not in the general sense in which all human characteristics and relations may be considered social, but in the more historically concrete sense of socialism as that term came into use in the nineteenth and twentieth centuries. The corporate stage of capitalist development may be understood, in essential respects, as encompassing the codevelopment and interacting of capitalist and socialist modes of production and exchange, or, a property-production system consisting of a mix of both capitalist and socialist characteristics. Not by capitalism alone has twentieth-century America been decisively shaped, in its property-production and class relations, and in policy-formation and law, but also by socialism – and by populism oscillating between the two.

That this viewpoint may seem odd attests to the tyrannical power of ideological – indeed, *sectarian* ideological – thought in the twentieth century over the minds of most people, including not least the minds of intellectuals and scholars of all outlooks and persuasions – left, right, and center, liberal, conservative, and radical, Marxist, non-Marxist, and anti-Marxist alike. In particular, it attests to the power of Lenin's, or Leninist, ideology – a rather powerful vestige of the religious (faith-centered moralist) mentality in secular guise – in convincing people, including most of the learned, to equate socialism with a sociopolitical ideology or system that came into being in largely nonmarket, noncapitalist, and nonpolitical societies (in the sense of the terms as used here), although then imposed by military force upon other societies in more, or less, advanced stages of market-society development. Aside from such an equation being at profound variance with the thought of most socialists of the late nineteenth and early twentieth century, including that of Karl Marx and his closest professing colleagues and followers, and aside from such an equation being fundamentally ahistorical, if for nothing else in taking one "model" as sufficing for the understanding of the evolutionary course of all societies, it is similar to the fallacy of equating capitalism with its course of development in, say, Germany, or Japan, or Italy, or Chile, or South Africa, or to the fallacy of equating Christianity with, say, Anabaptism, that is, with only one strain of it, or with Anglicanism, or, to make the analogy more poignant, with the Russian Orthodox Church.[13]

8

In the course of his own scholarly studies, Marx himself, whose credentials as a prosocialist thinker are not negligible, again and again empha-

13. It might also be noted that many professing socialists who have rejected "Leninism" in part or completely, including social democrats, have held nevertheless to a variation on the ahistorical theme, that is, to a special vision or faith, according to which "true" socialism, conceived as a secular (or Christian, or Islamic, etc.) Kingdom of God on earth, would at some time, whether relatively abruptly or gradually, replace or preempt capitalism, and according to which nothing too far short of this could be regarded as "really" socialism. Even self-professed nonsocialists and antisocialists have embraced such a notion of socialism as suppressing and replacing capitalism, and at any rate as being incompatible with and exclusive of capitalism, not like socialists in happy assent but either in disdain or in determined opposition, or in resigned expectation (with respect to the latter mood, think, for example, of Schumpeter).

sized his rejection of ahistorical or "utopian" ideas and enthusiasms in comprehending the historical character of society and its likely patterns of change and development. At length, he arrived at a more complex, and less linear, understanding of the relation between capitalism and socialism in highly developed market (industrializing-capitalist) societies such as, in his time, England and the United States, than he is usually identified with, and than he had expressed in his earlier writings or even at times in his later politically engaged statements.[14]

Marx saw the rise of "joint-stock companies," or large corporations, in modern industry and the modern economy in general, coupled with the corresponding rise of modern capital markets and credit systems, as representing the beginnings of the evolution of the industrializing mode of production from capitalism to socialism, or more precisely, as

14. It was an understanding that he derived from historical study and that he duly recorded in a scientific spirit, however much it may have departed from, revised, or even offended, his own ideological predilections, political presuppositions, or ethical preferences, and even his own earlier evolutionary anticipations – as befit the mind of probably the greatest analytical historian of capitalism in its competitive-industrializing stage of development: a mind immersed in evolutionary method in studying and comprehending human development, and that crafted theory that was, not simply deterministic, but in essence, complexly probabilistic, centered upon identifying trends from variable conditions, as well as the conditions of variability themselves, hence the interplay of determinism and contingency, certainty and chance, necessity and freedom. One might say that in his studies of capitalism, Marx was a pioneer in the discovery and applicability of probability theory in the social sciences, predating as well its emergence in the physical sciences with Heisenberg and quantum physics. Although Marx had long held to an evolutionary view, according to which socialism would succeed capitalism at a certain stage in the latter's development, by a process involving an abrupt displacement via the "overthrow" of the capitalist class by the working class, and although it is reasonable to believe that he never entirely relinquished entertaining such sentiments, his studies impelled him away from expecting such a clear-cut, or simple, linear procession as adequate to an understanding of the evolution of modern capitalist society. He is perhaps best known for his published statements embodying the linear expectation encapsulated, for example, in his and Engels's "Workers of the world, unite!" and in his "the expropriators are expropriated." But even as he penned and published such thoughts as these, he was drawing different conclusions and devising different ways of thinking about the modern world in his work in progress. As early as 1863, for example, the year of the publication of volume I of *Capital,* he wrote to Engels upon rereading the latter's *The Condition of the Working Class in England,* first published almost two decades earlier, how "regretfully aware of our increasing age" he had become (he was 45, aging perhaps by then current actuarial tables, but not so old by scholarly standards): "How freely and passionately, with what bold anticipations and no learned and scientific doubts, the thing is still dealt with here! And the very illusion that the result itself will leap into the daylight of history to-morrow or the day after gives the whole thing a warmth and jovial humor – compared with which the later 'gray in gray' makes a damned unpleasant contrast." Note that the contrast Marx emphasizes, however much he laments it, and however painful, is between the damned unpleasant "learned and scientific" and the warm and jovial "illusion." Marx to Engels, 9 April 1863, in *The Correspondence of Karl Marx and Friedrich Engels,* tr. Dona Torr (New York: International Publishers, 1936), p. 147.

representing a transitional mode of production containing both capitalist and socialist characteristics. The socialization – or deindividualization – of the form of property owning through widespread stock-ownership, the separation of ownership from management, the necessity of management in modern enterprise as a distinct function paid as highly skilled labor, quite apart from property ownership or property rights, the concentration of social as well as market power eliciting greater government involvement in the economy, the complex intermeshing or integration of many specialized functions and huge numbers of variously unskilled, semiskilled, and skilled workers – all these characteristics and developments Marx specifically noted, although at an early stage of their emergence and hence rather abstractly.[15]

In noting these characteristics and developments and their historical implications, Marx assessed the corporation as representing "the abolition of capital as private property within the framework of capitalist production itself," "the abolition of capitalist private industry on the basis of the capitalist system itself . . . [which] destroys private industry as it expands," and, more broadly, as representing "the abolition of the capitalist mode of production within the capitalist mode of production itself." Accordingly, he designated the rise of large corporations as therefore representing a "phase of transition to a new form of production." As the result of the workings of industrializing competitive capitalism, corporate enterprise entailed a *necessary* stage in the transition from capitalism to socialism: "This result [corporate enterprise] of the ultimate development of capitalist production is a necessary transitional phase towards the reconversion of capital into the property of producers, although no longer as the private property of the individual producers, but rather as the property of associated producers, as outright social property." The "capitalist stock companies, as much as the co-operative factories [of workers themselves]," Marx held, "show how a new mode of production naturally grows out of an old one, when the development of the material forces of production and of the corresponding forms of social production have reached a particular stage," and hence "should be considered as transitional forms from the capitalist mode of production to the associated one." The "associated mode of production" was Marx's synonym for socialism.[16]

15. Marx, *Capital* (Moscow: Foreign Languages Publishing House, 1959), Vol. III, pp. 427–432.
16. Marx, *Capital*, III, quotations at pp. 427, 428, 429, 431. The point here, it may be noted, is not the "necessity" with which Marx endowed the evolutionary developments in question but the mixture of capitalist and socialist characteristics he attributed to them. It may also be noted, as of particular significance, that Marx observed in passing that in making possible an "enormous expansion of the scale of production and of enterprises, that was impossible for individual capitalists," the corporation also made it possible for "enterprises that were formerly government enterprises, [to]

Marx still thought in terms of a linear transition *from* capitalism *to* socialism and was unable entirely to disentangle his comprehension of corporate capitalism from the grip of the broader nineteenth-century European linear evolutionary conception. But this conception of evolution, and so Marx's, was cumulative as well as linear, and it is clear that Marx perceived corporate capitalism as representing a hybrid – or an evolving "dialectical unity of opposites" – of capitalist and socialist modes of production, in which the very development of the one generated the development of the other, and in which the two developed together both antagonistically and symbiotically. As such, corporate capitalism represented a "progressive" development, or as he put it, "a necessary transitional phase," and one marked, by its very nature, by intensifying interaction – marked by both conflict and complementarity – between capitalist and socialist relations, ideas, values, movements, politics, as well as between capitalists and workers as great classes of society.[17]

Implicit in Marx's formulation, if not clearly and quotably articulated, is a use of the term socialism, like that of the term capitalism, to mean an evolving set of property-production and class relations, and corresponding evolving modes of consciousness, not a party or a "movement," and the idea that socialism so conceived does not simply or suddenly displace or replace capitalism (as a prosocialist party or

become public." (*Capital*, III, p. 427.) That is, the associated or socialist mode of production was to be distinguished from government ownership. Current trends toward "privatization" of government-owned enterprise in many countries may be understood instead as "publicization," corresponding with a society's greater developmental maturity allowing associated people to do what had before been done "in trust" for them by government.

Also, I would like to note here that the passages quoted in the text from Vol. III of *Capital* (and others like them not quoted), though undoubtedly known to scholars and hagiographers, have generally been treated with a benign neglect by procapitalists and proscocialists alike. Procapitalists may not like to admit their complicity in the Devil's work by being themselves, and prosocialists may not like to admit that the Devil is doing their work or is one of them, at least in part. Procapitalists may not like to think Marx might have been right about the "historical necessity" of capitalism evolving toward socialism precisely in and through its own developmental processes. Prosocialists, especially those of the "radical" or "populist" or "fundamentalist" kind, whose thinking is farthest from Marx's historical method, however much they may revere or invoke him, may not like to think there is anything "good" or of "redeeming social value" about modern corporate-capitalist society.

17. Cf. Marx, *Capital*, III, pp. 430–431: "In the last analysis, it [the spread of corporate enterprise] aims at the expropriation of the means of production from all individuals.... However, this expropriation appears within the capitalist system in a contradictory form, as appropriation of social property by a few.... There is antagonism against the old form in the stock companies, in which social means of production appear as private property; but the conversion to the form of stock still remains ensnared in the trammels of capitalism; hence, instead of overcoming the antithesis between the character of wealth as social and as private wealth, the stock companies merely develop it in a new form." A new form, nevertheless, that Marx, as we have seen, designated as a necessary one in a process of progressive transition.

government officials may replace a procapitalist party or officials in government), but necessarily evolves as a function of capitalism's own development as a mode of production.[18] This would cohere with – if not serve to certify – Marx's own requirement that only if inhering in evolutionary necessities or conditions could socialism be "believed in" or anticipated on scientific grounds as consistent with "laws" of human historical development. At the same time, it also means that the emergence of a socialism so conceived, in modern society, is a matter of broadly developing social relations, institutions, modes of behavior and consciousness, involving the activity and variability of all classes of society, and not the exclusive province of any one class or of any particular party or "movement": As capitalist property-production relations change, and in particular, as they develop from their proprietary-competitive to their corporate-administered stage, they generate, and in some degree themselves transform into, socialist property-production relations, in processes shaped by and involving the activity and the alteration of all classes of society – capitalists, proprietors, workers, farmers – as well as other groups and associations in society, and their various and interrelated modes of consciousness.[19]

9

In the context of the discussion in this essay, it may be said, from the standpoint of periodization, that the essence of the Progressive Era in the United States, the years from the depression of the 1890s to World War I, resided in its having been the time when capitalism and socialism, as modes of production in an early phase of codevelopment, entered into "dialogue," not only in the economy as such, but also in American political, intellectual, and cultural life, and in that dialogue became the major forces – both contending and intermixing – shaping American life. The more corporate capitalism developed, the more socialism, the more administered market relations, the more nonmarket associative rela-

18. Or, as the Mensheviks warned Lenin, and to paraphrase: "Vladimir Ilyich, you can't skip stages," a warning that has come home to roost.

19. The foregoing discussion of Marx's formulations is not to invoke "authority" in aid of the general view offered here, but simply to indicate some of the thinking of an eminent prosocialist, regarded by many socialists as a principal – or the principal – founder of modern prosocialist thought, and to suggest that the authority of Marx may not be invoked to bar such a view, but that, on the contrary, Marx's own scholarly thought moved along similar lines. More important, however, it is to acquit one's responsibility to the thought of others, that is, to give credit to another thinker where it is due, as it is here, and to acknowledge one's intellectual debt, especially in a case like this, where the thinker, Marx, may be considered to have been both exemplarily pioneering and astutely incisive. Ultimately, however, the only authority properly to be invoked is that of sustained inquiry disciplined by reason.

tions. Corporate Liberalism, the prevalent outlook in the nation's politics, as it evolved from Theodore Roosevelt's "Square Deal" to Wilson's "New Freedom," to Hoover's "New Era," to Franklin D. Roosevelt's "New Deal" and beyond, gave expression to the evolving mix – or codevelopment – of capitalism and socialism in society at large.

The 1920s witnessed the quickening of the tempo of codevelopment, as corporate capitalism began its passage from accumulation to disaccumulation in goods production – both agricultural and industrial – that is, the passage from rising to declining requirements of labor-time as the condition of growing productivity in goods-production spheres, thereby releasing more and more people from traditional labor tasks for new kinds of labor in human services, the professions, and the arts, in both governmental and nongovernmental sectors. (See Chapter V of this book.)

If the depression of the 1890s was the last great crisis of the industrializing competitive-capitalist order, issuing in the corporate reconstruction of capitalism, the great depression of the 1930s was the first great crisis (and so far, the last) of the corporate-capitalist order, issuing in qualitatively new departures in government involvement in market relations, the first firm founding of the "welfare state," and the coming-of-age of trade unions and workers' power in both market relations and the nation's major party politics. It was the disaccumulation process, requiring massive shifts in capital and labor from goods production to other spheres for the resumption of high or full employment, and the complex sociopolitical, legal, intellectual, and cultural changes and conflicts that needed to be transacted in the eventual making of those shifts – not tariff, monetary, or fiscal policies as such – that explain the depth and longevity of the depression of the 1930s. The depression was so deep and long in the United States, more so than in other industrial societies, precisely because the United States was the society most advanced in the transition from industrial to "postindustrial" society, presided over by the codevelopment of capitalism and socialism in a nonstatist political environment, (See Chapters II, V, and VII of this book.)

Whatever our ethical preferences or ideological predispositions, nevertheless, in the history of the twentieth century, capitalism and socialism have not excluded each other in the developmental process, but have needed and embraced each other, both within markets and outside them, both within government and outside it, both within nations and among them. Other potent forces in shaping the twentieth century there have been: nationalism, imperialism, anti-imperialism, militarism, totalitarianism, liberalism, populism, racism and the struggles against it, religion, feminism, applied science and technology, and so on, but each of these has had to adapt to, and operate as modifying components of, or influences on, capitalism and socialism. The latter two terms are convenient abbreviations in referring to complex matters. It is not as if, here stands society like an impassive geophysical mass, and then along come these external "forces," like storms hurling themselves upon and remolding the inanimate terrain. Rather, the terms capitalism and socialism signify the characteristic ways in which people within an industrializing society like that of the United States have organized and reorganized, or sought to organize and reorganize, their political-economic activity, including their class relations, and have expressed their prevalent sociopolitical ideas, theories, values, and ideological propensities.

Like other societies undergoing industrialization and the passage to a postindustrial condition, the United States has been decisively shaped by the two great "forces" of the modern world – capitalism and socialism. No industrializing society has been able to avoid either of these "forces." The United States – in all its wondrous uniqueness – has been no exception.

II

Studying American political development in the Progressive Era, 1890s–1916

Today the questions that are uppermost, and that will become increasingly important, are not so much political as economic questions. The age of machinery, of the factory system, is also the age of socialistic inquiry.
To me it seems that we are approaching a pivotal point in our country's history.

Frederick Jackson Turner, 1891

The present finds itself engaged in the task of readjusting its old ideals to new conditions and is turning increasingly to government to preserve its traditional democracy. It is not surprising that socialism shows noteworthy gains as elections continue.

Frederick Jackson Turner, 1911

Sometimes when I am asked to define myself, I say that I am a socialist-anarchist-communist-individualist-collectivist-cooperative-aristocratic-democrat, for . . . the very complicated thing we call society is rolling forward along all these lines simultaneously.

Henry Demarest Lloyd, ca.1900

In keeping with the social character of the advancement of knowledge, and in spite of a strong competitive impulse among scholars to magnify small differences into warring schools of thought, the leading historical writings in the past four decades have yielded substantial agreement on the identification of critical trends that were transforming U.S. society in the period of the 1890s to 1916. Implicitly, at least, they may well have been anticipating the way to resolving some latest of these small differences before they get too far out of hand, such as that between "social history" and "political history" and, in a variation upon the theme,

The Fall 1991 issue of the journal *Studies in American Political Development* includes this essay essentially as it appears here, except that the version the journal is publishing includes the paragraphs that now make up Section 1 of Chapter 1 of this book.

that between "society-centered" (or "movement-centered" or "interest-centered") and "state-centered" history. The common acknowledgment of critical trends has served newcomers and veterans alike, including partisans on either side of these differences, and historians in the various genres, in the selection of authoritative frameworks of continuing research into the period. In this respect, the historical discipline shares with other disciplines, including those in the physical sciences, attributes held to be common to a "normal science."[1]

The consensus on critical trends reinforces the longer-held, if more general, agreement among scholars that the 1890s marked a turning point in the nation's history, that developments thenceforward to World War I made U.S. society into something significantly different from what it had been before the 1890s, and that accordingly, the years from the 1890s to 1916 marked a distinct period in American history.[2] The period may be stretched back several years before 1890 and forward beyond 1916, although before 1890 many of the formative trends had remained latent, and without the developments in the period proper the subsequent shape of U.S. society is hardly conceivable. It may, therefore, be taken as generally agreed upon as well that the events of the period 1890s–1916 were directly formative – a birth time – of basic institutions and social relations of twentieth-century U.S. society as it evolved toward midcentury.

Long-term trends generally recognized as having distinctively emerged in the period occurred in those areas historians and social scientists widely agree upon as constituting basic social relations, institutions, out-

1. Concerning political-history/social-history schools, see, e.g., William E. Leuchtenburg, "The Pertinence of Political History: Reflections on the Significance of the State in America," *Journal of American History*, 73:3 (December 1986), pp. 585–600, and the works cited in Leuchtenburg's notes. For discussion of the concept "normal science" and its antecedents, see Thomas S. Kuhn, *The Structure of Scientific Revolutions* (Chicago: University of Chicago Press, 1962), also published as Vol. II, No. 2 of the *International Encyclopedia of Unified Science* by the University of Chicago Press. One need not subscribe to Kuhn's theory in its entirety or in general to acknowledge the cogency and value of the concept of "normal science" in the sense suggested by Kuhn (although not necessarily original with him) and as used here.
2. Samuel P. Hays's statement is representative: "In foreign as well as in domestic affairs . . . , the decade of the 1890s was a dividing point in American history, separating the old from the new and setting a pattern for much of the future." *The Response to Industrialism: 1885–1914* (Chicago: University of Chicago Press, 1957; 1973 paper ed.), p. 192. For broad cultural, intellectual, and governmental spheres, in addition to the technoeconomic sphere, cf., e.g., Henry F. May, *The End of American Innocence: A Study of the First Years of Our Own Time, 1912–1917* (1959; New York: Oxford University Press, 1979); Henry Steele Commager, *The American Mind* (New Haven, Conn.: Yale University Press, 1950), pp. 41–54; Peter Conn, *The Divided Mind: Ideology and Imagination in America, 1898–1917* (Cambridge: Cambridge University Press, 1983), pp. 1–17; Stephen Skowronek, *Building a New American State* (Cambridge: Cambridge University Press, 1982), pp. 3–5.

looks, and movements of twentieth-century U.S. society. Among these trends, the more salient included the following:

The emergence of the large corporation as the dominant form of business organization and the establishment of central banking (the Federal Reserve System), which together constituted the basic structural framework of the economy in its subsequent development.

An intensification of the long-term trend away from localism in markets, political power, and social identities, and toward intercity, intersectional, and national and international associations and identities.

A significant extension of the role of the federal government in regulating market relations, with a noticeable shifting of initiative, power, and prestige from the legislative to the executive branch and its administrative agencies.

The accelerated introduction and spread of bureaucratic standards and forms of organization not only in private industry but also in the federal executive departments, in the armed forces, and in state and local governments.

The beginnings of the adaptation of agriculture, via farmers' cooperatives and regulatory and banking legislation, to administered market structures, correlated with an increasing ideological accommodation of farmers to the corporate-capitalist economic order.

The definitive adaptation of work to mass production and mass distribution technique, and a corresponding adaptation of the labor movement to an ascendant collective-bargaining outlook as against opposition in principle to the wages system.

The emergence of modern woman-suffrage and feminist movements and modes of thought.

The emergence of the major integrationist, separatist, nationalist, and urbanizing trends in modern African-American political, social, and cultural movements.

The incipience of social work and "welfare-state" reform movements across class, gender, and political lines.

The rise of modern socialist and social-democratic movements.

The emergence of modern trends in transportation, communications, and the arts.

The emergence, in critical mass and social significance, of a "new middle class" of independent and salaried professionals and technicians, employed in both the private and public sectors.

The emergence of the modern university, with specialized graduate schools oriented to the training of the new professionals and technicians.

The assumption by the U.S. government of new roles and alignments in the international economy and world politics, which proved to exert an enduring impact on the nation's subsequent domestic and foreign relations alike.

1. Periodization and the Progressive Era

However much amended in detail, this list of trends or one essentially similar would elicit broad assent as indicating a scholarly consensus on the distinctiveness of the period of the 1890s to 1916, and on the major developments that constitute its distinctiveness. Indeed, even in a matter that touches upon impassioned partisan sensibilities, works of widely different political and philosophical outlooks have established the view beyond serious dispute that support for, and opposition to, most of the legislated reforms of the Progressive Era did not simply correlate with a division between anti–big business (or antibusiness) and pro–big business (or probusiness) movements, outlooks, or sentiments, nor with such divisions as capital versus labor, metropolis versus countryside, or "the interests" versus "the people."

The greater knowledge of the period in its parts, however, and the widespread agreement on its several trends, have yielded an embarrassment of scholarly riches that has dissolved older and more recent crystal clarities alike in a consensual acid of new facts, analyses, and skeptical second thoughts. Among the older periodizing efforts, the term "Progressive Era" no longer conveys a concept of interpretive precision. Nor does "Progressive Movement." Similarly, terms like the "Rise of Finance Capital," the "Money Trust," "Monopoly Capital," and "Imperialism" (the "Highest Stage of Capitalism"), long ago lost their power convincingly to designate a comprehensive periodizing concept, and in any case, such terms too readily conjured up, or became entangled with, simplistic diabolus-ex-machina models of explanation. Terms like the Square Deal, the New Nationalism, and the New Freedom, though inspirational contemporary shibboleths, can no more suggest a conceptual framework of inquiry than similar terms applied to subsequent times, like the New Era, the Age of Normalcy, the New Deal, the Fair Deal, the New Frontier, or the New Beginning.

Among the more compelling periodizing terms of more recent vintage, the contrapuntal "Triumph of Conservatism" invites conflicting as well as shifting meanings, and in either case it is vulnerable to ideological or presentist bias. As prevalently conveyed, the idea embedded in the term tends to equate Conservatism with Business (Big Business, the Interests,

Entrepreneurs), and Liberalism, or Radicalism, or "Social Movements," or "Social (Good) Reform," with the People – farmers, workers, small proprietors, and other designated vessels of virtue – and hence with the Common Good or the General Welfare. However fervently one would wish it were true, this is a dichotomy that fails too many empirical tests, that makes it impossible to understand U.S. history in general and the Progressive Era in particular, and that historical writings by the late 1950s and early 1960s had already brought seriously into question, if not utterly invalidated, and that writings since have not rehabilitated.[3] In addition, to characterize the era as one of ascendant conservatism when it was filled with so much change and reform, heading both to the right and to the left, may serve more as a provocative opinion inciting fruitful discussion and thought than as an analytical or synthetic conception suited to guiding research and reflective generalization.

In the sense that reforms, singly or together, may not properly be considered revolutionary in direct tendency or effect, and may therefore be considered to have been "conservative," the reform-liberalism of the

3. E.g., Louis Hartz, *The Liberal Tradition in American* (New York: Harcourt, Brace & World, 1955); Richard Hofstadter, *The Age of Reform* (New York: Vintage Brooks, 1955); Hays, *Response* (1957); Robert H. Wiebe, "Business Disunity and the Progressive Movement, 1901–1914," *Mississippi Valley Historical Review*, XLIV:4 (March 1958), pp. 664–685; Wiebe, "The House of Morgan and the Executive, 1905–1913," *American Historical Review*, LXV:1 (October 1959), pp. 49–60; Hays, *Conservation and the Gospel Efficiency: The Progressive Conservation Movement, 1890–1920* (Cambridge, Mass.: Harvard University Press, 1959); Martin J. Sklar, "Woodrow Wilson and the Political Economy of Modern United States Liberalism," *Studies on the Left*, I:3 (Fall 1960), pp. 17–47; William A. Williams, *The Contours of American History* (Cleveland: World, 1961), pp. 345–438; James Weinstein, "Organized Business and the City Commission and Manager Movements," *Journal of Southern History*, XXVIII:2 (May 1962), pp. 166–182; Wiebe, *Businessmen and Reform: A Study of the Progressive Movement* (Cambridge, Mass.: Harvard University Press, 1962); Samuel Haber, *Efficiency and Uplift: Scientific Management in the Progressive Era, 1890–1920* (Chicago: University of Chicago Press, 1964); Hays, "The Politics of Reform in Municipal Government in the Progressive Era," *Pacific Northwest Quarterly*, LV:4 (October 1964), pp. 157–169. For "Triumph of Conservatism" and "Political Capitalism" (the latter discussed later in this chapter), as interpretive concepts, see Gabriel Kolko, *The Triumph of Conservatism: A Reinterpretation of American History, 1990–1916* (New York: The Free Press of Glencoe, 1963), pp. 1–10, 279–305. For "Organizational Society" (discussed later in this chapter), see note 19. Let it be noted here that in discussing certain terms that also serve as titles of works or lending thematic terms therein, I do not assume a necessary equation between the ideas I am treating and the precise beliefs of the authors of the works. I am concerned with these concepts and their use and impact in scholarly writings, teachings, and discussions, which may or may not accord with the meaning intended by authors whose works may be associated with the terms or concepts. I wish also to emphasize that criticism of the terms and concepts in question is in no way meant to detract from the great value of the associated works; on the contrary, the importance of the works in extending and deepening our historical understanding is evidenced by our continuing interest in critically deliberating over the works' leading terms or concepts.

Progressive Era may be judged to have been "conservative." But changes short of revolution are not necessarily best understood as conservative. To think that they are is a philosophical, or ideological, judgment of a different order from the term's application to historically specific political movements and political events, which in empirical outcome portend or yield circumstances inconsistent with conserving those of the established past or present. Indeed, in the philosophical sense, radical or revolutionary movements themselves may be cogently discerned as profoundly conservative in certain fundamental respects – for example, in the yeai....ng for a real or supposed lost community, for economic order and social stability, for public morality and consensual authority. Recent events in the Soviet Union, Eastern Europe, China, Cuba, Iran, and elsewhere would seem to corroborate this formulation.

The conceptions embedded in such continuingly current terms as "Age of Reform" (or a variant like "Social Forces" or "Social Movements"), "Businessmen and Reform," "Response to Industrialism," "Search for Order," "Political Capitalism," and "Organizational Society," convey meanings that either can not be held peculiar to a period generally agreed to have been distinctive, or fail to encompass critical components of the distinctive trends. For example, many periods of U.S. history, involving as it does a society undergoing incessant capitalist development, and thus continuous change, and having responsive representative political institutions, may be fairly described as ages of reform, driven by "social forces" or "social movements." Such change, moreover, in most cases either being bourgeois in character or including among its formulators and advocates people of bourgeois sensibility or interest, very little change or reform can be pointed to in U.S. history with which "businessmen" – including capitalists or entrepreneurs – were not intimately involved. The idea that there is something unusual about capitalists or business interests being associated with, or divided over, reforms, and that if capitalists favor a measure or a change it is necessarily something less than reform, or if it is a reform, then an anomaly, is one that is strongly represented in the American political culture, especially in some of its populistic, or professedly radical, strands, but it is not empirically well founded. To the extent that American historians and social scientists indulge such an idea, they would seem to be offering corroboration of Louis Hartz's criticism that they tend more to replicate than to explicate American political history.

On the other hand, changing status and rising status anxiety among upper and middle social strata, a concept associated with a seminal variant of the Age of Reform idea, may be and has been readily applied to several periods in U.S. history; so with a drive for economic or social efficiency; so with movements for social justice. Similarly, a "search for order" can be detected as a major theme in various periods of U.S. history, all the more so as various periods have also been ones of significant change. A "response to industrialism" may be said to characterize not only late nineteenth- and early twentieth-century U.S. history, but also a good portion of antebellum U.S. history, in both North and South.

"Political Capitalism" and "Organizational Society" equate the rising importance of bureaucratic structures in both the private and public sectors and their increasingly intricate intersecting, with "political" and "organizational," respectively. On the one hand, however, bureaucratization and administration by executive or independent commissions or agencies may be better understood as oriented to *de*politicization, in the sense of removing the determination of decisions from the sphere of party, electoral, or legislative politics, while precorporate capitalism, and the market itself, can not be described as anything but political throughout U.S. history, in their relation to government, the law, party politics, and ideology. Among the purposes professed by some of those favoring greater government regulation of the market, in the Progressive Era, one of the more prominent was precisely that of taking issues of economic relations "out of politics." This is not to say that capitalism became less political than before, only that it was no more political than before, however much national politics and the capitalist political economy were indeed changing. On the other hand, nonindustrial, noncorporate capitalist, or nonbureaucratic, society – nonmodern (or traditionalist) society all the more so – may be very highly organized. Bureaucratization is simply one form of social organization, and by no means necessarily the most complex or totalistic. In many ways, moreover, the rise of corporate capitalism and bureaucratic economic, administrative, and governmental structures in the United States has permitted individuals to be subject to less overt organizational affiliation or constraint than in earlier or other forms of society. Under some historical circumstances, at least, bureaucratization may release, or may be associated with, strong tendencies toward *dis*organization, and at any rate, may go hand in hand with rising individualization, privatization, or depoliticization of social life.

In recent years, studies of workers, farmers, immigrants, African-Americans, women, professionals, and reformers, and their associated intellectual, political, and cultural trends and social movements, have emphasized and greatly enriched our knowledge of the role that these people, trends, or movements played in the shaping of U.S. history in the late nineteenth and early twentieth century, but such studies as yet have offered no distinctive periodization concepts beyond those indicated above; they essentially tell their stories within the framework of one of the established or disestablished concepts, or some mixture of them.[4]

Within this social history genre, as it is called by many of its eminent practitioners, there is a supposition, gaining currency especially among historians professing to be "radical," or "on the left," that distinguishes "elite history" from "people's history" or "movement history." But movements and leaders among workers, women, African-Americans, "radicals," farmers, and such others, no less involve elites (and ranks-and-files) than those among capitalists, high-ranking politicians, government officials, "conservatives," racists, and such others. The tendency on the part of these historians is to confuse "elite" with questions of class, hierarchy, authority, and power, and in large part to disdain, denounce, or renounce these aspects of relations among people, but to ignore historically analyzing or studying them, on the grounds that they wish to avoid "elite history," or that they are seeking an alternative to it. Aside from their attaining neither an avoidance nor an alternative, however, their ignoring a large, not to say a critical, range of the empirical record,

4. Occupation, sex, race, nationality, religious denomination, or ethnicity will affect our understanding of periodization with corresponding dimensions of inquiry and meaning, but so far none per se nor some combination of them constitutes or represents itself as an adequate periodization concept. Rather than supply the reader here with what would amount to a considerably extensive bibliographical note, with the embarrassing hazard of neglecting one title or another, let me instead cite the following works and symposia, including their extensive notes, as good guides to the most recent literature (as well as some of the older) in the fields mentioned in the text: Daniel T. Rogers, "In Search of Progressivism," in Stanley I. Kutler and Stanley N. Katz, eds., *The Promise of American History: Progress and Prospects* (Baltimore: The Johns Hopkins University Press, 1982), pp. 113–132; "A Round Table: Labor, Historical Pessimism, and Hegemony," *Journal of American History*, 75:1 (June 1988), pp. 115–161; J. Carroll Moody and Alice Kessler-Harris, eds., *Perspectives on American Labor History: The Problems of Synthesis* (DeKalb: Northern Illinois University Press, 1990), with a useful introduction by Moody, and essays by Leon Fink, Michael Reich, Mari Jo Buhle, Sean Wilents, Alan Dawley, David Brody, and Kessler-Harris; Karen Orren, "Organized Labor and the Invention of Modern Liberalism in the United States," *Studies in American Political Development*, 2 (1987), pp. 317–336; Lawrence Goodwyn, *The Democratic Promise* (New York: Oxford University Press, 1976); James Green, *Grassroots Socialism* (Baton Rouge: Louisiana State University, 1978); Steven Hahn, *The Roots of Southern Populism* (New York: Oxford University Press, 1983); Norman Pollack, *The Just Polity* (Urbana: University of Illinois Press, 1987); Linda K. Kerber, "Separate Spheres, Female Worlds, Woman's Place: The Rhetoric of Women's History," *Journal of American History*, 75:1 (June 1988), pp. 9–39; Ellen C. DuBois, "Working Women, Class Relations, and Suffrage Militance: Harriot Stanton Blatch and the New York Suffrage Movement, 1894–1909," *Journal of American History*, 74:1 (June 1987), pp. 34–58; John Hope Franklin, "Afro-American History: State of the Art," *Journal of American History*, 75:1 (June 1988), pp. 162–173; "Perspectives: The Strange Career of Jim Crow," *Journal of American History*, 75:3 (December 1988), pp. 841–868; "A Round Table: Synthesis in American History," *Journal of American History*, 74:1 (June 1987), pp. 107–130.

seems inconsistent with sound historical method, however noble one may regard their motivating sentiment.

The older and newer terms, and their underlying concepts, though still useful for many purposes of inquiry, and the differences of the new knowledge from the old, though destructive of familiar certainties, may nevertheless point to the reaffirmation of a comprehensive and objective periodizing conception for U.S. history in the years 1890s–1916. For the older and newer work taken together suggests thoughts about periodization that may be of aid in the specific problem at hand.

2. Modernization: Common ground of classical and postclassical thought

In accordance with the strong interdisciplinary trend in recent times among historians in search of sound interpretive frameworks, theoretical conceptions about the historical evolution of U.S. society have shifted from idea clusters peculiar to U.S. political history to concepts derived from the social sciences and applicable in principle to inquiry into various societies. Insofar as it represents a trend away from parochialism or ethnocentrism, or a doctrinaire "American exceptionalism," this shift is unobjectionable, even salutary, although it displays a tendency toward abstraction from concrete characteristics of American historical experience, to which at least in part the social history genre is a response, and a healthy one certainly in intent, if not always in execution. Hence, in the above listing of periodizing terms that historians have applied to the pre–World War I era, one may note in recent scholarship a trend away from the use of "Americanist" terms like "Progressivism" and "New Freedom" to terms like "Industrialism," "Modern," and "Organization." A parallel trend has taken hold among historians of other periods of U.S. history, most notably the colonial, early national, and Civil War eras. By and large, this trend of interpretation, unquestionably the most dynamic, influential, rich in results, and still prevalent, has drawn heavily upon social science modernization theory.[5]

5. The historical literature along these lines on U.S. history from colonial times through the Civil War era is by now legion. The trend-setting works include Richard L. Bushman, *From Puritan to Yankee: Character and Social Order in Connecticut, 1690–1765* (Cambridge, Mass.: Harvard University Press, 1967); Richard D. Brown, *Modernization: The Transformation of American Life, 1600–1865* (New York: Hill & Wang, 1976); Ralph Lerner, "Commerce and Character: The Anglo-American as New-Model Man," *William & Mary Quarterly*, ed Series, XXXVI:1 (January 1979), pp. 3–26; Jack P. Greene, "The Social Origins of the American Revolution: An Evaluation and an Interpretation," *Political Science Quarterly*, LXXXVIII:1 (March 1973), pp. 1–22; Kenneth A. Lockridge, "Social Change and the Meaning of the American Revolution," *Journal of Social History*, VI:4 (Summer 1973), pp. 403–439;

46   *The United States as a developing country*

The application of modernization theory to the late nineteenth- and early twentieth-century period preceded, at least in its exerting a decisive impact, its application to other periods of U.S. history.[6] It can be found, for example, in Richard Hofstadter's *The Age of Reform* (1953), Samuel P. Hays's *The Response to Industrialism* (1957), and his essay, "The Social Analysis of American Political History, 1880–1920" (1965), William A. Williams's *The Contours of American History* (1961), Alfred D. Chandler, Jr.'s "The Beginnings of 'Big Business' in American Industry" (1959), and his subsequent works, and Robert H. Wiebe's *Businessmen and Reform* (1962) and his *The Search for Order* (1967).[7] The

Leonard P. Curry, *Blueprint for Modern America: Non-Military Legislation of the First Civil War Congress* (Nashville: Vanderbilt University Press, 1968); Raimondo Luraghi, "The Civil War and the Modernization of American Society: Social Structure and Industrial Revolution in the Old South before and during the War," *Civil War History*, XVIII:3 (September 1972), pp. 230–250; Eric Foner, "The Causes of the American Civil War: Recent Interpretations and New Directions," *Civil War History*, XX:3 (September 1974), pp. 197–214; James M. McPherson, *Ordeal by Fire: The Civil War and Reconstruction* (New York: Alfred A. Knopf, 1982), esp. ch. 1: "American Modernization, 1800–1860," pp. 5–22.

6. Perhaps the first sustained application to U.S. history of social theory oriented to development or modernization came with studies in nineteenth-century sectional conflict as distinct from studies of specific time periods as such. For example, the issue of the *Journal of Economic History*, XVI:4 (December 1956), devoted to "The American West as an Undeveloped Region" (and it also includes materials on the South as an undeveloped region). It may be no exaggeration to say that it began with Turner: "The problem of the West is nothing less than the problem of American development. . . . The West, at bottom, is a form of society, rather than an area." "The Problem of the West," reprinted from *Atlantic Monthly*, LXXVIII (September 1896), pp. 289–297, at Billington, ed., *Frontier and Section*, p. 63. Indeed, it is plausible to believe that Turner is better understood as an historian of development, as it applies to societies in general, than as an historian of a "Frontier" peculiar to the United States. For this and discussion of a similar outlook of Woodrow Wilson, closely associated with that of Turner, see Martin J. Sklar, *The Corporate Reconstruction of American Capitalism, 1890–1916: The Market, the Law, and Politics* (Cambridge: Cambridge University Press, 1988), pp. 383–392. Cf. Lee Benson's essay on Turner in his *Turner and Beard* (Glencoe, Ill,: Free Press of Glencoe, 1960).

7. Williams is probably the first U.S. historian to apply in a systematic conceptual manner key elements of both classical and postclassical social-science modernization theory to the sweep of U.S. history both in its domestic and foreign relations. See, as well as the works themselves, his acknowledgments in *The Tragedy of American Diplomacy* (Cleveland: World., 1959), pp. 217–219, and in *The Contours of American History* (Cleveland: World, 1961), pp. 493, 495–496. His attention to the relevance of social theory to the study and teaching of U.S. history, including the sociology of knowledge and theory of modernization, development, and bureaucracy, which subsequently became *de rigueur* among many historians in the 1960s and 1970s, was markedly evident in his lectures at the University of Wisconsin, Madison, in the late 1950s. In this connection, the impact of Hans Gerth on young intellectuals like Williams, C. Wright Mills, Warren Susman, Herbert Gutman, and Gabriel Kolko, and through them on U.S. historical, social, and political studies, in his lectures and seminars in the Department of Sociology at the University of Wisconsin, in the 1940s and 1950s, can not be overstated. A similar impact by Fred Harvey Harrington may also be noted, especially with respect to the reinterpretation of U.S. foreign relations and understanding U.S.

broad-ranging application of modernization theory to the period of the 1890s to 1916, prior to its similar application to other periods, should come as little surprise: A rich culmination of classical social theory, centered upon defining "modern civilization," or "modern society," emerged around the turn of the century, and many of its basic elements can be found, empirically, in the thought of leading *personae dramatis* of American intellect and politics in the period.

The essential elements prominent in recent modernization theory can be traced back to David Hume and Adam Smith and to the rationalist legacy upon which they drew, to such Americans as Benjamin Franklin, Tom Paine, John Adams, James Madison, Alexander Hamilton, and Albert Gallatin, although they are less routinely admitted to the social-theory pantheon than they deserve to be[8]; to such early- and mid –

history in the larger context of world history. Williams was one of Harrington's graduate students, as were later such prominent "revisionist" historians as Lloyd Gardner, Walter LaFeber, Thomas McCormick, and Carl Parrini. See Williams's acknowledgments in *Contours*, p. 490; and his commentary on the sources of his own thinking in "The Confessions of an Intransigent Revisionist," *Socialist Revolution*, III:5 (September-October 1973), pp. 87–98. C. Wright Mills's close relation to Gerth – he had been Gerth's graduate student at Wisconsin – is perhaps better known. Louis Hartz may also be noted here as among the first to apply systematically the theoretical concept of the bourgeois society-type to the interpretation of the history of prevalent American political thought: *The Liberal Tradition in America: An Interpretation of American Political Thought since the Revolution* (New York: Harcourt, Brace & World, 1955); see also Hartz et al., *The Founding of New Societies* (New York: Harcourt, Brace & World, 1964), chs. 1–4, pp. 3–122. The tendency to label Hartz a "consensus" histsorian has obscured the significance of his work. Earlier, Richard Hofstadter drew upon the concept of the bourgeois society-type decisively, though less systematically, in *The American Political Tradition* (New York: Alfred A. Knopf, 1948). Williams was indebted to Hartz and Hofstadter, and the three were indebted to Turner, Beard, and Parrington, and although less explicitly apparent, to Lewis Mumford and Van Wyck Brooks and other "Young Intellectuals"of the 1920s. Cf. Chapter V of the present book, esp. Section 4.

8. Thomas Jefferson should be included here. But in Jefferson's thought may be discerned an intense conflict between preindustrial (or nondevelopmental) and industrial (or developmental) bourgeois values, which he never resolved to his own satisfaction. As a policymaker, however, he rather consistently supported proindustrializing (or prodevelopment) policies. This was not necessarily, and probably not in fact, a matter of hypocrisy: His inconsistency flowed from an intense and honest perplexity. Of Jefferson it might be said that in his personal preferences, he was an apostle of arrested development, or arrested modernization. Cf. Daniel J. Boorstin, *The Lost World of Thomas Jefferson* (Boston: Beacon Press, 1948), esp. p. 241, concerning Jeffersonian futurism. See also Talcott Parsons's assessment of "the Jeffersonian picture of a system of economic production consisting mainly of small farmers and artisans, with presumably a small mercantile class mediating between them and consumers": "Clearly this is not a situation compatible with high industrial development. . . . First, the order of decentralization of production where the standard unit is a family-size one is incompatible with either the organization or the technology necessary for high industrialism. Second, the 'Jeffersonian' economy is not one in which economic production is differentiated from other social functions in specialized organizations; instead, the typical productive unit is at the same time a kinship unit and a unit of citizenship in the

nineteenth-century thinkers as Jeremy Bentham, St.-Simon, Auguste Comte, Herbert Spencer, John Stuart Mill, Henry Maine, Walter Bagehot, and Karl Marx; and to the galaxy of historical-sociological thinkers in the later nineteenth and early twentieth centuries, such as Werner Sombart, Emile Durkheim, Ferdinand Tönnies, and Max Weber in Europe, and William Graham Sumner, Lewis Henry Morgan, Lester F. Ward, Brooks Adams, and Thorstein Veblen in the United States, to name only a few.

The many philosophical differences, some fundamental, among these thinkers, make the common ground of their discourse all the more significant. Whether ostensibly in advocacy, criticism, or dispassioned analysis, and whether from a standpoint of natural-law, evolutionary, or institutional premises, the developing body of thought associated with these thinkers converged upon the attempt to define the type of society and the corresponding modes of consciousness that had been emerging and evolving since about the sixteenth century (perhaps earlier) in Britain, Western Europe, and the Anglo-American New World, and to distinguish the emergent society from past society and from other current societies of different types. These thinkers were, in effect, periodizing Western societies as representing "modern" civilization, in contrast with "premodern," "medieval," or "traditional," societies.

The common ground extended, moreover, to the substance of the definition or periodization. With terminological differences, though less than might be expected over so long a period of great social change, their works disclose a comprehension of Western society, insofar as it was modern or becoming so, as a market society, capitalist in its political-economy and bourgeois in its ascendant values or broad culture. That is, they disclosed a type of society in which, over time, the following characteristics were becoming or became dominant:

Land, goods, property rights in general and, of critical importance, labor-power, became freely salable or mobile, and subject to diminishing restraint from religion, custom, or other prescriptive norms. Market and contractual relations displaced kinship, communal, and older status relations as the paramount mode of social organization. A market-directed division of labor generated both specialization of function and complex patterns of integration in the sphere of production and exchange, as well as in the sphere of politics and government. As national and international markets superseded local markets, and as urban-industrial life increasingly dominated rural-agricultural life, nation-states promulgating uniform codes of law supplanted localistic or loosely federated governing

community." Parsons, "The Distribution of Power in American Society," *World Politics*, X:1 (October 1957), pp. 123–143, at p. 129.

authority. Class distinctions based upon relations to property in the market displaced status by birth or title and created new status orders. Social relations devoted to production and exchange of goods and services, and to the accumulation and reinvestment of surpluses, resulting in rising productivity and sustained economic growth, increasingly subordinated and significantly modified all other social relations. Future-oriented pursuit of individual self-interest, defined in terms of economic efficiency or the maximization of value (utility) in exchange relations, supplanted other standards of emulative behavior. The obligatory use of money (the "cash nexus") permeated society as the means of exchange, the measure of value, the instrument of income allocation, and the legal claim upon employment of labor and other assets. A stable monetary and banking system assumed importance in securing and extending the predictability necessary to a calculable pursuit of self-interest in the market, and became essential to the development of credit instruments that further facilitated specialization, market integration, and accelerated economic growth. Capitalists, as the owners of productive property, employers of wage-labor, managers of the functions of investment, production, and exchange, and carriers of the new attitudes of self-interest in the production, accumulation, and disposal of wealth, displaced the landed aristocracy and clergy in the exercise of the dominant economic and moral authority in society. The law and statecraft increasingly conformed to the norms and requirements of the market and capitalist property relations, whatever the particular form of government and whatever the social origin of the elites presiding in government office. Forms of consciousness corresponding with market relations attained ascendancy over older ones, with worldly religious, secular, instrumental, self-interested, and economic modes of thought, infused with a technoscientific outlook, displacing other-worldly, sacred, customary, and traditionally prescriptive modes of thought. Personality or character traits and values changed accordingly, with reinforcement by education, emulative standards, and the law. All these developments tended to become interrelated and, whether in severe conflict or mutual support, to generate relatively rapid change.

Eighteenth-century thinkers like Hume and Smith evoked the market society in its preindustrial and early industrial stage (those like Burke evoked it with deep critical reservations); nineteenth-century thinkers like Mill and Marx in its midindustrial stage; late nineteenth- and early twentieth-century thinkers like Weber and Veblen in its transition from the proprietary-competitive stage to its large bureaucratic, administered, or corporate, stage.[9] As E. A. Wrigley concluded, with respect to the

9. For Weber's conception of the intimate relation between modern bureaucracy and

general historical process of modernization and industrialization in the western world, and its salient components, "Smith, Marx, Weber, and many lesser men are in substantial agreement here although their descriptive vocabularies differ."[10]

Modernization theory of more recent social-science vintage has produced many new insights and perspectives on past and present, including a salutary elaboration of the behavioral, intellectual, psychological, cultural, and administrative concomitants of economic development. Its achievements in these respects go far to explain its power of attraction. But as this theory touches nineteenth- and twentieth-century history of the political economy, broad social relations, prevalent modes of consciousness, and governmental structure and policies of the industrial-capitalist societies of the Western world, it has added little in principle to the basic conceptions of modernization and development as they had evolved from Smith's time to Weber's. The major difference lies in the tendency to celebrate what some of the classical theorists viewed with critical ambivalence, and to replace socially textured and historically situated concepts and terms with those of a more abstractly evolutionary and functionalist character that carry a greater implication of universal

capitalism, see Max Weber, *Economy and Society: An Outline of Interpretive Sociology*, ed. Guenther Roth and Claus Wittich (New York: Bedminster Press, 1968), Vol. III, ch. XI, "Bureaucracy," pp. 956–1005, esp. pp. 963–975; see also Weber, *The Theory of Social and Economic Organization*, tr. A. M. Henderson and Talcott Parsons, ed. T. Parsons (New York: Free Press, 1964; originally published in German, 1925), pp. 168–202, 246–250. Weber regarded a developed money economy as a precondition of an enduring, fully articulated bureaucratic organization of social relations on a broad scale; he designated the capitalist corporation (not organs of the state) as representing the ideal type of bureaucracy. Cf. Robert A. Brady, *Organization, Automation, and Society: The Scientific Revolution in Industry* (Berkeley: University of California Press, 1961), p. 415: "Long ago, Max Weber made it clear that the generalization of bureaucracy throughout modern society was engendered by the rise of capitalist enterprise...." Also, Maurice Zeitlin, "Corporate Ownership and Control: The Large Corporation and the Capitalist Class," *American Journal of Sociology*, LXXIX:5 (March 1974), pp. 1077–1078, 1114–1115. EMILE DURKHEIM, in his 1902 Preface to the Second Edition of *The Division of Labor in Society* (1893), judged the corporation to be the logical outcome of the development of national and international market relations, and hence the basic form of social organization in modern societies,; he went so far as to predict, and also to recommend, its becoming the basic representative unit of government. Durkheim, *The Division of Labor in Society*, tr. George Simpson (Glencoe, Ill.: The Free Press of Glencoe, 1964), pp. 1–31, esp. pp. 3, 4, 24, 27.

10. E. A. Wrigley, "The Process of Modernization and the Industrial Revolution in England," *Journal of Interdisciplinary History*, III:2 (Autumn 1972), p. 244, also pp. 228–229. For a comparative study of differences and similarities in the thought of Marx, Durkheim, and Weber, emphasizing the historical approach of each to the study of society and to the study of capitalist society in particular, see Anthony Giddens, *Capitalism and Modern Social Theory: An Analysis of the Writings of Marx, Durkheim, and Max Weber* (Cambridge: Cambridge University Press, 1971), pp. xi–xvi, 185–247.

validity. In the process, universal natural-law concepts gave way to utilitarian principles, then to the more ethnocentric idea of "westernization," and then back to a different order of universal terms rooted in evolutionary positivism, rather than either the old natural law or utilitarianism, terms such as "industrialization," "modernization," and "development."[11]

Accordingly, what in earlier terms had been class became, in postclassical thought, function or role. Capitalist became executive, manager, goal-integrator, or purpose-defining leader. Capital and wage-labor became factors of production. Division of labor became functional specialization displacing traditionalist functional diffusion. Capital- and labor-mobility or immobility became inclination or aversion to change or achievement. Proletarianization became an aspect of functional specialization and demography. Market activity, profit-making, and pecuniary pursuit became rational behavior, or the maximization of utilities and marginal efficiencies. Capital accumulation became exponential growth. Class distinctions based on ownership or nonownership of property became role assignment and role definition. Bourgeoisie and nation-state, and later, bureaucratic capitalist corporations and the bureaucratic nation-state, became complex, integrated structures representing universalism as against particularism. The "class situation" and "price wars" (Weber) of the market society became pluralistic differentiation and interest-group competition. Class consciousness became values or belief

11. Cf. Dean C. Tipps, "Modernization Theory and the Comparative Study of Societies: A Critical Perspective," *Comparative Studies in Society and History,* XVI (1973), pp. 199–226, esp. pp. 200–201, 204, 208. Tipp's essay encompasses a review and criticism of the major concepts of modernization theory and some of their origins; it surveys the work of leading theorists and provides a comprehensive bibliography of their work. Although expressed differently, Tipps's findings corroborate Wrigley's. Wrigley believes that notwithstanding the great differences in other respects among the schools of thought associated with Smith, Marx, Tönnies, Weber, Freud, and Parsons, nevertheless a pattern of broad agreement is evident respecting the elements of modernization and industrialization and their interconnections: "Not all analyses of modernization contain all the elements. . . . In part, this is an accident of chronology. Marx's analysis, for example, obviously could not be cast in a form which took account of the insights of Freud. . . . In part, it is a matter of terminology rather than substance. Unquestionably differences remain, . . . but there is at least tolerable unanimity that the several changes were closely interlocked and that they tended to reinforce each other. . . . Smith used a less technical and more telling prose than those who write of modernization today, but there is little in recent discussions of the topic which does not find a parallel in the *Wealth of Nations.*" Wrigley, "The Process of Modernization," pp. 236, 238; and see the extended discussion (with citation of relevant works) of, in effect, the essential similarities between classical and postclassical theorists, at pp. 226–239. Cf. David S. Landes, *The Unbound Prometheus* (Cambridge: Cambridge University Press, 1969), esp. c. 1–3, for the treatment of the interrelations of industrialization, modernization, and capitalism in the history of Western Europe and Great Britain since 1750.

systems. Anticapitalist (antimarket) theory or belief became traditional-ism, irrationalism, or ideology. Capitalist or bourgeois society became modernization and developed society. Decoded, much of the apparent difference over the characteristic social relations and modes of con-sciousness of Western industrial society recedes. Yet, there is a change of emphasis in the translation. Relations of power and domination fade into structure and function. Historically specific diagnoses and prescrip-tions concerning social relations and modes of consciousness in Western societies become in the newer terminology universalistic norms that traverse numerous historical contexts.[12] These norms are useful for cer-tain analytical and comparative purposes but misleading when severed in meaning from their roots in classical social theory. One of the striking attributes of latter-day theory is its heavy resort to instrumental and economistic terms (e.g., self-interest, group interest, materialistic acqui-sition, calculative advantage) in describing character formation, politics, and sociocultural phenomena, and to functional terms (e.g., decision making, rationalization, efficiency) when describing wealth, property, authority, and power.[13]

12. Cf. Anthony Giddens, *The Class Structure of the Advanced Societies* (London: Hutchinson, 1973, 1981), pp. 16–17. The tendency toward universalization has to some extent been a response to changing historical conditions, that is, to the spread of capitalism to nonindustrial societies via the agency of imperialism, to the commit-ment to development by governments in the growing number of independent nations in the non- and semiindustrial world since World War II, and to the development presided over by noncapitalist authority in Communist-governed countries. Some modernization theorists have therefore allowed for different patterns of moderniza-tion embracing, however, many common phenomena. Cyril E. Black, for example, has allowed for seven patterns, with Britain and France and their new world off-shoots comprising the first two patterns, which nevertheless "set the pattern to a sig-nificant degree for all other societies." Black, *The Dynamics of Modernization: A Study in Comparative History* (New York: Harper & Row, 1966), quotation at p. 106. Others, like Joseph J. Spengler, have preferred to view noncapitalist or non-market, patterns of development as cases of incomplete or ideologically thwarted modernization. Spengler, "Theory, Ideology, Non-Economic Values, and Political-Economic Development," in Ralph Braibanti and Joseph J. Spengler, eds., *Tradition, Values, and Socio-Economic Development* (Cambridge: Cambridge University Press, 1961), pp. 3–56, esp. pp. 22–23, 31–33, 36–37, 55–56. In light of recent events in the Soviet Union, Eastern Europe, and China, this view may gain a greater author-ity among theorists and policymakers alike, cutting across previous ideological lines.

13. E.g., David E. Apter, *The Politics of Modernization* (Chicago: University of Chicago Press, 1965), esp. pp. 26 et seq. (Apter identified his method or theory as structural-functional in the tradition of Parsons and Marion J. Levy, Jr., to the latter of whom he dedicated the book, p. viii.) Apter, like Black, regards Western industrial society as having become "a model (or at least a standard) for the comparison of countries elsewhere" (Apter's parenthesis). Apter sees intensive intellectual concern with the problem of modernization as having begun in Europe in the latter part of the nine-teenth century "after the consequences of industrialization had become apparent" (p. vii). Also, exhibiting strongly instrumental, functional, and economic conceptual tendencies are Black, *Dynamics of Modernization*, esp. pp. 7–26; Parsons, "The

Some postclassical social scientists who have engaged in the study of modern Western society have adhered to the terms and concepts of the classical social theorists. For them, capitalism as a system of social relations, class stratification, and distribution of power, has remained a central reality. While influential, they did not represent the prevalent trend in the social sciences in the United States in the three decades or so after World War II, but in recent years their work and its followers have contended for prevalence with growing impact in the academy.[14] Among other social scientists, some like Charles Lindblom, who had prominently contributed to the prevalent postclassical trends, have returned for guidance to Smith and Marx as more realistic and historically concrete than they had previously thought. Some of the reassessments have noted distortions often arising in latter-day thought from a strong tendency to equate modernization necessarily with industrialization, or with specific Western liberal-capitalist forms. Some have criticized the tendency to separate power in the socioeconomic sphere from power in the political sphere, and to dissolve questions of power in conceptions of structure and reciprocal function.[15]

Distribution of Power," pp. 123–143; Spengler, "Theory, Ideology, Non-Economic Values," Wilbert E. Moore, "The Social Framework of Economic Development," and Bert F. Hoselitz, "Tradition and Economic Growth," in Braibanti and Spengler, eds., *Tradition, Values, and Socio-Economic Development*, pp. 3–56, 57–82, 83–113. In all these works, modernization and development are seen as based upon a series of interconnected trends amounting in effect to a transformation in the mode of production.

14. E.g., Joseph Schumpeter, Karl Polanyi, John Kenneth Galbraith, Paul A. Baran, Robert S. Lynd, Hans Gerth, Hannah Arendt, C. Wright Mills, Barrington Moore, E. Digby Baltzell.

15. E.g., Wrigley, "The Process of Modernization." Also Charles E. Lindblom, *Politics and Markets: The World's Political-Economic Systems* (New York: Basic Books, 1977), pp. 7–8: "The two heroes of this book are Adam Smith and Karl Marx. . . . the market remains one of the new institutions capable of organizing the cooperation of millions of people. We owe to his [Smith's] *Wealth of Nations* . . . much of our understanding of what markets can and cannot do. . . . To the genius of Marx we owe more than can be listed. . . . Even at this late date in the history of social science, we must still turn back to Marx to understand, for example, the adverse effects on democratic government of property rights and of their grossly unequal distribution. . . . " It might also be noted here that William A. Williams's *The Great Evasion* (Chicago: Quadrangle, 1964) was an essay on the interpretation of U.S. history in terms of the leading ideas of Smith and Marx. See also John Hicks, *A Theory of Economic History* (Oxford: Clarendon Press, 1969), pp. 2–3: "In what sense can one attempt a 'theory of history'? . . . My 'theory of history' will quite definitely not be a theory of history in their [Toynbee's and Spengler's] sense. It will be a good deal nearer to the kind of thing that was attempted by Marx. . . . What remains an open question is whether [drawing upon general ideas in ordering historical material] . . . can be done . . . for special purposes, or whether it can be done in a larger way, so that the general course of history, at least in some important aspects, can be fitted into place. Most of those who take the latter view would use the Marxian categories, or some modified version of them; since there is so little in the way of an alternative

While latter-day modernization theory has been undergoing a critical reassessment among social scientists, it has continued to exert a powerful influence among American historians engaged in interpreting U.S. society in the period from the 1890s to 1916.[16] Indeed, much of the contention in the interpretation or periodization of this era has centered on differences between those who have drawn more heavily upon latter-day and those who have drawn more heavily upon classical terms and con-

version that is available, it is not surprising that they should. It does, nevertheless, remain extraordinary that one hundred years after *Das Kapital*, after a century during which there have been enormous developments in social science, so little else should have emerged. . . . " Cf. Tipps, "Modernization Theory and the Comparative Study of Societies," for a wide-ranging reassessment of modernization theory; Wrigley, "The Process of Modernization," pp. 237, 242, 248 et seq., for discussion of British and Dutch development, showing that modernization (the rise of the bourgeoisie and capitalism) can not be simply equated with industrialization, and that industrialization does not necessarily bring with it broader cultural attributes generally associated with modernization. Also Richard L. Sklar, "On the Concept of Power in Political Economy," in Dalmas H. Nelson and R. L. Sklar, eds., *Toward a Humanistic Science of Politics: Essays in Honor of Francis Dunham Wormuth* (New York: University Press of America, 1983), pp. 179–206, for an assessment of tendencies in political science theory toward evading the question of power in society and toward economistic models of political systems. For similar assessments among historians comparing the relative value of older and newer theoretical approaches, see *Daedalus*: "Historical Studies Today," C:1 (Winter 1971): Jacques Le Goff, "Is Politics Still the Backbone of History?" pp. 1–19; E. J. Hobsbawm, "From Social History to the History of Society," pp. 20–45; Felix Gilbert, "Intellectual History: Its Aims and Methods," pp. 80–97.

16. See, e.g., Louis Galambos, "The Emerging Organizational Synthesis in Modern American History," *Business History Review*, LXIV:3 (Autumn 1970), pp. 279–290; Galambos, "Technology, Political Economy, and Professionalization: Central Themes of the Organizational Synthesis," *Business History Review* LVII (Winter 1983), pp. 471–493; Samuel P. Hays, "The New Organizational Society," in Jerry Israel, ed., *Building the Organizational Society: Essays on Associational Activities in Modern America* (New York: Free Press, 1972), pp. 13 et seq.; Robert D. Cuff, "American Historians and the 'Organizational Factor,' " *Canadian Review of American Studies*, IV (Spring 1973), pp. 19–31; Ellis W. Hawley, "Herbert Hoover, the Commerce Secretariat and the Vision of an 'Associative State,' 1921–1928," *Journal of American History*, LXII (June 1974), pp. 116–140; Hawley, *The Great War and the Search for a Modern Order* (New York: St. Martin's Press, 1979); Robert H. Wiebe, *The Search for Order, 1877–1920* (New York: Hill & Wang, 1967); Stephen Skowronek, *Building a New American State*; and titles by Wiebe, Hays, and Haber cited in notes 2 and 3 of this chapter; also, William L. O'Neill, *The Progressive Era: America Comes of Age* (New York: Dodd, Mead, 1975); John W. Chambers II, *The Tyranny of Change: America in the Progressive Era, 1900–1917* (New York: St. Martin's Press, 1980); John D. Buenker, John C. Burnham, and Robert M. Crunden, eds., *Progressivism* Cambridge, Mass.: Schenkman, 1977); Alexandra Oleson and John Voss, eds., *The Organization of Knowledge in Modern America, 1860–1920* (Baltimore: The Johns Hopkins University Press, 1979); David Thelen, *The New Citizenship: Origins of Progressivism in Wisconsin, 1885–1900* (Columbia: University of Missouri, 1972); Alfred L. Thimm, *Business Ideologies in the Reform-Progressive Era, 1880–1914* (University: University of Alabama Press, 1976); David D. Danborn, *The Resisted Revolution: Urban America and the Industrialization of Agriculture, 1900–1930* (Ames: Iowa State University Press, 1979).

cepts. Those dubbed "revisionist" tend to be those least revisionist with respect to classical social theory, while those considered "antirevisionist" tend to be those most revisionist with respect to classical social theory. The periodization suggested here returns to the soil of classical social theory without excluding the fruits of postclassical theory. It seeks, that is, to offer an adequate periodization concerning U.S. history in the Progressive Era in terms of the nation's development (or modernization) as a capitalist society.

3. Periodization and capitalism

As the foregoing suggests, periodization in terms of capitalism seems to be warranted, and is certainly not excluded, by a large body of social science theory, both classical and latter-day, and by the general trends enumerated at the outset here and generally agreed to among historians as characterizing the period. Such periodization corresponds, accordingly, with a broad range of empirical evidence, including that concerning prevalent currents of political and social consciousness at the time. Periodization in terms of capitalism may serve, therefore, as an adequate framework for posing the essential questions of historical context: What general type of society was it, and in what historically specific phase of its evolution? What were the prevalent social relations and modes of consciousness, their requirements, capacities, pattern of authority, and structure or relations of power?

Periodization in terms of capitalism may be taken to be a "mode-of-production" theory of history. As such, it has evoked several objections, at least in the American historical profession. Four of these, which seem to carry most weight, may be briefly considered here: (1) Such periodization is Marxist. (2) It smacks of a "grand" theory of history. (3) It is an obsolete materialist conception of history. (4) It is economic determinist.

The first objection, that it is Marxist, rests on sentimental, not scholarly, grounds; but as an inhibition against acceptance, it may exert more force than all other objections combined, and underlie them. As already indicated, however, this objection lacks accuracy: Periodization by mode of production accords with Marx's theory of history, but with respect to Western industrializing societies, and in the taxonomic sense, it is, as we have seen, by no means exclusive to Marx.[17]

17. Cf. George Lichtheim, *Marxism: An Historical and Critical Study* (New York: Frederick A. Praeger, 1962), pp. 139–140. It may be noted here, also, that Marx himself and Engels made far more modest claims to "uniqueness" than have subsequent Marxists and anti-Marxists alike. See e.g., Karl Marx and Friedrich Engels, *Correspondence, 1846–1895*, tr. Dona Torr (New York: International Publishers, 1934;

Concerning the second objection, it is not necessary to assent to periodization by mode of production as a *general* theory of history applicable to all societies and in all times, in order to assent to it as a special theory adequate to late nineteenth- and early twentieth-century U.S. history (or to Western industrializing society more broadly). In effect, whatever their other differences, scholars have indeed drawn upon it, with or without explicit acknowledgment, as a special theory. Marx based his own claim for mode of production as the basis of a general theory of history on what he took to be the implications of the principle of cumulative evolution, explicitly drawn in Darwinian terms, but with strong roots in his own Hegelian background. To Marx and other scholars then and since, in capitalist societies the mode of production, based on private property and commodity exchange, was generating continuous and accelerated transformations in the means of production and exchange, in the ownership and disposal of land and resources, in the forms and conditions of labor, and was becoming the transparently paramount complex of social relations, palpably subordinating to itself, and shaping and reshaping, all the others: *Gesellschaft* replaced *Gemeinschaft*. But what further differentiated the capitalist from previous epochs, or modes of production, was that for the first time, the dominant property-owning class itself was not only directly engaged in, but also proclaimed, the sphere of production and market relations as paramount over all other spheres, and made economic and instrumental modes of consciousness prevalent over all others. It did so not only in the name of efficiency and material progress, but also in the name of human freedom, civil liberty, and ethical and religious sanction in the here and now. Freedom became a matter of worldly history expressed in a society-type overtly devoted to economic activity – or the "work ethic." It was this development that led Marx, who apprehended the principle of evolution to certify the cumulative nature of human development, both social (or material) and intellectual, to conclude that what bourgeois society revealed as essential to its own character also disclosed, as a general principle of scientific inquiry into human history, what was essential to all societies. It disclosed, that is, that although in precapitalist societies, social relations and their expression in ideals, religion, ethics, custom, law, and government appeared to determine and control the mode of production, in reality they were the particular forms or expression of modes of production or were

1936 ed.), pp. 56–57, 518. At one point, Marx exclaimed with some exasperation: "Since the thought process itself grows out of the conditions, is itself a *natural process*, thinking that really comprehends must always be the same, and can only vary gradually according to maturity of development, including that of the organ by which the thinking is done. Everything else is drivel." Marx to Kugelmann, 11 July 1868, *Correspondence*, p. 247 (Marx's italics).

variably determined by them.[18] It may well be that to derive a general theory of history from a special theory of Western capitalist society amounts to ethnocentrism, or to the fallacy of presentism, with little more than speculative value, but that is a different question from that involved here.[19]

18. Marx expressed the evolutionary principle of cumulative knowledge, in part, as follows (1857): "The bourgeois society is the most highly developed and most highly differentiated historical organization of production. The categories which serve as the expression of its conditions and the comprehension of its organization enable it at the same time to gain an insight into the organization and the conditions of production which had prevailed under all the past forms of society, on the ruins and constituent elements of which it has arisen, and of which it still drags along some unsurmounted remnants, while what had formerly been mere intimation has now developed to complete significance. The anatomy of the human being is the key to the anatomy of the ape. But the intimations of a higher animal in lower ones can be understood only if the animal of the higher order is already known. The bourgeois economy furnishes a key to ancient economy, etc. This is, however, by no means true of the method of the economists who blot out all historical differences and see the bourgeois form in all forms of society. . . . " And: "the laws of abstract reasoning which ascends from the most simple to the complex, correspond to the actual process of history." "Introduction to the Critique of Political Economy," printed as appendix (pp. 265–312) to Marx, *A Contribution to the Critique of Political Economy*, tr. N. I. Stone (Chicago: Charles H. Kerr & Co., 1904), pp. 300, 296. It is in this "Introduction" that Marx wrote his comment on the ancient Greeks as representing the "social childhood of mankind" (pp. 310–312). It is in Marx's Preface of 1859 that is to be found his famous formulation of the concept of mode of production (pp. 9–15). The longer passage just quoted above is to be found, also, in slightly different English translation, at Karl Marx, Grundrisse: *Foundations of the Critique of Political Economy*, Tr. Martin Nicolaus (New York: Vintage Books, 1975), p. 105. As the quotation indicates, Marx directed (here as elsewhere) some of his sharpest criticism at the widespread presentist proclivity among economists and other theorists in their reading current Western bourgeois production relations back in history to past societies or across borders to other societies of a different type. The evolutionary idea that the higher, or more advanced, form reveals the lower, or less advanced, form was commonly held among historians and social scientists of the late nineteenth and early twentieth century. Woodrow Wilson, for example, applied the concept, in his exemplary and influential theoretical work, to understanding the regulatory role of government, stating that the "birth and development" of modern industry "reveals the true character of the part which the state plays" throughout history; that is, it revealed the "rule . . . that in proportion as the world's industries grow must the state advance its efforts." Wilson, *The State: Elements of Historical and Practical Politics* (1889; Boston: D. C. Heath, 1906), pp. 614–615, 626. For further discussion of Wilson's views along these lines, see M. J. Sklar, *Corporate Reconstruction*, pp. 404–406.

19. Stated differently, and more precisely, it may well be granted that the mode of production is essential to the understanding of all societies. The question remains, however, whether the mode of production determines a society's class formation and class stratification, and what relation class divisions bear to the system of power. For the type of society constituting the United States in the period under review, it may be reasonably hypothesized that the mode of production (or property-production system) did determine class formation and stratification, and that these in turn correlated with the hierarchy of power. For a critique of mode of production as the basis of class formation and class power in less developed and developing countries (as nonindustrial or less industrial societies have come to be called), as well as in Communist-governed countries (whatever their status of development may be taken

As to the third objection, regarding the question of a materialist conception of history: This touches the *causes,* not the *fact,* of the rise and development of Western capitalist societies, that is, societies in which market relations of production and exchange came to dominate, dissolve, or reshape all others. The division among theorists over whether material conditions or ideas were the ultimate *cause* of this historical development (or of historical development in general) was already becoming an anachronism among scholars by the turn of the twentieth century[20] – only to be revived in lay-political circles by Lenin's self-defense against charges of "idealism" by Mensheviks and other political adversaries. In any case, it touches a question, the interrelation of the subjective and the objective in human affairs, plaguing thinkers of various philosophical persuasions who seek to understand the interrelation of matter and mind, practice and thought.

As to the fourth objection: Rightly or wrongly, the mode-of-production concept often carries economic determinist or economic reductionist connotations. Many of its advocates themselves give strong reason for supposing such connotations. But this is a general problem for both classical and latter-day social theory in its interpretation of industrial capitalist societies. The question is, rather, how to interpret what social theorists and historians widely regard as an "economic" or "business" society, where market relations are taken to permeate society and comprise the major institution of social integration, without falling into economic reductionism. Indeed, the one general idea about the United States that enjoys as wide assent as any other, if not wider, among historians, social scientists, culture critics, novelists, and all other manner of thinkers, is that the United States in this period was the quintessentially "business" or "economic" society.

American historians have tended to use the terms "business," "business society," "business civilization," and "businessmen" in preference to "capitalism" and "capitalist," although this preference was not characteristic of scholarly or broader social discourse in the United States around the turn of the twentieth century.[21] But "business" tends strongly

　　to be), see Richard L. Sklar, "On the Concept of Power in Political Economy."
20.　See, e.g., Jacques Le Goff, "Is Politics Still the Backbone of History?" and Giddens, *Capitalism and Modern Social Theory,* p. xv.
21.　For example, in his translator's preface to Marx's *Contribution,* N. I. Stone (in 1903) explained that although Marx used the term *"bürgerlich"* in the work, subsequently in *Das Kapital* he used *"kapitalistische"* in corresponding passages. Hence: "the only liberty taken with Marx's terminology has been in the case of the work 'bürgerlich.' . . . As the English speaking reader is more accustomed to hear of the 'capitalist' system of production than the 'bourgeois' system of production, etc., the translator considered Marx's own change of this term . . . a sufficient justification for rendering the word 'bürgerlich' into 'capitalistic' wherever it seemed more likely to carry the

to connote a discrete function and a narrow interest-group formation: It is itself laden with economic reductionist implications. "Capitalist" and "capitalism" have the advantage of denoting at one and the same time a stage of history, a type of society in a particular mode of development, a historically defined property system, and a social formation with corresponding modes of consciousness. Together these denotations accord empirically with the broad range of the society's dominant social relations, while fully allowing for the narrower economic process as such, interest-group behavior, and functional differentiation.[22] Put another way, "capitalism" allows drawing upon classical and latter-day social theory alike.

Economics is misconceived if equated with property relations, and property relations are misconceived if reduced to economics. Economics denotes input-output functions, the calculation of efficiencies and inefficiencies in the production and distribution of goods and services, the allocation of labor and resources, and the like. Property relations denote how production and distribution are organized, the larger social framework and relations of power within which input-output and allocative functions proceed. The term "property-production system" may be invoked to denote the sociopolitical determination of "economics," at a given historical period. The term may therefore be used interchangeably with "mode of production." Capitalism is a property-production system in this sense. Periodization by "mode of production" or "property-production system" affords, accordingly, a social or sociopolitical interpretation of an economic order as well as the broader society, or in the particular case of the United States in the period of the 1890s to 1916, a social interpretation of an apparently "economic" or "business" society.

As in its other forms, property in its capitalist form is not a simple *thing*, nor is it simply an economic category, but a complex of social relations, including a set of class relations, that involves a system of authority inextricably interwoven with the legal and political order, as well as with the broader system of legitimacy, the prevailing norms of emulative morality and behavior, and the hierarchy of power.[23] Business,

meaning home to the reader." Marx, *Contribution*, p. 6.

22. "Capitalism" also has the advantage of designating what *kind* of market it is; that is, one based on predominantly capital-wage labor relations, with capital in the form of private property and private enterprise, rather than, for example, on worker-owned and -managed enterprise, cooperative enterprise, state-owned enterprise, or public service enterprise.

23. Cf. Lindblom, *Politics and Markets*, pp. 8, 26, 34–35, 116; James Willard Hurst, *The Legitimacy of the Business Corporation in the Law of the United States, 1780–1970* (Charlottesville: University Press of Virginia, 1970), pp. 58–60, 62, 65, 66, 153. In noting that in the United States market activity has served as the main arena for the pursuit of utility and for the accrual of legitimacy, Hurst (p. 153) points to

or economic activity as such – buying, selling, allocating resources, employing labor, making contracts, establishing and directing partnerships or corporations – is misconceived if understood simply as economic activity abstracted from the social and political spheres or from ideas and ideals, and corresponds to what Talcott Parsons, for example, designated as political power of the broader sort in a society.[24] It is activity that presupposes and is permeated by a complex mode of consciousness, that is, by ideas and ideals about deliberate calculation of ends and means with respect to other persons, about the shape of society, its goals and moral standards, and about the law and politics. Business activity presupposes and is permeated by expectations about one's own and other people's character-structure, values, and normal behavior, respecting broader social relations with others, some of whom are taken to be equals, some superiors, and some subordinates – about, that is, social hierarchy. It presupposes and is permeated by expectations about the law and jurisprudence, politics, and the range and limits of government authority. All these expectations, ideas, and values are integral to activity pursued with a view to pecuniary gain, to making and accumulating profit through private discretionary investment, and in more generic terms, with a view to growth and development of the enterprise and nation. All this is here taken to mean, however, that what is often regarded as an "economic aspect" of society is, rather, the paramount web of social relations and modes of consciousness of that society, appearing as "economics."[25]

It follows that periodization by mode of production conceives capitalists, not less than workers, under the dignity of class, as a broad social formation, with political implications respecting the exercise of authority and power, and not as simply representing an economic function, nor simply as personifications or aggregations of "special interests" or interest groups. Their activity, outlook, and authority cut across lines of func-

---

"our long-term reliance on the market as an institution of social control." Also, from a somewhat different outlook, see Douglas Sturm, "Property: A Relational Perspective," *Journal of Law and Religion*, IV:2 (1986), pp. 353–404.

24. Parsons defined "power in a political sense" as "the capacity to mobilize the resources of the society for the attainment of goals for which a general 'public' commitment has been made, or may be made. It is mobilization, above all, of the actions of persons and groups, which is *binding* on them by virtue of their position in society. . . . " (Parsons's italics.) Parsons, "The Distribution of Power," p. 140.

25. For more detailed discussion of this point, including a critique of the "base-superstructure" concept, see M. J. Sklar, *Corporate Reconstruction*, pp. 4–14, and in particular, n. 7, p. 9. Cf. Thorstein Veblen, "The Preconceptions of Economic Science. II, *Quarterly Journal of Economics*, XIII (July 1899), pp. 396–426.

tion and discrete interests. This concept, accordingly, does not view the society as composed of various coequal functions, merely one of which is "economics" or "business." "Business" is not taken as one among numerous interest groups competing in a larger society otherwise not more concretely defined than as "modernizing," "industrial," "pluralistic," "democratic," "organizational," or "bureaucratic." The term "capitalist class" denotes not simply "business interests" that labor, lobby, and league for immediate gain, although it includes such interest-centered activity. It also denotes associated individuals (and their families) constituting a more or less functionally heterogeneous and hierarchically stratified social formation, which, on the basis of established property rights embedded in the law, exercises the broad range of authority that governs in the market as the paramount institution of social organization. The market's ever-evolving (changing) requirements and capacities, along with their prevalent values, govern the norms or effectively limit the nature and scope of authority in other major spheres of society, that is, not only in the market-investment system, and in the determination of vocations and subsistence, but also in the law, in politics and policymaking, in applied science and technology, in philanthropy, in religion, in education and exemplary morality, in communications and the arts. In a capitalist society, the capitalist class and its modes of consciousness play – in latter-day social science terms – the regulative "purpose-defining" or "goal-integrating" role in society at large. This is what Marx and other classical theorists called a dominant or "ruling" class. In recent years, social historians have tended to use the term "hegemonic," perhaps because it suggests an erudition appropriate to academic usage, but it is all the same as far as dictionary meaning is concerned. In American English, I believe "dominant" or "ruling" is preferable, or at least crisper. Ultimately, I suppose, it is a matter of taste.[26]

In summary, periodization of U.S. history in terms of capitalism conceives of capitalism as a distinct type of society, not as an "economic aspect" of society. It conceives capitalism as a complex of social relations,

26. Cf. Lindblom, *Politics and Markets*, pp. 116, 172, 175–176, 193, 204, 226, 230, 347. A leading architect (along with Robert A. Dahl, with whom he often collaborated in publication) of pluralist political theory, Lindblom represents a current trend among social scientists toward reassessing and rejecting the view of business as simply one among many interest groups. He also notes (p. 8) that "liberal democratic thought remains insensitive to problems of that authority which is embodied in property rights." Also (p. 356): "It has been a curious feature of democratic thought that it has not faced up to the private corporation as a peculiar organization in an ostensible democracy." He notes that in a "polyarchy" (pluralist) society like the United States, where there may be many centers of power, business and government exercise

a dominant dual leadership, but with business exercising an effective veto power over government, without an equal reciprocal veto power in the other direction. See also Henry S. Kariel, *The Decline of American Pluralism* (Stanford, Calif.: Stanford University Press, 1961), ch. 7, et passim, and M. S. Baratz, "Corporate Giants and the Power Structure," *Western Political Quarterly*, IX (June 1956), pp. 411–412, et passim, for earlier critiques of pluralism that Lindblom in part now accepts. Lindblom believes that the corporation is replacing "class indoctrination" as manifested in older values of acquiescence, deference, compliance, and the work ethic: But, as he states it: "It is possible that the rise of the corporation has offset or more than offset the decline of class as an instrument of indoctrination. . . . That it has risen to prominence in society as class lines have muted is clear enough. That it creates a new core of wealth and power for a newly constructed upper class, as well as an overpowering loud voice, is also reasonably clear. The executive of the large corporation is, on many counts, the contemporary counterpart to the landed gentry of an earlier era. . . . " The trends Lindblom points to may be taken to manifest new forms of "class indoctrination" superseding older forms, rather than the displacement of class indoctrination as such. It may also be that, in Lindblom's terms, this new form represents a crepuscular stage in class indoctrination based on corporate power. Be that as it may, it is a question more pertinent to periodization of U.S. society since World War II than in the period around the turn of the twentieth century, although it is not without some significant relevance for the earlier period.

Much of the debate over the existence and power of a capitalist class in the United States has revolved around the question of the corporate division of ownership from control of property, or between formal owners and controlling managers. This division constitutes a characteristic of the change in the form of capitalist property inhering in the corporate reorganization of property ownership, but in the period, 1890–1916, it was still in an emergent state. In any case, Lindblom's view of an upper class based on corporate wealth and power, which he sees as "newly constructed," corresponds with Baltzell's concept in *An American Business Aristocracy* (New York: Collier Books, 1962), and more recently in *Puritan Boston and Quaker Philadelphia* (New York: Free Press, 1979), esp. chs. 1 and 2, and with that in Williams, *Contours*, pp. 343–478, upon which I also draw. But Baltzell's work, and Williams's, and my own studies, indicate the emergence of this corporate "upper class" at around the turn of the twentieth century and its development since. See also James Livingston, *Origins of the Federal Reserve System: Money, Class, and Corporate Capitalism, 1890–1913* (Ithaca, N.Y.: Cornell University Press, 1986), and David F. Noble, *America by Design: Science, Technology, and the Rise of Corporate Capitalism* (New York: Alfred A. Knopf, 1977). On the question of the relation of the business corporation to the capitalist class, with a comprehensive discussion of the literature and a full bibliography by the early 1970s, see Zeitlin, "Corporate Ownership and Control: The Large Corporation and the Capitalist Class," *American Journal of Sociology* (1974); and see Alfred D. Chandler, Jr., *The Visible Hand: The Managerial Revolution in American Business* (Cambridge, Mass.: Harvard University Press, 1977), esp. ch. 1; Richard L. Sklar, "On the Concept of Power in Political Economy," in Nelson and Sklar, eds., *Toward a Humanistic Science of Politics*, pp. 179–206; and M. J. Sklar, *Corporate Reconstruction*, ch. 1, esp. pp. 11–14, n. 11 on p. 14, and pp. 20–33.

As to the prevalent tendency among social scientists and historians to avoid the study of the power of capitalists as integral to the interpretation of U.S. society, William Letwin, the economic and legal historian, has observed: " 'This Nation's business is business' instantly identifies the nation as the United States. . . . Business has been the national work of the United States . . . ; and the top of American society is occupied largely by businessmen. Historically, this status is unusual, perhaps unique. . . . All this should stir the curiosity of historians more than it has. How did American businessmen get to the top? How have they stayed there? And who are 'they' anyway? . . . " Letwin, "The Past and Future of the American Businessman," in *The American Business Corporation: New Perspectives on Profit and Purpose*, eds., Eli Goldston, Herbert C. Morton, and G. Neal Ryland (Cambridge, Mass.: MIT Press, 1972), pp. 17–18.

expressed in evolving class formations and relations, modes of consciousness, patterns of authority, and relations of power.[27]

Periodization in terms of capitalism is by no means necessarily the only valid one for this period in U.S. history. Rather, it is *a* valid one, but also it is, at least provisionally, a *necessary* one, for research into the political economy, social stratification, power relations, various social movements and modes of consciousness of the first significance in public life, and a broad range of decisive nongovernmental and governmental policy formation in both domestic and foreign affairs. It is necessary in the sense that without its theoretical implications for empirical inquiry, such spheres as just indicated would not be adequately comprehended, and in the sense that other periodizations could not be basically inconsistent with this one without excluding its validity.

Indeed, few if any historians would dispute the central role of capitalism in U.S. society in this period. In general, historians concerned with this period in U.S. history tacitly or explicitly acknowledge some such periodization in terms of industrial capitalism and corporate capitalism as critical to the shape and development of U.S. society from the 1890s to 1916. But the regulative implications of the concept of capitalism as a type of society, or a complex of social relations, instead of as an "economic aspect" of society, or as an "economic interest" within society, are often ignored or evaded, no less by the concept's advocates than by others, and it is often enough not applied in a consistent manner in research strategies or in general interpretations of the period.

For example, it is not uncommon to find among historians and social scientists professing themselves radicals or Marxians a formal

27. This periodization would not necessarily hold for societies that contained capitalist enterprise but that did not develop historically as capitalist societies in a manner similar to the United States or Western European societies. For those societies a different periodization would be appropriate. Some modernization theorists consider such societies as cases of incomplete or arrested development due to effective intercession by anticapitalist or alternatively by antirevolutionary (e.g., "traditionalist," clerical, ideological, socialist, or imperialist) forces, which are oriented precisely against *societal* development along capitalist lines or along fully "modern" capitalist lines. To view a society in terms of incomplete or arrested development, however, may be considered inordinately ethnocentric, if not ahistorically teleological, whether it appears among liberal, conservative, Marxist, or radical thinkers, including those associated with "dependency," "world-systems," or "core-periphery" theories. See note 12 and, for a critique of this view, R. L. Sklar, "On the Concept of Power in Political Economy," and his essay, "The Nature of Class Domination in Africa," *Journal of Modern African Studies*, XVII:4 (1979), pp. 531–552, and David G. Becker, Jeff Frieden, Sayre P. Schatz, and Richard L. Sklar, *Postimperialism: International Capitalism and Development in the Late Twentieth Century* (Boulder, Colo.: Lynne Rienner, 1987). At any rate, the United States in the period 1890–1916 corresponds with neither a case of arrested development nor of anticapitalist intercession in the sense indicated above.

acknowledgment of, or even an emphatic insistence upon, corporate capitalism as central to the character of U.S. society in the period under discussion, but then a treatment of capitalists, especially those associated with the larger corporations or investment banking houses, as illegitimate usurpers, or as improper intriguers, plotters, or manipulators, in their efforts at protecting or pursuing their enterprise or class interests, rather than as members of a class integral to the society and therefore exercising power and authority, including that involving exploitation, appropriate to their position in the mode of production. There is, also, to be found a corresponding treatment of capitalism's historical development from the competitive to the corporate stage as somehow illegitimate, or a "monopolistic" or "political" usurpation, as deviate and unethical, rather than as a historically intelligible evolution of the capitalist mode of production, its property and class relations. In the name of rejecting a "false necessity," but without designating a credible alternative periodization, demonization takes command. Holding individuals or groups morally responsible for the choices they make and the things they do is necessary and proper – indeed, it is critical to human evolution, not to mention to being human – but it should not be allowed to become the basis for caricaturing, and hence dehumanizing, people, or for ignoring or distorting the evolving social relations as members of which they live, breathe, and work.

Or, among such scholars may be noted a presentation of what they regard as "good" reform or "radical" or "revolutionary" movements – for example, movements identified with appropriately conscious or well-intentioned workers, farmers, women, African-Americans, socialists, critics, dissenters, or social reformers – as decisive, or at least as potent, shapers of society, without some rigorous reference, however, to the acknowledged corporate-capitalist context of property and market relations and corresponding patterns of authority and relations of power, within which, or against which, these designated movements sought to work their will: that is, without such reference beyond a vigorous empathetic disaffection with corporate capitalism in the abstract. On the other hand, although arguing the effective impact of such movements in shaping the lives of the participants themselves and therefore, presumably, U.S. society, or some significant aspect of the society, there is nevertheless to be found the tendency to assume an essentially unchanged corporate-capitalist society somehow persisting into the next era, and the next, and the next, unto the present era of U.S. history.[28] The people

28. For a good introduction to these and related historiographical issues, see the insightful views of Herbert G. Gutman in "Interview with Herbert Gutman," conducted by Michael Merrill, *Radical History Review*, 27 (1983), pp. 203–222, and the indis-

are incessantly changing the tunes, but the same corporate-capitalist melody lingers on. Social history in this key eats its cake of movements – people *making* their own history – and has its unbreakable cake of corporate-capitalist custom, too. *Pace* Bagehot – and Bakunin.

At a different location on the political or philosophical spectrum, in the work of historians or social scientists professing themselves "free-market" advocates, there may be found an idealization of market relations abstracted from their social context and consequences, along with the demonization of those people and movements opposed to, resisting, or seeking to modify or abolish, capitalistic market relations. In the case of these scholars, capitalists (or entrepreneurs) can do little or no wrong, and with respect to them angelicization takes command. Also, in the case of historians or social scientists professing themselves conservative or liberal, or professing a realism in interpretation or theory without reference to a particular political or philosophical outlook, there may be found institutional, legislative, or technoeconomic descriptions and analyses without relating them in some detail to capitalist property and market relations and corresponding modes of consciousness, although these latter are, on empirical grounds, very much a part of the story. The result is structural-functional descriptions and analyses of U.S. economic organization, society, and politics, often excellent in technical quality and useful knowledge, but displaced or sifted from the historical context of concrete social relations.

4. The United States, 1890s–1916

The proposed periodization for the United States in the years 1890s–1916 may be briefly indicated as follows: In its general historical formation, it was a market society, based on private property, that was undergoing capitalist industrialization and, in its political dimension, the development of liberal democracy in a republican form. In its historically specific stage of evolution, it was a relatively mature industrial capitalist society in an early phase of the corporate reorganization of capitalist property relations. Since social relations in general and government in particular were adjusting to the corporate reorganization of the property system, the period may also be designated as the time of the corporate reconstruction of American society.[29]

pensable and penetrating critique of the "social history" genre in some of its more prominent recent manifestations by Elizabeth Fox-Genovese and Eugene D. Genovese, "The Political Crisis of Social History" ch. 7, pp. 179–212, in their book, *Fruits of Merchant Capital* (New York: Oxford University Press, 1983).

29. For further detail in definition, application, and implications, respecting this period-

As already suggested, this periodization refers to the emergence of a social order in the broadest sense, not simply to "economic" developments. Among its general implications, two are particularly pertinent to the present purpose.

1. As a regulative principle of inquiry, the concept, "the corporate reconstruction of American capitalism" (or of American society), does not explain the period, but identifies terrain that needs to be explored and explained. To begin with, for example, what was the nature of this capitalism and of this reconstruction? The corporate reorganization of industry that crystallized in the merger movement of 1898–1904 and developed thereafter can not be taken for granted as a self-evident fact, whether as a natural outcome of economic evolution, as a logical defensive reaction to the depression of the 1890s, as an objective consequence of technological development or market stimuli, or as an aspect of some inevitable bureaucratic-organizational glacial drift. It may have been all these things, but the rise of corporate capitalism may still not be best understood as essentially a "business" aspect of a response to the opportunities or disorders of industrialism. Industrialism itself was a way in which Americans throughout the nineteenth century responded to the opportunities and insecurities of capitalism, or to their nonindustrial (or preindustrial) ideas and aspirations, not to mention other motivating circumstances. Similarly, the corporate reorganization of industry might be viewed as a way in which some Americans, not only capitalists, but also professionals, political leaders, jurists, intellectuals, workers, farmers, reformers, and others, along a broad range of society, were making industrialism respond to their changing respective views of, or positions in, the market or society at large.[30]

Both capitalist industrialism and its corporate reorganization, accordingly, are better comprehended not simply as an "external force," or an "objective" structural phenomenon, but no less than, for example,

ization, see M. J. Sklar, *Corporate Reconstruction*, chs. 1 and 2, et passim. Cf. Skowronek, *Building a New American State*, p. 4, referring to "institutional innovations around the turn of the century" as comprising in general a response to industrialism, and as involving a "pivotal turn" amounting to a "governmental reconstruction."

30. It may be that a concept of industrialism as a fixed given, to which people passively respond, has contributed to depriving less industrial and nonindustrial countries, including the Communist-governed, of thinking in new ways about industrialization or development, in that it has presented industrialism as a relatively fixed idea, or a prescribed route, embodying an indefeasibly forged wisdom, largely in its Western capitalist form and its derivative bureaucratic statist ("Marxist-Leninist") form – that is, in having made of industrialization a finished *thing* to be responded *to*, as well as development in general, rather than a process of discovery, creation, experimentation, and re-creation, or in the broadest sense, on a society-wide scale, what John Dewey might have designated instrumental democracy.

populism, trade unionism, suffragism, African-American nationalism or equalitarianism, or socialism, as a social movement, or a set of social movements. If we treat these other trends and their respective intellectual and organizational expressions as political and social movements among farmers, workers, women, African-Americans, radicals, or reformers, so may we treat the corporate reorganization of capitalism and its related intellectual and organizational expressions as a political and social movement (or movements) among capitalists and corresponding groups of intellectuals, politicians, and reformers, among others. Capitalism's historical evolution is as much social and political as economic in its dimensions. The tendency to regard "business" as economics, or as economic history, or as "interests," or as technoeconomic structures and functions, *in contrast to* "ideas" or social movements and politics, has obstructed the adoption of this rather obvious approach, and its application as a framework of research outside of special studies of "business" history, or "businessmen" as special-interest agents, or the "business mind."

2. The terms "early phase" and "emergence" of the corporate reorganization or corporate reconstruction, are intended to convey a periodization that recognizes conflict within and between empirically observable, not preordained, ascending and declining trends, ascending and declining forms or stages of the capitalist property-production system, or mode of production. The periodization refers to an era when the extant political system of power, including the legal order, fell out of phase with the changing pattern of authority – that is, with the changing forms of capitalist property, and hence with property and market relations as they expressed and affected both trends of thought and class relations (interclass and intraclass relations). Party alignments, the law, governmental policy and structure, and broad currents of ideology and culture, consequently, were drawn into the vortex of conflict among those movements favoring the preservation or restoration of proprietary capitalism, those favoring the realization of the emergent system of corporate-capitalist authority, and those movements representing efforts at attaining a mixture of, or an alternative to, both. The movements for and against the transformation of the system of power proceeded in several spheres at once – in the legal order, in party politics, in the structure and functions of government, in market and property relations, in foreign affairs, and in scholarly and popular modes of thought.

The periodization, accordingly, does not mean that corporate capitalism came on the scene as a finished product or a pure "ideal type"; nor that corporate capitalism "took over" society and muscled out everything else. On the contrary, although tending toward relative decline and a permanent position of subordination, nevertheless property and market relations, modes of thought, political movements, and cultural patterns associated with the proprietary-competitive stage of capitalism, and although still less fully formed those associated with trends of socialism or social democracy, remained or became widespread, influential, and strongly represented in national politics, in Congress, and at the state and local levels of politics and government. They continually exerted a large impact, moreover, in party politics, in the electoral arena, and in legislative activity at the national, state, and local levels. Throughout this period and well beyond it, the large corporations lacked anything near full legitimacy in the minds of a considerable segment of the people and their political representatives.

The social relations, institutions, forms of thought, and policy preferences associated with corporate capitalism embodied what may be understood, without violence to the words, as developmental, future-oriented, and hence "progressive" social trends, but they reached ascendancy, nevertheless, in and through accommodation to and modification by those in opposition, including those on the decline and rooted in the past. Programs and outlooks originating in socialist and social democratic movements or thought became components of the corporate-capitalist order. At the same time, small enterprise attained ample room within the rising corporate-capitalist order, and in law, politics, administration, and jurisprudence, received regulatory assistance and protection, credit and finance facilities, subsidies and exemptions, as well as a fair share of ideological favor and obeisance, even if not as much on all these fronts as small enterprisers wanted and demanded. Corporate capitalism came into the world, grew, and developed with continual, heavy, lasting, and habit-forming dosages of both populism and socialism. It was receptive to, and integrative of, a diversity of evolving social relations and developmental trends, in ways and to an extent that proprietary-competitive capitalism could not be. By the same token, accordingly, within and among trade and civic associations, not to mention the major and minor political parties and movements, the conflict among variations of the corporate, proprietary, and socialist outlooks characterized the entire period. Differences over government regulation, market power, investment authority, capital-labor relations, gender and race relations, and social amelioration, divided people not only across but also within classes, strata, groups, and movements, including for example, capitalists within one and the same enterprise, corporation, banking house, club, trade organization, or civic association, or for example, workers and trade unionists, suffragists and feminists, African-Americans and civil rights advocates, socialists and anarchosyndicalists, within the same organization, association, or movement.[31]

As this implies, an older evolutionary conception, embracing a rather neatly linear procession, must be set aside: Corporate capitalism is not to be understood as simply succeeding to and vanquishing small-scale enterprise and the populism associated with it, and socialism is not to be understood, putatively, as succeeding to and vanquishing corporate capitalism. Rather, corporate capitalism as a mode of production or stage of historical evolution of a modern capitalist society is to be understood as containing, mixing, and by degrees progressively integrating or synthesizing capitalism, populism, and socialism, ultimately moving toward a new stage of historical evolution beyond corporate capitalism, a stage the United States (and other "postindustrial" societies) may well have already entered. This may indeed explain why the social history genres prosper and resonate so strongly in current scholarly work and popular appeal, emphasizing as they do the role of people making their own history – not only people of wealth and power, but also populists, radicals, socialists, feminists, farmers, workers, small enterprisers, African-Americans, Native Americans, and others – a strong testimony, precisely in its not necessarily being intended, to corporate capitalism's intermixing, integrative, and synthesizing character.[32]

The recognition of sustained and multifaceted conflict as integral to the rise and development of corporate capitalism may therefore be viewed from another perspective. The conflicts themselves were increasingly defined by new patterns of consensus, and hence were different from the conflicts of the past. The conflicts over regulation of the market, for example, proceeded within a new consensual framework, which by the 1890s was beginning to displace the old consensus that had favored the largely competitive domestic market. Manufacturers, bankers, farmers, workers, reformers were variously reacting against the competitive market and its consequences. The regulatory consensus established the ground of conflict over the purposes, character, and methods of regulation, for example, over the extent to which regulation should serve "small business" or "big business," and over how much and what kind of regulation might be left to arrangements in the private sector (among parties in the market), how much and what kind assigned to government, and how arrangements in the two sectors might best interact or intermesh.

31. See M. J. Sklar, *Corporate Reconstruction*, pp. 14–20, and esp. n. 12, p. 16.
32. This idea is further explored in Chapters I and VII of this book.

Corporate reorganization, trade associations, supply and marketing contracts, agricultural cooperatives, trade unions, and social work projects, were among the regulatory trends in the private sector, each with roots in the past but now assuming a new significance. They involved or immediately called into play proposals for government regulatory roles, for it was one of the cardinal principles not only of the competitive market regime, still ideologically potent now as before, but also of the American republican tradition tracing back to Madison and Adams, that great regulatory authority could be safely reposed in private hands if at all only under the check and balance of public supervision or control. Conflicting proposals for government regulation of the market derived from small producers' fears of both competition and monopolistic oppression, from adversarial market interests such as those of shippers against carriers, interregional or national against local suppliers, owners against tenants, creditors against debtors, utilities against customers, and also from positive and defensive corporate initiatives, as well as from investors in negotiable securities seeking greater stability and lesser risk in the capital markets – that is, from all manner of business sources within the market, as well as from the efforts of political leaders, intellectuals, trade unionists, agrarian populists, feminists, social reformers, Christian gospelers, and socialists, within and outside of the market.

The pervasive conflict, and the wide-ranging regulatory and reform legislation that resulted from it at the local, state, and national levels, constitute the realistic grounds for interest-group, sectional, reform-movement, status-displacement, and other such special-angle interpretations of the period. Whatever their incongruities, however, regulatory and reform law and practices, and the various movements and their outlooks, tended ultimately at very least to address, and more commonly to recognize and legitimize, even where they may have resisted or curbed, the new corporate order, its form of property, its leading underlying assumptions, and corresponding new or changing social relations, cultural patterns, ideas, and values. This is why so much of the reform and legislative efforts of the period, however diverse in interest, motivation, or goal, directly or indirectly had to relate to, regulate, or reshape the market – property and exchange relations – as it was undergoing its corporate reorganization. This is a measure of the type of society the United States was at the time, as well as of the corporate ascendancy and the rising power of the corporate sector of the capitalist class; it registers a change in the property-production system, or mode of production, which expressed itself as changes in the legal, political, economic, cultural, and intellectual spheres. It indicates, in short, a distinctive periodization.[33]

In general, periodization with reference to the emergence of the corporate reorganization of American capitalism assumes broad social change engendered by the extended conflict between two major forms of capitalist property relations and their corresponding modes of consciousness, or, between two historical stages of capitalist society, the proprietary-competitive market stage, and the corporate-administered market stage, the one receding before, but having generated and therefore leaving its indelible marks upon, the ascendancy of the other.[34]

5. Corporate capitalism and corporate liberalism

The transformation of market and property relations and of thinking about them gave the period 1890s–1916 its distinctive character in U.S. history. The transformation included changes in the organization

33. The emergence of corporate capitalism as the latest evolutionary stage in the history of capitalism was a common theme by the early twentieth century among historians and social scientists on both sides of the Atlantic, its American chroniclers and theorists since then ranging from Thorstein Veblen, Charles A. Conant, and Jeremiah W. Jenks, to Wesley Clair Mitchell, Adolf A. Berle, and Gardiner C. Means, to Paul Sweezy, John Kenneth Galbraith, and Alfred D.Chandler, Jr. But William A. Williams (*Contours*, pp. 343–478) established the concept of corporate capitalism as an essential periodization of U.S. political, social, and intellectual (not only economic) history since the 1880s. (Williams's phrase was "The Age of Corporation Capitalism," and he dated the period from 1882 to the present.) Other historians, either independently or drawing upon Williams, have contributed works based upon such a periodization, touching both general surveys or interpretations and specific spheres of study. Singly and as a substantial body of scholarship, these works may be taken to indicate the fruitfulness of the periodization for historical inquiry, however much they may differ in consistency, subtlety, complexity, or in understanding the concept in a genetic and dynamic rather than a static sense. For a listing of some of the better known and more frequently cited works in the genre, see M. J. Sklar, *Corporate Reconstruction*, n. 13, pp. 17–19.

34. Cf. Woodrow Wilson's perception of the general situation of American society in the first decade of the twentieth century: "The contest is sometimes said to be between capital and labor, but that is too narrow and too special a conception of it. It is, rather between capital in all its larger accumulations and all other less concentrated, more dispersed, smaller, and more individual economic forces. . . . " Also: "the things that perplex us at this moment are the things which mark, I will not say a warfare, but a division among classes; and when a nation begins to be divided into rival and contestant interests by the score, the time is much more dangerous than when it is divided into only two perfectly distinguishable interests, which you can discriminate and deal with. . . . " Wilson, "The Banker and the Nation," address delivered at the Annual Convention of the American Bankers' Association, Denver, 30 September 1908, and "Abraham Lincoln: A Man of the People," address on the occasion of the celebration of the hundredth anniversary of the birth of Abraham Lincoln, Chicago, 12 February 1909, in *The Public Papers of Woodrow Wilson*, eds., Ray S. Baker and William E. Dodd (New York: Harper & Bros., 1925, 1926), II, pp. 55, 99.

and management of labor, production, distribution, and administration, changes that affected not only manufacturing, but also agriculture, banking and finance, transportation and communications, education and recreation, and not least of all, government – that is, the political economy and the society all along the line. By their very nature, therefore, they found expression in, or called forth, new labor, technical, professional, management, and administrative functions with their corresponding social strata, and in turn their values, attitudes, and ideological dispositions, along with institutions providing for the training of these strata and the propagation of appropriate modes of consciousness. The new market and property relations also generated movements for the alteration of government roles in social and economic affairs, that is, new governmental functions and administrative structures. These developments both in the market and society and in government, or, in the "private sector" and the "public sector," correspond with what historians take social science theory to designate as structural-functional characteristics with systemic tendencies toward administration, bureaucratization, and professionalization, or in short, toward modernization in a mature or highly developed industrial society. In this sense, the changes in the market, in property relations, in class relations – in the mode of production – that transpired in the late nineteenth and early twentieth century in the United States may be understood as having constituted the substance, the causal or motive force, of the nation's historical evolution, or maturing "modernization," and hence of the reforms and thought that affirmed, shaped, or modified the corporate reorganization of the political economy, the new government regulatory roles – the reforms and the thought that, taken together with the nation's liberal-democratic political tradition and institutions, became associated with "Progressivism," or modern Liberalism, or Corporate Liberalism, in the United States.

The transformation, therefore, was not simply a matter of technoeconomic structural change that occurred behind people's backs and over their heads. It was a matter of social movements and movements of thought, in the market, in politics, in the society at large, in which, however wide the disparity between intent and result, people transformed not only their relations of production and exchange, not only class relations, both between capital and labor and among sectors within capital and labor, but also – as might be expected in a society in which market relations constitute the dominant social relations – the law of the market, the structure and role of government, party politics, international relations, and basic forms of thought.

The regulatory, tax, banking, conservation, capital-labor, clean-government, electoral-reform, and other great political debates of the Progressive Era gave expression, on the one hand, to the conflict among representatives of two stages of American capitalism – the proprietary-competitive and the corporate-administered – in which those on both sides sought to regulate the market and property relations and the corresponding distribution of power, but in different ways and for different purposes. On the other hand, and at the same time, the debates gave expression to differences within the ranks of partisans of proprietary-competitive capitalism and those of corporate capitalism over the coexistence or intermixing of the one kind of capitalism with the other (which came to be the actual outcome, on the basis of the ascendancy of corporate capitalism), or the annihilation of the one or the other (a fancied but not the actual outcome). The debates also generated differences that cut across all these lines, over *how* to regulate the market, whatever the purpose, that is, for example, over the respective roles of the executive and the judiciary, and the extent to which government or private parties should regulate the market. Fundamentally, the debates revolved around the relation of the state to society in resolving the general questions of whether the corporate reorganization of the political economy was to be permitted or prevented, and in either case whether along statist or nonstatist lines.

A statist resolution might have taken hold had the American capitalist class, or its corporate sector, been less developed in its market powers and proficiencies and hence more dependent on the state for its wealth and power; had the liberal republican tradition of the supremacy of society over the state (the sovereignty of the people) been weaker; had the working class been less imbued with that republican ideology, less developed, and hence more inclined to statist rather than associative-constitutional ideas and principles; had the corporate sector of the capitalist class sought and found alliance with a statist oriented sector of the working class or a statist oriented petty bourgeoisie especially in the farm and rural population; had the corporate sector of the capitalist class sought and found alliance with civilian or military professionals, technicians, administrators, and manager – or a "managerial class" – looking to the state as a base of power. None of these circumstances was strongly rooted in the American historical soil at the turn of the century, and none found politically significant expression in the national mainstream, whatever the eddies of literary expression.[35]

35. Cf. Ellis W. Hawley, "Herbert Hoover, the Commerce Secretariat, and the Vision of an 'Associative State,' 1921–1928," *Journal of American History,* LXII (June 1974), pp. 116–140, and Hawley, "The Discovery and Study of a 'Corporate Liberalism,'"

Instead of a statist route, a broad proregulatory consensus around the affirmation of strong positive government defined the common ground of the great debate over the reorganization of market and property relations. Upon this ground, disagreement proceeded over precise roles of government, the status of organized labor, and not least of all the prospects of small enterprise in the emergent corporate order.

The emergence of corporate capitalism in the years 1890s–1916 coincided with the rise of a "corporate" outlook affecting thought about society, politics, and economic organization. The prevalent American corporate current, however, differed from contemporary or subsequent European (or Japanese, or Latin American) corporative trends. The prevalent American trend was "corporate *liberal*": It assigned to the corporation and other private entities the primary task of managing the market, and to the state the secondary task of regulating the corporations and other private entities, along with complementary distributive, credit and financial, social service, even some allocative or productive, functions and roles that private entities alone could not or, it was thought, best not, fulfill. In renouncing laissez-faire for positive government, corporate liberalism nevertheless affirmed the supremacy of the society over the state and the subordination of state policy to the dominant forces in society that composed the evolving capitalist property-production system. But at the same time, accordingly, it sustained the separation of state powers from private authority, which meant in particular not conferring upon private entities, whether trade association, corporation, or political party, coercive powers of the state, and subjecting all authority to judicial process and review.

In the prevalent political trend, there was no special corporatist doctrine in any meaningful sense of the word, beyond the view, with its implications and corollaries, that the corporate mode of capitalist enterprise was the historically evolved vehicle of progressive efficiency and modern development that was taking the place of individual enterprise as the dominant form of property relations in the economy. This called into play new government regulatory roles and hence an expanding field for positive government. But corporate capitalism in the United States did not generate or assume the form of "corporative" social relations, law, or modes of thought, in its characteristic trend. The prevalent forms of extrafamilial social relations remained associative and bureaucratic

Business History Review, LII (Autumn 1978), pp. 309–320; M. J. Sklar, *Corporate Reconstruction*, n. 1, pp. 4–5, n. 32, p. 394, and pp. 431–439; and see Richard Schneirov, *Labor's Quest for Power: Knights, Unions and Politics in Late Nineteenth-Century Chicago* (Urbana: University of Illinois Press, forthcoming).

rather than corporative in any real organicist, state-command, or total-itarian sense. The prevalent forms of thought and politics among American partisans of the corporate reorganization of capitalism were not in essence collectivist, but associational.[36] That is, the prevalent mode of consciousness associated with corporate capitalism in its period of emergence in the United States was not a communitarian, or a traditionalist or *volkisch*, or a paternalistic or authoritarian, but a liberal, form of thought adapted to the corporate stage of capitalism.

The prevalent procorporate thought did affirm the growing displacement of the individual by the organization or group as the basic functional unit of a modern capitalist economy, but it was an organization or group that the individual was conceived to join or quit according to opportunity and circumstance, and not to belong to as a matter of kinship, custom, coercive assignment, or binding obligation other than contractual. Hence, although corporate-liberal thought saw the organization or group as becoming the basic functional unit of the economy, it still defined the individual as the basic unit of the body politic and the society. Rights and obligations were still to remain, in concept and at law, fundamentally individual, not corporative. Incentive and choice, moreover, navigated by contractual relations, floated on legislated limits and opportunities, and anchored in market disciplines, rather than collectivist coercion and state command, played the dominant roles as organizing principles.[37]

As the American corporate-liberal outlook was not "organicist" in the conservative, or "traditionalist," sense, so neither was it simply or statically oriented to "organizational" order or social stability. It highly valued growth, innovation, the reordering or reforming of economic and social relations as well as the physical landscape, and the instabilities of development ("modernization"), both at home and in the nation's engagement in world affairs. The perennial "search for order" emanated from the incessant impulse of American corporate capitalism to

36. Hawley, "Herbert Hoover, the Commerce Secretariat, . . . "; and Hawley, *The Great War and the Search for a Modern Order.*
37. The systematic de facto and de jure exclusion of African-Americans from the applicability of these organizing principles until the 1960s (and substantially declining but persistent de facto exclusion for many since then) ranks as an obscene and grave injustice, and it also of course underlies African-American civil rights movements, on the one hand, and nationalist or race-centered politics, on the other, as well as the frequent intersecting or mixture of the two currents. Similarly, the exclusion of women underlies the women's and feminist movements throughout much of U.S. history, movements that since the early twentieth century have had growing impact in bringing women increasingly within equal applicability of these principles as compared with men.

disruption and change. The quest for countercyclical stabilizing mechanisms in the economy, for example, as in central banking and administered markets, proceeded as a function of the corporate reorganization and transformation, that is, the disruption, of the older proprietary-competitive political economy, as well as of the recurrent disruption of conditions generated by corporate-capitalist development itself.

The prevalent corporate-liberal outlook was committed to, while it refashioned, the democratic political tradition as it had developed in the United States. It gave expression to the dominant power of the capitalist class in society, by validating a revised definition of property at law and in practice, and by affirming a change in the rules of the market, while it embraced the political tradition of defining society as superior to the state in accordance with the constitutionalist principle of limited government under law and the inviolability of specified individual rights. In particular, while oriented to the expansion and development of positive government, and of executive power within government, the prevalent corporate-liberal outlook affirmed the limitation of government power in general and executive power in particular by constitutional and statute law, and in the last analysis by the authority of an independent judiciary. It affirmed, that is, strong positive government without embracing state command or a corporate state. Corporate liberalism thereby gave expression to the movements for the mutual accommodation of corporate capitalism and the American liberal tradition.[38] In a period of history when in much of the world large-scale industrial capitalism and liberalism did not go easily together, this was of no mean significance.

At every step of the way, the movement (or movements) for corporate capitalism had to contend with, and also accommodate to, and in so doing contain, in the inclusive as well as the exclusive sense, the small-producer tradition and the rising demands of a modern diversified working class – hence, both populism and socialism. It was in the age of reform largely brought on by the age of the corporate reconstruction of American capitalism that the period of the 1890s to 1916 found its distinctive character. To put it another way, the advent of corporate capitalism in the United States, under the auspices of corporate liberalism as the general outlook of the nation's prevalent social movements, signified the shaping of American society in the twentieth century by the contending, and at the same time the complementary and intersecting, trends of capitalism, populism, and socialism. In its liberal democratic form, in other words, corporate capitalism denotes a highly complex society of changing, conflicting, intersecting, and complementary economic, polit-

38. M. J. Sklar, *Corporate Reconstruction*, ch. 1.

ical, and cultural relations that require, in Heinz R. Pagels's words, a "science of complexity" for its adequate study.[39]

The United States in its twentieth-century corporate-liberal mode became the quintessential nation of the evolving mix of capitalism, socialism, and populism that constitutes the "pluralist" substance of what the postclassical theorists called modernization and development. As Hegel had pronounced from an astute naivete, and as Marx later concurred from some fuller historical perspective (having earlier designated England), the United States was becoming in the late nineteenth century, and by the Progressive Era had become, the land of the future. Whether it may still be remains to be seen.

39. See also Peter F. Drucker, *The New Realities* (New York: Harper & Row, 1990), Parts III and IV, et passim.

III

Dollar Diplomacy according to Dollar Diplomats: American development and world development

For an accurate understanding of events, the historian can not exclusively rely upon the conception that the participants had about themselves and about the nature of their actions. It appears, however, that in neglecting an examination of the ideology of the Dollar Diplomats, historians have often enough attempted to see Woodrow Wilson's intentions in foreign affairs through his own eyes, but have rarely extended the same courtesy to the Dollar Diplomats. The assumption, apparently, is that as a "business diplomacy," Dollar Diplomacy functioned in the manner of a reflex, as it were, to practical "interests," and therefore involved no underlying considerations beyond the immediate profit calculus; but that President Wilson's diplomacy, as one based upon moralism and vision, however sound or misguided, sprang from a complex body of thought transcending the marketplace mentality, and consequently requires analysis in light of the underlying ideology, philosophy, or outlook.

The respective foreign policies of Dollar Diplomacy and President Wilson have therefore been differentiated less in their results, which historians agree were in many respects essentially similar, than in their motives, the one springing from "interests," the other from "ethics." With so wide an agreement on results, it might seem best to leave the question of motives to novelists, poets, and politicians – Clio, after all, like the law, becomes cross-eyed when stripped of her blindfold. But the currently prevalent differentiation according to motives conceals a neglect of an inquiry into the substantive content and objectives of the diplomacy and foreign policies in question.

It is useful, therefore, to review the theory and practice of Dollar Diplomacy as stated by some of its leading, self-avowed advocates and

Written 1961–1962; slightly edited by the author for publication here.

78

practitioners. In particular (although not exclusively), Willard D. Straight, William J. Calhoun, and Francis M. Huntington Wilson stand as three major protagonists of the outlook.[1] The relevance of their thinking stems from the key role they played in formulating and implementing the Far Eastern policy of President William Howard Taft and Secretary of State Philander C. Knox, and their direct or indirect association with large banks and corporations interested in Chinese trade and investment. They may be considered representative of the interrelations between large corporations and the government insofar as the shaping of U.S. foreign policy was concerned. It is precisely for this reason that it is important to see that they functioned not as slide rules registering a profit calculus, not as narrow "economic men," not as lobbyists or tools of lobbyists, but as individuals consciously possessed of a world-view centered upon the affirmation, preservation, and growth of the capitalist political economy in the United States.

Straight and Calhoun were the ideologues, the practical intellectuals, among the practitioners of Dollar Diplomacy in corporate and government circles. Straight's thinking fell in closely with that of intellectuals like Herbert Croly, but he preferred to practice, rather than to write about, his ideas.[2] He respected ideas, however, and financed the launching (in 1914) and maintenance of the *New Republic* as a vehicle for Croly, Walter Lippmann, and Walter Weyl. Calhoun, who served as

1. "The chief architects of that modification of the open door from the emphasis on trade to the emphasis on investment were not the secretaries of state Root and Knox themselves, but rather two subordinates, Willard Straight and Francis M. Huntington Wilson. . . . " Raymond A. Esthus, "The Changing Concept of the Open Door 1899–1910," *Mississippi Valley Historical Review*, 46:3 (December 1959). Cf. Charles Vevier, *The United States and China, 1906–1913* (1935), pp. 88–89.

2. Having decided against a career as a poet and writer, Straight served under Root and Knox as U.S. Consul-General at Mukden, Manchuria, and later as chief of the Far Eastern Division of the Department of State. Variously, during and after serving in these capacities, he acted as agent of the Schiff-Harriman interests in Manchuria, and of J. P. Morgan & Company and the American Banking Group in China. Shortly after returning from China, he became, in 1914, the president of the American Asiatic Association succeeding its former perennial president, Seth Low. Seth Low, himself prominent in the National Civic Federation, is symbolic of the intricate interlocking of membership and leadership among such organizations as the Civic Federation, the Asiatic Association, the American Manufacturers Export Association, the Pan American Society, the New York State Chamber of Commerce, the U.S. Chamber of Commerce, and the National Foreign Trade Council. By the latter part of the first decade of the twentieth century the National Association of Manufacturers (NAM) no longer appears to have been so important among large corporate interests, its conventions (whatever else may be said of its self-perpetuating executive committees) being essentially release time for smaller industrial interests, and their importance, with respect to participation of the large corporate interests, declining in proportion as the NAM concerned itself less and less with foreign affairs.

Minister to China under President Taft, replacing William W. Rockhill,[3] liked to describe himself "not [as] a trade expert, or even a practical business man": "I must classify myself among the theorists."[4] Huntington Wilson, a career diplomat, served in the U.S. embassy in Tokyo before becoming Third Assistant Secretary of State under Root and then Assistant Secretary for Far Eastern Affairs under Knox.

To these men the phrase "Dollar Diplomacy" was somewhat distasteful, because, whether used in derogation or with approval, it concealed fuzzy and imprecise thinking.[5] As Straight put it in 1912, there "has been too much unjust criticism, too much unwarranted praise, and too general a lack of candid exposition and intelligent comprehension of the reasons for, and possibilities of, 'Dollar Diplomacy.' " On the one hand, some critics accused Taft and Knox of having "formed an unholy alliance with the Octopus; and Wall Street, the property scape-goat of our national political drama, is accused of seducing a reluctant and hitherto well-domesticated government into the maelstrom of international financial adventure"; while other "sober and intelligent" critics "have demanded why American capital should seek foreign fields when there is so much work to be done at home." On the other hand, a section of the press approving Dollar Diplomacy "hails each and every oversea venture with indiscriminate enthusiasm and rhetorically preens the feathers of the Bird of Freedom, sneering at or condemning our rivals, and lauding American enterprise with an impartial disregard for the real facts."

3. Taft's reasons for dismissing Rockhill reveals to a significant degree his own views on U.S. policy with respect to China, as well as those of Calhoun, the man he appointed. Said Taft in explanation of his dismissal of Rockhill: "He has not the slightest interest in American trade or in promoting it. He is pessimistic and not optimistic in his views of what can be done, and he is not a man of strength and force of action such as what we need at Peking. . . . I regard the position at Peking as one of the most important diplomatic positions that I have to fill, and it is necessary to send there a man of business force and perception and ability to withstand the aggressions of the Japanese, the English, and the Russians. China is very friendly to us, and. . . . anxious to encourage American trade and the American investment of capital, because she does not distrust our motives. The opportunities it seems to me, therefore, for the development of the Oriental trade are great if we can only have a man on the ground who realizes the necessity and has the force and pluck and experience to take advantage of the opportunity." (Taft to Rollo Ogden, 24 April 1909, Taft Papers, quoted in Vevier, *U.S. and China,* pp. 90–91.)

4. Calhoun at the Fifteenth Annual Dinner of the American Asiatic Association, 26 January 1914, *AAA Journal,* XIV, 1 (February 1914), p. 13. (Hereafter cited as Speech of 26 January 1914.)

5. Straight preferred to use the words only between quotation marks, and Calhoun claimed, "Just what is meant by that phrase I hardly know." For Calhoun, see his address at luncheon in his honor, attended by officers of industrial and finance corporations and intellectuals such as Charles A. Conant, and presided over by General Thomas A. Hubbard, president of the International Banking Corporation, 28 May, 1913, *AAA Journal,* XIII, 5 (June 1913), p. 137. (Hereafter cited as Luncheon Address, 28 May 1913.)

Straight's reply to such critics and enthusiasts offered a succinct and pre-cise statement of the general framework of thought underlying Dollar Diplomacy:

> "Dollar Diplomacy" is a logical manifestation of our national growth, and the rightful assumption by the United States of a more important place at the council table of nations. Our export trade is constantly increasing and foreign markets are becoming each year more and more necessary to our manufacturers. The new policy aims not only to protect those Americans already engaged in foreign trade but to promote fresh endeavor and by diplomatic action pave the way for those who have not yet been, but who will later be, obliged to sell capital or goods abroad.

European diplomacy, he observed, had "for years been of the 'Dollar' variety," engaged as it was in "solving a maze of complicated questions immediately political, ultimately commercial in character. . . . " The ob-jective was the acquisition of "fresh fields for colonization" or the cre-ation of "preferential markets." The "international rivalry" resulting from diplomacy of "the 'Dollar' variety," was to be found "only in those countries whose native administrations are either decrepit or which are still militarily too weak to secure that consideration, which, unfortu-nately, depends not upon international equity, but upon the power of self-protection. . . . " For in such lands the government of an industrial power seeking to secure markets for its nationals, "must because of the pressure of its competitors either acquire territory or insist on an equality of commercial opportunity. It must either stake out its own claim, or in-duce other interested powers to preserve the 'open door.' . . . " There was, Straight insisted, "no middle course." This was a matter not of "be-nevolent theories, but of political facts." In Dollar Diplomacy, the U.S. government chose expansion through the open door rather than through formal colonialism:

> The people of the United States do not desire fresh territory over seas. The policy of our government has been to secure for American merchants the "open door." American industry has until recently been too much engaged by our own domestic expansion seriously to set about the establishment of foreign markets. A far-seeing admin-istration has therefore inaugurated a new policy, the alliance of di-plomacy, with industry, commerce and finance. This is "Dollar Diplomacy."[6]

6. For quotations in this and previous paragraphs, Willard Straight, "China's Loan Ne-gotiations," address delivered to conference on recent developments in China, 13–16 November 1912 (14 November 1912), at Clark University, Worcester, Mass., in George H. Blakeslee, ed., *Recent Developments in China* (1913), pp. 120–122. The

If, as is evident from Straight's exposition, Dollar Diplomacy meant the implementation of the open door for economic expansion into agrarian areas of the world, applied to China it meant an insistence upon the nation's "territorial and administrative entity." For, without it, participation of the United States in China's development faced sharp delimitation, if not total exclusion. Accordingly, China's "integrity" assumed the character of a means and an end: It was the means of sustaining the open door for U.S. investment and trade, while the latter were the means of maintaining China's "integrity." *Mutatis mutandis,* investment also became a means and an end. Stating it reveals the formulation's less than useful nature. As conceived by the Dollar Diplomats, the question was not of the chicken-egg, means-end, variety; it was not politics on the one hand, economics on the other. It was a question of political economy, where, far from assuming separate entities, politics and economics were inextricably interrelated. The objectives involved were not of a purely diplomatic nature divorced from political economy, such as securing a political balance of power for its own sake by strategically "using" bankers (dollars); rather, they involved the establishment of an international system of political economy required by the expanding U.S. capitalist system, in which the nation's investing power might be used as "a political instrument in the great diplomatic struggle in which all are engaged to secure the markets for their foreign trade." As President Taft informed Congress in 1912, "modern diplomacy is commercial."[7]

Accordingly, it was precisely by a political stratagem that Secretary of State John Hay, in his open door doctrine, had "induced the Powers to accept . . . a new definition of rival interests [in China] in financial and commercial, no longer in territorial, terms. . . . "[8] This amounted to internationalizing the noncolonial form of expansion in China, which the United States itself pursued there and elsewhere. It operated to preserve China's formal territorial and administrative entity, while serving the United States' own developmental imperatives. As the *Journal of Commerce* defined the issue in 1913, it had "become plain even to the least reflective that the integrity of China was a vital necessity not only for the

text of this address may also be found in *AAA Journal,* XII, 11 (December 1912), pp. 330–339.

7. Straight, "Foreign Trade and Foreign Loans," 27 May 1914, *Official Report of the National Foreign Trade Convention,* 1914, p. 179. (Hereafter cited as NFTC, *Proc.,* year.) Taft's message to Congress, 3 December 1912, U.S. Department of State, *Papers Relating to the Foreign Relations of the United States,* 1912, p. x. (Hereafter cited as *For. Rels.*)
8. Straight, "American Friendship for China," address at Fourteenth Annual Dinner of the American Asiatic Association, 2 November 1912, *AAA Journal,* XII, 10 (November 1912), p. 298. Cf. Straight, "China's Loan Negotiations," in Blakeslee, *Recent Developments,* p. 124.

Name DOVIAK/JOSEPH M
Card type: VISA
Card #4621203019374330   EXP:0406
Date 09/12/01   0053282
Time 11:38:18
RETURN -45.00
Approved: 000001
Clerk:

X _____
  Signature

RECTO & VERSO BOOKSHOP
90 ALBANY STREET
NEW Brunswick NJ 08901-1227
732-247-2324
Transaction No: 0053282
Customer ID:

Station: 1
09/12/01 11:38:18   CLERK:

1*@ 16.00 0306803623   25%   -12.00
   Stomping the Blues
1*@ 15.00 0226511731   -15.00
   Screening Out the Past : T
1*@ 18.00 0300042280   -18.00
   The Grounding of Modern Fe
UBTOTAL   -45.00
AX @ 6.000%   0.00
OTAL   -45.00
ISA Credit   462120301937433
06/04
                                -45.00

THANK YOU!
LL TEXTBOOKS RETURN DEADLINE 09/14/01
NO REFUND WITHOUT RECIEPT.

full development of the material resources, and the industrial and commercial energy of the United States, but for the adequate fulfillment of its manifest political destiny."[9] Or in the words of American Asiatic Association secretary John Foord in 1911:

> [It] has from the first been insisted upon by the American Asiatic Association that our commercial interest in China was reinforced by political considerations of acknowledged potency by reasons of policy, which are founded on a due regard for the full and free development of our national greatness. In short, this association has held from the first that the place which the United States occupies in the world and the place which it should occupy in future ages was equally challenged by every step made toward the dismemberment of China. . . . [10]

To its advocates and practitioners, and in Huntington Wilson's words, Dollar Diplomacy was "common sense diplomacy . . . in the highest sense of that term"; for given the underlying evaluation of the character and requirements of the U.S. political economy, it was "a diplomacy determined by the application of scientific principles and sound thinking to plain facts studied and understood as they really are; a diplomacy preferring to build for the long future, rather than to dogmatize for the moment's expediency. . . . " Significantly, in discussing the objectives and instrumentalities of Dollar Diplomacy, Wilson made it clear that they could not be segregated into political and economic categories. The "division of political from economic advantage," he pointed out, "so gradually merge into one another as to make clear cut classification difficult," in a process whereby nature "takes its inexorable course [in international affairs] with private enterprise and diplomacy as its instruments. . . . "[11]

9. "The Friendship of Japan," *New York Journal of Commerce*, in *AAA Journal*, XIII, 4 (May 1913), p. 105.
10. Editorial, *AAA Journal*, XI, 10 (November 1911), p. 290.
11. Francis M. Huntington Wilson, "The Relation of Government to Foreign Investment," *The Annals of the American Academy of Political and Social Science*, LXVIII (whole no. 157), November 1916, 300, 301–302, 306–307. See also Straight's remarks before the first National Foreign Trade Convention, 27 May, 1914: "The balance of power in the Far East, to which China owed and still owes her continued existence as a nation, has for some years, and is now, largely maintained by the nice adjustment of the financial and commercial, and therefore political, interests of the great powers. . . . It is to their mutual interest to maintain the 'open door' and share in the general Chinese trade, rather than by the seizure of territory to endeavor to monopolize the commerce of any particular region. President Taft desired to assist in the maintenance of the 'open door', by securing for the United States a voice in this council of nations, the weight of whose influence depends primarily upon the extent of their material interest. He wished also to gain for American manufacturers a share in the profits of China's industrial development. . . . " NFTC, *Proc.*, 1914, p. 183.

Wilson, Calhoun, and Straight each appealed to different justifications for U.S. expansion. Wilson spoke of "a sort of 'international biology'," whereby the strong nations must dominate the weaker ones. Calhoun referred to the *Volk*-instinct sociology of Benjamin Kidd, whereby the continental, colonial, and economic expansion of the United States, in that order, expressed the nation's "destiny by instinct."[12] Straight emphasized the necessities of modern economic conditions that promised, however, beneficent results for the rest of the world. In this respect, Straight most closely represented the ascending open door ideology of his contemporaries and of more recent corporate and government policymakers. Yet, whatever the specific justification, all were concerned with the condition of chronic surplus of capital and goods in relation to effective demand, and assumed that economic expansion abroad was both a natural culmination of the nation's historical development and an indispensable condition of its continued economic stability and growth, and hence of its continued historical development as a nation or modern society.

Calhoun, for example, argued that while in "olden times," diplomacy revolved primarily around the territorial ambitions of monarchs, which he described as political in nature, in modern times "the great forces that are moving in the world are economic rather than political. . . . The struggle is for markets and for trade."[13] American participation in this struggle became necessary with the end of the continental frontier. While expansion westward proceeded, the problems and dangers of overproduction and economic dislocation could work themselves out, absorbed in the tasks of continental development. "As long as we had the virgin market, a growing, expanding and absorbing market, a great demand was made upon the energies of our people to supply it. . . . " But with industrialization "the volume of production increased so rapidly that the supply was greater than the demand." The "old ideal competitive condition that once existed . . . wherein small units of production might grow and expand" depended upon the continually expanding frontier; it "no longer exists, because . . . [the] virgin, growing, expanding and absorbing market no longer is there." For survival, capitalists resorted to two equally undesirable alternatives – first, destructive competition,

12. F. M. H. Wilson, "Relation of Government," pp. 306–307. For Calhoun, see Luncheon Address, 28 May 1913, *AAA Journal*, XIII, 5 (June 1913), p. 138.
13. Ibid., 137. The luncheon was arranged in Calhoun's honor upon his return from China, by corporate leaders and Asiatic Association members. Upon Calhoun's introduction by General Hubbard, the diners greeted him with "Loud and prolonged cheers." Ibid., p. 133. Corporate leaders expressed sotto voce agreement of this type time and again during the semiprivate talks by Calhoun and Straight. For list of diners at this luncheon, see ibid., p. 132.

then monopoly. Not that the nation was "fully developed," nor that its population might not double within the next generation, renewing consumer demand, "but the producing power will keep even pace therewith, and the strain between supply and consumption will still exist and may possibly be more intensified as time goes on." The solution, according to Calhoun, lay in economic expansion abroad into the agrarian areas, where the new "virgin, growing, expanding and absorbing" territories awaited development: an expansion based upon the assertion of the open door for U.S. investment and trade, but facilitated by the modest modicum of annexationist colonialism already achieved (the Panama Canal, Guam, Puerto Rico, Hawaii, Midway, Wake Island, Samoa, the Philippines).[14]

Given these basic assumptions about the nature of the national economy and the corresponding expansionist objectives, the specific content of Dollar Diplomacy revolved around the role of the state in implementing effective policy in the name of the national interest. For, implicit in the pursuit of a national interest so defined was the coming to grips with certain necessities and circumstances. The most crucial were (1) the central role of investment in fostering the economic expansion in view; (2) the absence of a developed and receptive domestic market in the United States for foreign securities, bonds, and commercial acceptances; (3) the precapitalist nature of the societies and governments of the agrarian areas, and the importance of such governments as agencies of economic development within those areas; (4) the severe competition among the capitalists of the various industrial nations for control of the markets and investment opportunities in these areas. It was to these necessities and circumstances that the advocates and practitioners of Dollar Diplomacy invariably addressed themselves when expounding its theory and practice.

Their settled conviction that the trade they sought was the function of investment flowed from their concern not merely to find more markets

14. Speech of January 26, 1914, ibid., XIV, 1 (February 1914), pp. 14–15, 18. Calhoun emphasized that "No dream of far-flung imperialism lures me," and in proceeding to the type of economic expansion he envisioned he evoked from his audience of corporation executives and other Asiatic Association members cries of "Go on, do not stop; keep it up!" Cf. Calhoun's reference to the Canal and the Pacific possessions as "so many stands that have come to us as bases for our commerce, as steps toward its development," in his Luncheon Address, 28 May 1913, ibid., XIII, 5 (June 1913), p. 138. Straight, for his part, explicitly praised William H. Seward's "prophetic words regarding our future on the Pacific." The "barriers of industrial exclusiveness" were "fast disappearing," he said, and he went on to argue that just as the era of westward continental expansion was one of national economic development, so the new era of expansion across the Pacific Ocean "must be one of Pacific development as well . . ." Speech as president of the American Asiatic Association, 26 January, 1914, ibid., XIV, p. 1 (February 1914), p. 8.

in which to sell, but to expand the sphere of enterprise for industry and finance largely in terms of the needs of the capital goods sector of the economy. This may be seen, for example, in the Asiatic Association *Journal's* comment on the Taft administration's vigorous efforts on behalf of the participation of U.S. interests in the Hukuang railway project in China. The *Journal* declared that the administration had "done well in basing its unprecedented action . . . for the preservation of the Eastern market for American trade upon the menace existing in the monopolizing of trade through foreign loans to China. . . . "[15] For, it was "customary, in making loans to China, for the lenders to benefit by the expenditure of the money. In this way for three years China's orders for steel and railway machinery, mining machinery, arsenal equipments, woolen, cotton and silk spinning and weaving machinery, leather making and minting machinery, and also equipment for steel plants and iron works, have been placed in Europe. . . . " Recognizing this, the Taft administration "obviously does not intend that the markets of China shall be closed to American industry, and has promoted the investment of American money there as one of the surest means of securing the same profitable returns of trade that are secured by European nations by this process. . . . "[16]

If the open door for trade in agrarian areas such as China was a function of the open door for investment, it was, as John Foord observed, "in fact impossible to separate these two forms of business activity, since it is axiomatic that trade follows the loan and that in China, as elsewhere, capital borrowed abroad comes in the shape of merchandise. . . . "[17] In this way, investment abroad was seen primarily as the handmaiden of expanding the sphere of enterprise and markets of the industrial corporations, with the emphasis placed on direct investments. (After World War I and in the 1920s some of the larger banking houses pursued portfolio investments independent of the industrial corporations, involving both a conflict of interests between the expansionism of finance and that of industry, and divisions over government policy in the State and Commerce departments that occupied the attention of men such as Hoover.) This was the meaning of Taft's explanation of his administration's in-

15. Ibid., XI, 1 (February 1911), p. 2.
16. Fredrick McCormick, "American Defeat in the Pacific," ibid., pp. 8–9. At the same time, the Asiatic Association's *Journal* was printing such reports as "How to Develop Trade in China," from the U.S. vice-council general in Shanghai, W. Roderick Dorsey, who emphasized the "possibilities for flour, beet sugar, oil, and paper mills; cotton, mining, and agricultural machinery; along lines of progressive internal development, electrical light and water plants are to be supplied, and railways, both steam and electric, to be laid down. . . . This field is expanding and American commerce should increase with it." Ibid., XI, 2 (March 1911), p. 41.
17. Ibid., XIII, 10 (November 1913), p. 293.

tervention in the Hukuang affair, when he stated that "this railway loan represented a practical and real application of the open door policy"; it was as "a matter of broad policy urgent that this opportunity should not be lost," and "the indispensable instrumentality presented itself" in the form of "a group of American bankers" who agreed to share in the loan "upon precisely such terms as this Government should approve," the "chief" of which "was that American railway material should be upon an exact equality with that of other nationals . . . in the placing of orders for this whole railroad system." The administration, therefore, "deemed American participation to be of great national interest"; for, "Americans will thus take their share in this extension of these great highways of trade, and . . . such activities will give a real impetus to our commerce and will prove a practical corollary to our historic policy in the Far East."[18]

Discussing in some detail the relation of investment to foreign trade, Straight distinguished clearly between "ordinary merchandising," for which short-term credit sufficed, and the type of trade sought by Dollar Diplomacy. Accordingly, "in the great development schemes, such as railways, where vast quantities of materials are required; in the construction of arsenals and electric lighting plants, street railways, etc., the community or the country which is being developed, in all probability, has not the funds with which to meet the expense involved and must, therefore, borrow." Such a country could not borrow from the bank for these purposes, "because the bank must make a turnover of its capital"; it must borrow instead from "the public," through the issue of bonds and securities. In view of this and of the competition of capitalists from other industrial nations, there was, therefore, "absolutely no chance for American manufacturers to sell their goods to railway or other government or industrial undertakings, which are constructed or operated with foreign money. This after all is but natural. . . . " Quite aside from the question of foreign competition, insofar as China itself could not finance and organize such undertakings, U.S. interests could not hope to share in China's development without the appropriate investment of U.S. capital. Thus, in China, "more than in almost any other country perhaps, trade follows the loan." The "financing the sale of our materials abroad," Straight emphasized, "that is the question of foreign trade and foreign loans."[19]

18. Message to Congress, December 7, 1909, *For. Rels.*., 1909, pp. xviii–xix. Cf. Straight, "The Politics of Chinese Finance," *AAA Journal*, XIII, 6 (July 1913), pp. 165–166; and Straight, "China's Loan Negotiations," in Blakeslee, *Recent Developments*, pp. 127–128. See also Frederick V. Field, *American Participation in the China Consortium* (1931), pp. 34–35, and Vevier, *U.S. and China*, p. 216.
19. Straight, Speech at Fifteenth Annual Dinner of the American Asiatic Association, 26

In the same way, Calhoun, addressing himself to the general question, "Where shall we find markets?" and specifying South America and China, pointed out that China's "possibilities" were "immense." "You go to China. How is trade expanded there? That is a new country. Practically it needs to be opened up. That can only be done by building railroads and that requires foreign money, and the people who are loaning money to build railroads, to reorganize their finances get naturally and justly a preference which will serve to their economic advantage and to our disadvantage unless we participate therein. . . . " Consequently, "in establishing trade relations with an undeveloped country, capital plays a very important part. . . . "[20]

Dollar Diplomacy, therefore, referred to the government's role in "establishing trade relations with *undeveloped* countries"; it did not apply to relations among industrial capitalist countries (although it would to some extent during and after World War I, and on a rather larger scale during and after World War II). Shortly after his return from China, Calhoun took the occasion to make this distinction quite clear. When U.S. capitalists borrow money from European capitalists, for example, he told his corporate friends, "you don't say anything to your Government about it," and they "say nothing to their government." They know "our business experience and standing," and are assured of "a well-established system of laws and . . . well organized courts . . . to which the foreigner can appeal for protection of his rights and the enforcement of his contract." In relations between industrial nations, therefore, there was no necessity for the capitalists of the lending nation to appeal to their government. But, "in a country like China it is different." Because there the laws and courts give no such assurance, the foreign capitalist's "only protection is to appeal to his government for diplomatic support. That is a necessity growing out of this situation."

The natural result was that "the practice has grown up, . . . the rule has been enacted that the support of the government shall be invoked . . . and its approval secured." In this manner, "diplomatic influence has become usual in those countries which make it necessary for the protection of the individual." On the other hand, with respect to the question of

January 1914, *AAA Journal*, XIV, 1 (February 1914), pp. 8–9; Straight, "Foreign Trade and Foreign Loans," and preliminary remarks, NFTC, *Proc.*, 1914, pp. 174–175, 177.

20. Calhoun described South America as a "great field for commercial development," "a virgin territory," whose resources had "hardly been touched," and with which the United States still had "comparatively little trade connection." Speech of 26 January 1914, *AAA Journal*, XIV, 1 (February 1914), p. 16, 17; and Luncheon Address, 28 May 1913, ibid., XIII, 5 (June 1913), p. 138. Calhoun delivered the latter address shortly after returning to the United States from his post as U.S. Minister to China. Cf. ibid., p. 130, for editorial endorsement of Calhoun's analysis.

business practices and techniques, including government fiscal policy, industrial engineering, and business management, the Chinese lacked "the experience, the education or training to make them efficient. Therefore they do not command credit." This too made diplomatic support necessary; it substituted sufficiently for the credit rating, as it were, that investors would normally require in placing their capital, and it aided in persuading the Chinese government to adopt appropriate business methods and submit to unusual measures of supervision and control. In the absence of diplomatic support, then, for capitalists "who seek to establish trade relations with backward countries . . . there will be no stimulus in that direction."[21]

Calhoun provided the analysis of the government's role from the point of view of the diplomat. Straight did so from that of the corporations and banks. He explained that outlook, in 1912, not long after returning from China where he had been representing the American Banking Group. "It is not the bankers themselves who provide the money to finance a foreign loan, though they may for a time advance from their own resources certain preliminary payments." The bonds "are sold to the public," and the bankers, therefore, could float them only on a "business," and not a "sentimental," basis.[22] At the same time, the bankers were seeking to encourage and develop a foreign bond market in the United States. "Reputable American bankers cannot afford to purchase Chinese bonds unless their ability to sell them is reasonably certain, and the American investor is not willing to buy Chinese bonds unless he believes that the American government will protect him by all possible diplomatic means in case the Chinese Government, through difficulties of its own should fail for a time to meet its obligations."[23] Though the bankers' interest in a particular loan did not necessarily terminate with the completion of the bond issue, the banks were determined not to tie up their capital in such bonds. There was more profit to be made from domestic and other foreign investments that assured frequent and easy turnover. Their concern for the investing public, therefore, derived from the immediate, practical urgency of establishing the confidence in foreign bonds sufficient to the development of a broad public market for them, as well as from the more long-term, general considerations concerning

21. For quotations in this and previous paragraphs, Luncheon Address, 28 May, 1913, *AAA Journal*, XIII, 5 (June 1913), p. 137, and Speech of 26 January, 1914, ibid., XIV, 1 (February 1914), pp. 17–18. Cf. endorsement of Calhoun's views by the *Journal of Commerce*, reprinted in ibid., XIII, 9 (October 1913), p. 272, and by the *AAA Journal*, XIV, 1 (February 1914), p. 2.
22. Straight, "China's Loan Negotiations," in Blakeslee, *Recent Developments*, p. 155.
23. Straight, Speech at Fifteenth Annual Dinner of Asiatic Association, 26 January, 1914, *AAA Journal*, XIV, 1 (February 1914), p. 9.

the indispensability of foreign loans and investments to the type of international economic system the bankers and corporations sought to build.

In essence, the private corporations and banking houses found it necessary to call upon the state for help in the allocation of accumulated capital to foreign investment. At that time, as Straight pointed out, foreign bonds had "never been a popular investment in this country." Its investment markets lagged far behind those of Paris, London, and Berlin. And because of "the necessity of obtaining this public support for foreign loans . . . the Government has been brought into the situation." The question in the investing public's mind was "whether our Government will back us up in case of default." The government was not expected to give a "blanket assurance" that it would; nor was it expected to "send battleships to collect interest." But, Straight continued, "if the American public is to be educated to the point of financing the sale of our materials abroad . . . the American Government must make some statement which will reassure the public and give them the thought and the belief that in case of default, or in case of difficulty – not that the Government is going to act as a policeman and is going to collect their debts – but that the Government will act as the advocate of the public and in the international courts of diplomacy see that the American investor gets what is his due.[24]

Accordingly, neither the bankers nor the diplomats considered as desirable conditions that necessitated military intervention on behalf of bond holders. Such disturbances only undermined confidence in foreign bonds. Indeed, it was precisely the purpose of Dollar Diplomacy "to substitute dollars for bullets."[25] Military intervention was not, however, to be precluded as a measure of first or last resort where the objectives and instrumentalities of Dollar Diplomacy had yet to materialize or were threatened with disruption. Dollar Diplomacy either made military measures unnecessary or began where the latter successfully ended. "Investors do not want bonds," Straight explained, "if there is any chance that the interests thereon must be collected by war. Such bonds are not good investments, money can be placed much more safely at home. Investors in foreign securities do, however, desire some assurance of the support of their own govern-

24. Straight, NFTC, *Proc.*, 1914, 175 and ibid., 186–187. Cf. F. M. Huntington Wilson, "Relation of Government to Foreign Investment," *Annals*, LXVIII (November 1916), p. 302: "it is still true that there is not enough American capital yet available for foreign investment thoroughly to cover the duty of consolidating our economic position in the spheres where that necessity is most obvious. . . . "
25. Taft, Annual Message to Congress, 3 December 1912, *For. Rels.*, 1912, pp. vii–xvii; and Huntington Wilson, "Relation of Government to Foreign Investment," p. 305.

ment. . . . "[26] With respect to China, military intervention on behalf of the bankers as a probability or as an intention of the Taft administration was particularly irrelevant. The matter was stated typically by Secretary Knox in his instruction concerning the Six-Power Consortium to the U.S. legation in Peking: The U.S. government, "while continuing to insist upon what it considers reasonable and general measures for the protection of the interests of all its nationals, . . . is not prepared to join in any coercive steps designed to compel China's acceptance either of the present loan or of any particular proposal as to advisers."[27] Or, as Straight stated, in China "it has never been necessary to collect interest by gunboats, and there is little likelihood that it will be necessary in the future. . . . "[28]

Just as the government's role was not conceived as that of policeman or debt collector on behalf of bankers by the Dollar Diplomats, so neither was its role conceived as that of guaranteeing contracts or sponsoring particular capitalists to the exclusion of others.[29] The government was to extend general support to bankers and corporations seeking investments, contracts, markets, upon the "axiomatic principle" that it "shall extend all proper support to every legitimate and beneficial American enterprise abroad."[30] By this definition, however, Dollar Diplomacy in its application was selective and not meant to respond automatically to pressures of private interests without regard to strategic, military, political, and economic circumstances. It was not intended to support every U.S. enterprise abroad. While protecting foreign investments and enterprises of its citizens, the government was considered obliged to reserve its authority to control the course of such activities by extending "great or little protection" and encouragement "or none at all." A given enterprise undertaken abroad by a U.S. citizen or corporation "may be legitimate so far as the interested American is concerned

26. Straight, Speech at Fifteenth Annual Dinner of Asiatic Association, 26 January 1914, *AAA Journal*, XIV, 1 (February 1914), p. 9.
27. Knox to Chargé d'Affaires E. T. Williams, 27 February 1913, *For. Rels.*, 1913, p. 166.
28. Straight, Speech at Fifteenth Annual Dinner, *AAA Journal*, XIV, 1 (February 1914) p. 9.
29. See, e.g., Calhoun's Speech of 26 January 1914, ibid., pp. 17–18: "I do not believe that governments should guarantee contracts or become a mere collecting agency . . ." Cf. endorsement of such views by the *Journal of Commerce*, reprinted in ibid., XIII, 9 (October 1913), p. 272, and by the Asiatic Association's *Journal*, XIV, 1 (February 1914), p. 2. The latter referred to the "characteristic lucidity and force" of Calhoun's exposition, and noted approvingly that he had "energetically disclaimed the idea that Governments should guarantee contracts, or become a mere collecting agency. . . . "
30. Taft's message to Congress, 3 December 1912, *For. Rels.*, 1912, p. x. Cf. H. Wilson, "Relation of Government," p. 303.

and beneficial to him individually, while not beneficial to the nation. Such would be the case if the dangers of seriously involving this country in fresh obligations outweighed any national advantage; if the investment diverted from channels of real national advantage money that might otherwise serve that advantage either abroad or at home; or if the project offended a valued friend among the nations. To merit the strongest governmental support the foreign investment or enterprise must be really beneficial to the nation."[31]

Thus, not every capitalist or firm and its contemplated enterprise constituted a suitable instrumentality of the national interest worthy of the government's support. By the same token, only particular corporations or banks were suited in certain cases for arrangements (such as fiscal reform or staking a claim to railroad development) supported by the government in its pursuit of the national interest prescribed by Dollar Diplomacy. These had to be reliable, reputable, and effective for the purposes contemplated. With respect to the projects for development in agrarian areas, this usually meant support of large banks and large corporations. In Straight's words:

> Americans cannot expect nor can they legitimately demand exclusive support for certain individuals, but if the principle of support for merchants, contractors and engineers abroad be enunciated, assistance must be accorded those who already have had the courage and enterprise to engage in foreign trade. If we are to build up our interests abroad, moreover, firms that have not as yet established foreign connections must be encouraged to do so. They must be regarded as national assets, not as special interests, and whatever our differences may be at home, we must all – diplomats and consuls, missionaries and teachers, merchants and bankers – stand together, as Americans; . . . for once we have seen the dock lights die, we become representatives of our country, trustees for its trade and of its reputation.[32]

But success depended upon the capitalists concerned "being of such standing as [to] command respect from financial groups abroad," and being willing and able to bear the expense of long and unremunerative negotiations. "Without these qualifications American bankers are not equipped to become the instruments which our government requires to assist in the extension of our foreign trade." In the matter of government

31.   Ibid., pp. 298, 299, 303, 305.
32.   Straight, Speech at Fifteenth Annual Dinner, 26 January 1914, *AAA Journal*, XIV, 1 (February 1914), p. 9.

support for business ventures abroad, "We must apply eugenics to international trade."[33]

Government support for accumulation of capital by the bankers from the investing public was one thing, government guarantee of contracts made abroad was another. The refusal of the government, as a general principle, to sponsor or guarantee contracts predated the Dollar Diplomats, and remained an effective precedent under them as well as under Woodrow Wilson subsequently.[34] At no time during the negotiations for the Manchurian railway and bank loan, the currency reform and industrial development loan, the Hukuang loan, or the Reorganization loan, did the State Department concern itself directly with the terms of the contemplated contract. The bankers and the Department maintained a strict separation between the financial and political aspects of the negotiations. Knox and Huntington Wilson repeatedly dissociated the Department from any intention of giving exclusive support to the American Group in the matter of loans to the Chinese government.[35] In practice, however, the principle of selectivity and the need to translate support for capitalists in general to support for particular interests undertaking particular enterprises, led in effect to the government supporting certain capitalists and not others. This provoked criticism of the State Department from unfavored capitalists such as happened in the case of the Hukuang railway project and in that of the Reorganization loan, where the Department actively discouraged the operations of U.S. interests outside the American Group.[36] But the contradiction and attendant

33. Straight, "China's Loan Negotiations," in Blakeslee, *Recent Developments*, p. 121; and Speech at Fifteenth Annual Dinner, *AAA Journal*, XIV, 1 (February 1914), p. 9.
34. See, e.g., Secretary Day's note to Minister Denby in the matter of the American-China Development Co., *For. Rels.*, 1897, pp. 56–58, and discussion of this matter by Foord in *AAA Journal.*, XIII, 10 (November 1913), p. 290. See also Straight's position on this matter expressed in his note to the Chinese official Tang Shao-yi while Straight was chief of the State Department's Far Eastern Affairs Division in 1908, discussed in Vevier, *U.S. and China*, p. 81.
35. Cf. Field, *American Participation*, pp. 35, 37. See also, e.g., H. Wilson to Ambassador of Great Britain, 16 March 1912. "The object, of course, should be to secure to the groups fair treatment without giving them a monopoly to the exclusion of other legitimate lenders with whom they might be unwilling to combine. The proposed formula might be somewhat as follows: An undertaking not to negotiate 'any subsequent loan that might conflict with the legitimate interests or weaken the security of the large loan, if consummated, which is at present being negotiated by the combined groups with the approval of their Governments, or of loans hitherto negotiated.'" *For. Rels.*, 1912, p. 114; and Ambassador of Great Britain to H. Wilson, 21 March 1912, ibid., p. 121, for British assent to the formula proposed by H. Wilson. See also to same effect H. Wilson to Calhoun, 19 March 1912, Knox to U.S. Ambassador to France (Herrick), 17 May 1912, Herrick to Knox, 13 June 1912, Knox to Herrick, 18 July 1912, and Knox to Chargé E. T. Williams, 27 February 1913, ibid., pp. 115–116, 128–129, 137, 147, and ibid., 1913, p. 166.
36. The Dollar Diplomats themselves became divided over this. See, e.g., the comments of

embarrassments were not the peculiar problem of the Dollar Diplomats; the Wilson administration, too, had to grapple with them.

   Taken out of context, certain statements of Secretary Knox might appear to justify the supposition that the State Department conceived of "using" bankers for discrete and pure diplomatic objectives. For example, in May 1911, Knox wrote to Paul S. Reinsch (then professor at the University of Wisconsin and later to become Woodrow Wilson's minister to China), requesting that Reinsch intercede with Senator Robert M. LaFollette on behalf of the administration's attempt to secure Senate ratification of the Honduras Convention, which included provisions for the reorganization of Honduran fiscal and customs arrangements under the supervision of U.S. diplomats and bankers. Referring to LaFollette's "strong disapproval of what is called 'Dollar Diplomacy'," particularly in the matter of the Honduran Convention, Knox insisted that the Senator's attitude could not "be based on anything else than a complete misunderstanding of the realities of the situation, and an idea probably that Wall Street is using the Department, instead of the realization that the Department is seeking to make American capital an instrumentality of

Lewis Einstein, who had served as first secretary of the U.S. Legislation at Peking under Taft and Knox. Soon after his return to the United States he wrote that though in his view the policy was "eminently sound," nevertheless from a domestic point of view, "a grave initial mistake had been made by unduly restricting the basis of our financial force, instead of making it representative of the country at large. This error had originated at the time of taking up the proposed enterprises in Manchuria and had unfortunately remained uncorrected when our policy changed and broadened. A semblance of justification was thereby given to attacks made against 'dollar diplomacy' and the supposed unholy alliance between the State Department and Wall Street. While the motives of both were above suspicion, yet the country ill informed as to the situation, and with insufficient attention paid to its legitimate demands for information, turned these into violent criticism. . . . "Einstein, "Japan at Tsingtau and American Policy," *AAA Journal*, XIV, 2 (January 1915), pp. 360–361. (See the reference of the *Journal's* editor to "The acumen and intelligence which Mr. Einstein brings to the treatment of a subject which he has had the advantage of being able to study at close range. . . . " Ibid., p. 354.) President Wilson and Secretary Lansing, in encouraging the organization of the second consortium did not make the same mistake. For the broad composition of the second consortium see Field, *American Participation*, pp. 144, 145, 165. Straight tacitly acknowledged the possible validity of such criticism as that made by Einstein, when in May 1913, he stated: "It is perhaps un-American for the government to request any particular banking group to undertake foreign business and thus even indirectly to guarantee a degree of diplomatic support which such a request might imply. . . . " But the problem was that such investments in China were urgent if the United States were to have a share of its trade, and given the absence of a developed foreign bond market in the United States, it was "doubtful if the United States has as yet developed to the point where, from a merely business point of view, American bankers will find it desirable (except at the instance of the Government), to embark on any very large operations in a country whose political future is as uncertain as that of China." "The Politics of Chinese Finance," *AAA Journal*, XIII, 6 (July 1913), p. 171.

American diplomacy, and that if one is going to use capital it must come from wherever it happens to be. . . . "[37] This letter must be read, however, alongside that Knox sent to Reinsch a week later thanking him for responding promptly to the Department's request by taking the matter up with LaFollette. "The people of Honduras," explained Knox, "have no basis for credit except through customs revenue and that is not good collateral unless its honest administration is assured. . . . [38]

The specific objective of "American diplomacy" involved was that of establishing the financial basis within such agrarian countries as Honduras for U.S. investment in their resources, and the smoothly functioning pattern of trade corresponding with such investment. Without adequate revenues, the governments of such countries, which were the foremost or only institutions capable of securing large loans and investments, and which played decisive roles in dispensing economic privileges, could not adequately facilitate the investments except by granting special "concessions" to foreign corporations. But concessions often permitted noneconomic considerations to assume commanding influence in the dispensation of investment opportunities; and such factors were not only a source of irritating corruption, but also facilitated penetration by European interests while interfering with the "natural" assertion of U.S. economic potential. A sound customs and fiscal system in these areas, on the other hand, by providing ample security for loans, would encourage U.S. investment there. With extraneous considerations thereby pared to the minimum, the United States' economic equality or superiority would quite naturally assert itself more easily in the development of these areas.

This principle applied alike to China and Latin America. In defending the administration's support of U.S. participation in international loans to the Chinese government, secured on its internal revenues, which comprised the chief available security for foreign loans in China, Knox pointed out that without the United States' participation "the control of the principal revenues throughout the heart of China would have been pledged to other foreign powers, and America would have been deprived of any voice at the council board at which the important questions involved in the disposition of these revenues were determined."[39] The

37. Knox to Reinsch, 3 May 1911, *Paul S. Reinsch Papers, Letters*, 1910–1911, Wisconsin State Historical Society (Madison).
38. Knox to Reinsch, 10 May 1911, ibid.
39. Quoted in *Journal of Commerce*, "The Administration and the Chinese Loan Question," reprinted in *AAA Journal*, XIII (April 1913), p. 71. Cf. Taft's message to Congress, December 3 1912, *For. Rels.*, 1912, pp. xi–xii. See Vevier, *U.S. and China*, pp. 175–176; "The powers had long hoped to assist their trade interests in China by stabilizing the nation's currency. . . . " The chief of the State Department's Division of Far Eastern Affairs considered currency reform "pressing," because necessary to fis-

matter may be seen more sharply in Willard Straight's analysis of government revenues in agrarian areas and their relation to the development of investment and trade patterns sought by corporate and political leaders in the United States.

According to Straight, the "great lending nations" utilized "their investing power as a national asset." By "building up the weaker nations through financial reorganization and the development of [their] resources, they create for themselves a financial and political influence which they convert to commercial advantage. In this task, Government, bankers, merchants and manufacturers, supported by the investing public, which the Government represents, and of which the bankers, merchants and manufacturers are an integral part, cooperate for the common good." Having thus established the democratic nature of the process, Straight cited the Platt Amendment as the "first instance" in which the U.S. government "took official cognizance of the political importance of foreign loans." In providing that the Cuban government "shall not increase its indebtedness until it has first satisfied the American Government that such increase will not, by creating an excessive charge upon the Cuban revenues, prejudice the financial stability of that Republic," the U.S. government "desired to preclude foreign financial domination and to safeguard the credit of the Cuban Republic, in order that the people of the United States, as well as the Cubans, might benefit by the development of the resources of the island." The same principle applied, noted Straight, to arrangements effected or proposed by the United States or the European powers, in the Dominican Republic, Honduras, Nicaragua, Turkey, Egypt, and China. Specifically, the finances of the Dominican Republic had been "reorganized and its foreign debt consolidated by means of an American loan, and the collection of the revenues hypothecated as security therefor was placed under American supervision. While similar arrangements were proposed, but not consummated, with Honduras, they were successfully effected with Nicaragua."[40]

Discussing President Wilson's speech before the Southern Commercial Congress in Mobile, in which the President denounced "concessionaires," Straight made clear how in supplementing the "Monroe" with what he called the "Wilson" doctrine, the president had asserted the same objectives as those pursued under Taft and Knox. Wilson "anticipated the day when, through the beneficent influence of the United States, the

cal reform and economic development, and to enable China "to increase her indebtedness to foreign capitalists." E. T. Williams to Rockhill, 11 March 1911, Rockhill Papers, cited in ibid., p. 176.

40. Straight, "Foreign Trade and Foreign Loans," NFTC, *Proc.* (1914), pp. 179–181.

weaker South and Central American States would be enabled to borrow on their national credit and no longer be obliged to grant concessions. . . . " Since these nations derived "practically their entire income from their customs dues," the president's objective could "only be attained by placing these collectorates under foreign supervision, as has already been done in Santo Domingo and Nicaragua. Such action would assure a regular revenue amply sufficient to meet the service of the loans which these republics now need. . . . " By assuring in this way the ability of such governments to meet their financial obligations, the United States could "avoid complications" with European powers in the Caribbean area "and develop our own export and import trade." It was therefore essential "by means of foreign loans, [to] establish ourselves as the guardians of the financial stability as well as the territorial integrity of some of our southern neighbors." Such considerations, as Straight pointed out, underlay the policy of the Taft administration with respect to international cooperation for currency and fiscal reform in China.[41]

Having examined the thinking of the Dollar Diplomats in some detail, the government's role should be clear: through "the alliance of diplomacy, with industry, commerce and finance," it was to help establish a smoothly flowing system of investment and trade between the United

41. Ibid., pp. 181–183. One of the major, and consistently pursued objectives of the Taft administration in its support of the American Group's efforts to conclude loans with the Chinese government for fiscal reform, was to put a final end to the concessions system in China. In early 1912, for example, when the Belgian syndicate seemed about to obtain a railway concession from the Chinese government, H. Wilson pointed out to his diplomatic colleagues and to the Chinese officials "the advantages to China's future welfare of some such arrangement, which would tend to obliterate preferential political rights and thus forestall any purely political loan from being forced upon China by any individual power." Later that year, after the Belgian syndicate had got an important railway concession from the Chinese government Calhoun complained in his report to Knox, "The Belgian concession evidences a return on the part of the Chinese to a policy which it was supposed they irrevocably abandoned, that is, giving concessions instead of making straight loans." *For. Rels.*, 1912, pp. 115–116, 158. See also Knox to Italian Ambassador, 18 February, 1913, Knox to Russian Ambassador, 26 February 1913, Knox to Chargé Williams, 27 February 1913, ibid., 1913, pp. 161, 165, 166. In this connection, the Asiatic Association in its statement of its history and origins, emphasized that it had "never ceased to advocate a reform of the currency system in China, and has used every effort to promote the kind of international agreement under which that reform can be most readily effected." It characterized such reform as "among the necessary aids to the promotion of American trade in the Far East. . . ." *AAA Journal*, XI, 4 (May 1911), p. 117. See also ibid., p. 98; ibid., editorial, XI, 6 (July 1911); Wang Ching-Chun, "The New Chinese Currency," ibid., p. 168; and "China and the United States," *Outlook*, in ibid., XI, 1 (February 1911), pp. 4–5, where reference is made to the need for the Americanization of Chinese finance. For Wilson's, Bryan's, and Lansing's policy of replacing European with U.S. capital in Latin America through a program of reorganizing customs systems under the supervision of U.S. diplomats and bankers, see Dexter Perkins, *Hands Off, A History of the Monroe Doctrine* (1941), pp. 257–259, and William Diamond, *The Economic Thought of Woodrow Wilson* (1943), p. 154.

States and the agrarian areas. In this process, the assurance of equal opportunities for U.S. capitalists as against those of other industrial nations, and the reform of the agrarian areas' governmental fiscal systems
assumed central importance. The government's diplomatic support was
expected to encourage U.S. investors to place their capital in foreign
bonds and thereby contribute to the development of a sufficient foreign
bond market in the United States. Where military intervention had been
resorted to, as in the Caribbean, it was not because this was part of the
objectives or instrumentalities that the Dollar Diplomatists had in mind.
They considered themselves obliged to resort to military measures in order to establish the conditions allowing those objectives and instrumentalities to operate. Those objectives and instrumentalities were the
imperatives dictated by the national interest conceived by Dollar Diplomacy, and in their view, no nation suited to their operation had the right
to deny them.

Some of the Dollar Diplomats may have been "wicked," "immoral,"
or "commercialistic," but neither their imperialist mentality nor their
policies are best comprehended in terms of such personal qualities. They
were upholding a system of political economy with an ideology (in its
variants) that assumed and affirmed as natural, necessary, and therefore
moral, not only that system, but also the satisfaction of its requirements,
brooking no further doubt or inquiry of a fundamental nature. As much
as did Woodrow Wilson after them, the Dollar Diplomats suffered from
the "paradox" between their peaceful ideals and the bellicose methods
they often used, between their intentions and the consequences they often reaped. No less with them than with Wilson, however, the paradox
lay not in a supposed conflict or estrangement between "moralistic" and
"commercialistic" considerations and intentions, nor in a superficial hypocrisy, but in the contradictions inherent in the pursuit of their expansionist objectives, in the frustration of their intentions by real conditions
over which they did not exercise decisive control, and in the unintended
consequences of their actions. The Dollar Diplomats and the men of
wealth wanted to stand astride the world, but like Studs Lonigan (who
unlike them only wanted to live in it with dignity), they faced a world
they didn't make.

The terms in which the Dollar Diplomats conceived the nation's economic expansion abroad possessed all the attributes of high moralism.
Development of the agrarian areas meant, as with the continental west,
the extension of "civilizing" processes, of the new technology and more
"advanced" standards of life, of Christianity, and of republican ideas and
institutions such as representative democracy, laws of contract, and so
on, down the hierarchy of principles and policies. As the Asiatic Associ-

ation put it, commenting in 1912 on the ostensibly republican revolution in China: "While the Association need relax none of its energies in the promotion of trade with China and the countries of the Far East, there is a field of ethical and political influence which it should be able to occupy. . . . " For, with the advent of the Chinese revolution, the "material interest of the United States in the development of China has been reinforced by a moral interest in the successful working out of the experiment of a republican form of government. The intelligent pursuit of the one demands a sympathetic and helpful attitude toward the other. . . . "[42]

To the Dollar Diplomats, the extension of the nation's political and ideological influence and of its commerce and enterprise meant also the extension of the realm of peace. Merchants were "the rank and file of the army of peace." Commerce resulted in greater international intercourse and better international understanding; it directed the nations' energies from military to business, and therefore constructive, channels. It was the moral equivalent of war. With commerce went also American ideals and great responsibility: "We as Americans must go out into the world and assume our full share of responsibility, and at the same time keep true to the ideals that have always characterized human life," Calhoun told his corporate colleagues to cries of "Hear! Hear!" and enthusiastic applause.[43] Or, as Taft had stated on an earlier occasion (1907, as Secretary of War), in the preoccupation with the extension of U.S. commerce and enterprise in the Far East, "our activities . . . none the less express a logical, worthy and beneficent programme altogether consistent with the principles and ideals of our Government, because of the fact that American dollars are made to perform a high moral duty."[44]

Moralism, as Huntington Wilson wrote, was not to be confused with sentimentality. Indeed, sentimentality often resulted in the most glaring immorality and fraud. Business ethics, on the other hand, provided a

42. *AAA Journal*, XII, 3 (April 1912), pp. 66, 68.
43. Straight and Calhoun at Fifteenth Annual Dinner of the Asiatic Association, 26 January 1914, ibid., XIV, 1 (February 1914), pp. 8, 9–10, 18.
44. Taft's "Shanghai Address," 1907, quoted in *Journal of Commerce*, in ibid., XIII, 3 (April 1913), p. 71. Cf. Taft's Annual Message to Congress, 3 December, 1912, where noting that the "diplomacy of the present administration has sought to respond to modern ideas of commercial intercourse," he explained, "This policy . . . is one that appeals alike to idealistic humanitarian sentiments, to the dictates of sound policy, and to legitimate commercial aims. . . . " *For. Rels.*, 1912, p. x. The idea was phrased somewhat picturesquely by a businessman who had just returned from his duties as manager of a U.S. company's branch in the Far East: "The United States sustains in the city of Shanghai a regular American post office, . . . and it has installed a letter box which has across the top of it the words 'Lift up.' I never see it that it is not an inspiration. It is what the United States is doing." NAM, *Proc.*, 1915, pp. 142–143.

sound basis for public and private morality. A beneficent political-economic system, service to its well-being, and the satisfaction of its requirements, therefore, embraced a higher morality than sentimentalism, and whatever extended the sphere of that society or its influence ipso facto served the cause of morality. Accordingly, the national interest as defined by the assumptions and objectives of Dollar Diplomacy could not be separated from "service to humanity," because "America, as a government, can amply serve humanity in spheres and in ways in which America also serves itself; and because if it does that, the service to humanity may be considered by diplomacy, which is not, by the way, an eleemosynary institution, as merged in the service of America. . . ."[45] In his letter of protest and resignation to the president, 19 March 1913, Huntington Wilson concisely summarized the component of the Taft administration's application of Dollar Diplomacy to China. It was perfectly clear, he argued, from the repeated utterances of the previous administration, that "the motive and purpose" of the abandoned policy (respecting the Six-Power Reorganization Loan to the Chinese government) were "first and primarily" protection of China's integrity and sovereignty, "the uplift" of her people, "morally, materially, and governmentally; the development of China's resources, and the maintenance of our traditional policy of the 'open door,' or equal opportunity for American enterprise."[46]

Their frequent use of such words and phrases as "legitimate," "beneficial," "honest and fair, and just to the foreigners concerned," testifies to the Dollar Diplomats' presupposition that their objectives and instrumentalities were by definition beyond moral reproach. True, it is not a sufficient method of analysis to judge the "moralistic" content of a body of thought by the number of times those who articulated it used "moralistic" words or phrases; but on that basis, the Dollar Diplomats did not lag behind Woodrow Wilson. Just as Woodrow Wilson's Mobile Address of 27 October 1913 may be considered none the less moralistic when understood in terms of the objectives and instrumentalities of Dollar Diplomacy, so it should not be supposed that because the Dollar Diplomats thought in terms of political economy, their theory and practice were devoid of moralistic considerations. Policymakers like Straight, Calhoun, Huntington Wilson, Taft, and Knox, did not view their theory and practice of Dollar Diplomacy, nor the concept of national interest it embraced, as divorced from morality.

45. H. Wilson, "Relation of Government," pp. 300–301.
46. Letter of Protest and Resignation of Assistant Secretary Huntington Wilson, 19 March 1913, *AAA Journal*, XIII, 3 (April 1913), p. 69.

They believed in corporate capitalism as the natural, inevitable product of evolutionary development; that which was natural and necessary could only be right and beneficent. Expansion of the system's domain (the westward movement of the frontier), and of its influence and enterprise abroad, comprised the fulfillment of destiny, the condition of the society's well-being, and the realization of its power. As the society's destiny and power were in themselves beneficent, it had much to offer the world, and the extension of its influence and enterprise abroad corresponded with the development and well-being of the world.

The question for the Dollar Diplomats was not one of "commerce" and "realism" versus "morality." It is doubtful that they were bothered by bad dreams or tortured consciences over this, they were not cynics, and it is safe to assume that they were serene in the righteousness of their convictions. They were very American. Others who oppose, or suffer guilt feelings about, the profit system and the satisfaction of its requirements, whether in its large-scale corporate form or otherwise, may feel morally indignant, or uneasy, in the presence of Dollar Diplomacy and its political-economic imperatives. But the Dollar Diplomats were not medieval Thomists; they were not seventeenth-century Puritans; they were not socialists; they were twentieth-century Protestants, and they believed.

IV

Woodrow Wilson and the developmental imperatives of modern U.S. liberalism

> Most persons are so thoroughly uninformed as to my opinions that I have concluded that the only things they have not read are my speeches.
>
> Woodrow Wilson, 1912

Perhaps the greatest source of historical misconception about Woodrow Wilson is the methodological compartmentalization of his mentality into two distinct components, the "moralistic" and the "realistic" or "commercialistic," as if they were discrete and mutually exclusive. From this point of departure, if one thinks or acts "moralistically," he cannot be considered capable at the same time of thinking and acting "realistically," at least not consistently: If one is a "moralist," his political behavior can be considered as deriving only secondarily, if at all, from an understanding of, or a serious concern for, the affairs of political economy.

According to this approach, wherever Wilson is perceived to have spoken or acted for the "little man," "democracy," "liberty," "individual opportunity," and the like, he was "liberal" and moralistic; wherever he is perceived to have spoken or acted for corporate interests, economic expansion abroad, and the like, he was "conservative," "commercialistic," "expedient," or realistic. Where Wilson supported measures pro-

This essay was originally published as "Woodrow Wilson and the Political Economy of Modern United States Liberalism," *Studies on the Left*, I:3 (1960), a journal of which I was a founding editor. I had begun working on the essay in 1957, and presented an early version of it at a University of Wisconsin graduate seminar presided over by Merle Curti, who was sitting in for an ill Howard K. Beale, my major professor. Professor Curti gave the essay generous praise at the seminar session and thereby strongly encouraged me to develop and complete it. It is printed here as it appeared in *Studies*, except for correction of typographical errors, and as it was subsequently reprinted elsewhere. The essay seems to me to "stand up" over time, except that I long ago came to believe that its concluding paragraph is unfair to Herbert Croly by imputing inaccurately to his thinking a statist predilection. As I have come to understand Croly, his *Promise of American Life* and some of his other works mark him as one of America's most sophisticated, nonstatist, social-democratic, or liberal-socialist, thinkers. My own latest understanding of Woodrow Wilson may be found in Chapter 6 ("Woodrow Wilson and the Corporate-Liberal Ascendancy") of my book, *The Corporate Reconstruction of American Capitalism, 1890–1916* (Cambridge University Press, 1988.)

moting large corporate interests at home or abroad, he is considered to have forsaken his moralism, to have been driven by political expediency, personal egoism, or implacable social and economic forces, or to have gathered the unintended consequences of a misdirected moralism. In this view, Wilson the moralist is generally considered the true type, and Wilson the realist, the deviant.

Aside from objections that may be raised against the naïveté and theoretical deficiencies of such an approach to social thought and ideology in general,[1] certain specific objections may be raised against such an approach to Wilson, particularly should the main ideological components generally attributed to Wilson's mentality be granted at the outset, and their implications accorded a modicum of examination.

First, the "Puritan ethic," to which students of Wilson have attached fundamental importance as basic to his mentality, made no such mutually exclusive distinction between a transcendent morality and the world of political economy. Puritanism embraced a morality applicable not merely to the world beyond, but as well to the living individual and existing society; it sanctioned, indeed posited, capitalist social and economic relations. The affirmation of capitalist society was therefore implicit in Wilson's Protestant morality. From the straightest-laced New England Puritan of the seventeenth century to Poor Richard's Benjamin Franklin, to Gospel-of-Wealth Andrew Carnegie, to "New Freedom" Woodrow Wilson, religious conviction and "marketplace materialism" were each practical, each the uplifting agent of civilization and Providence, each the necessary condition for personal salvation and general human improvement, each a function of the other, mutually interdependent and interwoven like the white and purple threads of the single holy cloth. To the extent, then, that Puritanism entered significantly into Wilson's world-view, the affirmation of the capitalist system in the United States (and throughout the world) was a function of his morality, not merely an auxiliary prepossession.

Second, Wilson's moral affirmation of capitalism sanctioned by Puritan conceptions found powerful confirmation in the economic writings of Adam Smith (himself a professor of moral philosophy), John Bright, and Richard Cobden; as student and professor he had become firmly grounded in their theories of political economy, which he admired and enthusiastically espoused, and it is not difficult to perceive that such writings would strongly appeal to one reared on Puritanism. In Smith,

1. See Karl Mannheim, *Ideology and Utopia* (New York: Harvest Book edition, 1955), pp. 59–70. Mannheim here distinguishes between the "particular conception of ideology" and the "total conception of ideology"; it is in terms of the latter that Wilson's world-view is comprehended in this essay.

Bright, and Cobden, Wilson found secular moral sanction for the bourgeois-democratic political economy as well as indefeasible economic principles. Private, competitive enterprise manifested natural law in the realm of political economy, and went hand in hand with republican institutions, comprising together the essential conditions of democracy, individual liberty, and increasing prosperity. To Wilson, much of whose economic thinking was based upon the assumption of the growing superiority of U.S. industry, the arguments of Smith, Cobden, and Bright were compelling: They, in their day, spoke for an industrially supreme Great Britain, and recognizing Britain's position, argued that the optimum condition for the nation's economic growth and expansion rested upon the "natural" flow of trade, a "natural" international division of labor, uninhibited by "artificial" hindrances.

Taken together, Puritanism and Smithian-Manchestrian economics instilled Wilson with the compulsion to serve the strengthening and extending of the politicoeconomic system he knew in the United States as a positively moralistic commitment, since that would strengthen and extend the sphere of liberty, democracy, prosperity, and Providence, and accorded with natural law. As William Diamond observed, such assumptions were to become "basic" to Wilson's "thought on foreign policy."[2]

Third and finally, the organismic view of society that Wilson derived from Edmund Burke and Walter Bagehot provided him with the concept that whatever social phenomena or social system evolved "naturally" from the traditions and customs of the past, from the working of natural law through "irresistible" social forces, were not only inevitable as prescriptively ordained but morally indisputable. They represented both the evolution of the genius of human custom and institutions and the assertion of God's will in human affairs. To Burke, whom Wilson revered and assiduously studied, the market economy manifested the working of natural law, which in turn manifested divine law. In Burke, Wilson could

2. William Diamond, *The Economic Thought of Woodrow Wilson* (Baltimore: Johns Hopkins Press, 1943), p. 29. As revealed in his life, speeches, and writings, Wilson's concern was to protect the private enterprise system, as beneficent in itself and in its effects, from those dishonest, unscrupulous men who threatened to misuse and pervert it (and from socialists who threatened to abolish it). It was in keeping with his intense commitment to his moral principles that Wilson, early and late in his life, viewed an activist political career as his "heart's *first* – primary – ambition and purpose," as opposed to pure academic pursuits. Wilson to Ellen Axson, February, 1885, cited in Arthur S. Link, *Wilson: The Road to the White House* (Princeton, N.J.: Princeton University Press, 1947), p. 19 (hereafter cited as Link, *Wilson*, I). Emphasis in original, cf. ibid., pp. 20, 23, 97, 123, 130; and Ray S. Baker, *Woodrow Wilson, Life and Letters* (8 vols., New York, various dates), Vol. I, p. 229, Vol. II. p. 98. It was therefore only natural that in the 1880s and 1890s and thereafter, far from being a head-in-the-clouds "idealist," Wilson made himself intimately conversant with the concrete political and economic issues of the day.

find a reverence for the market economy akin to religious awe: "The laws of commerce . . . are the laws of nature, and consequently the laws of God," Burke had said.[3] American Puritan doctrine, as developed by Jonathan Edwards, had itself become firmly anchored in the natural law of Newton and Locke; it required the intensive study of society's concrete development and condition, in order to comprehend God's work in the universe. In this respect, Puritanism and Burke stood on common ground. Here both religious and secular morality converged upon the affirmation of things as they were and as they appeared to be evolving. What was "natural" was moral. The part of wisdom, morality, and statesmanship was to comprehend, affirm, and work for the necessary institutional adjustments to, "natural" evolution and "the well-known laws of value and exchange."[4] This evolutionary-positivist or conservative-historicist[5] approach to society served to modify whatever predilections Wilson may have had for atomized economic relations; it provided him with philosophical ground for rejecting the doctrine of unrestricted competition, as did the institutional economists he encountered at Johns Hopkins in the 1880s, and for affirming, as an inevitable result of the laws of commerce and natural social evolution, the demise of the freely competing entrepreneur at the hands of the large corporation. As Wilson once remarked, explaining his approval of large-scale industrial corporations, "No man indicts natural history. No man undertakes to say that the things that have happened by operation of irresistible forces are immoral things. . . . "[6]

To the extent that the characterization of Wilson's mentality as "moralistic" connotes Sunday school platitudes or Pollyanna ingenuousness, therefore, it is not only irrelevant, but fundamentally misleading. Since Wilson's writings, speeches, policy decisions, and actions simply do not correspond with such "moralism" the tendency of those who view his mentality in this manner is to judge both Wilson's utterances and actions, and the great events with which he was concerned, either in terms of a Faustian personality torn between the forces of high idealism and

---

3. Burke, *Thoughts and Details on Scarcity* (World Classics edition), Vol. VI, pp. 22, also 6, 9, 10.
4. See, e.g., Wilson, "The Making of the Nation," *Atlantic Monthly,* LXXX (July 1897), in Ray S. Baker and William E. Dodd, eds., *The Public Papers of Woodrow Wilson* (4 vols., New York: Harper & Bros., 1925, 1926), Vol. I, p. 328 (hereafter cited as *P P W W*); and "Democracy and Efficiency," *Atlantic Monthly,* LXXXVII (March 1901), ibid., p. 400.
5. The term conservative-historicist is used in the technical sense defined by Mannheim, *Ideology and Utopia,* pp., 120, 121, and is not meant here to denote "conservatism" as against "liberalism" as those terms are conventionally used.
6. "Richmond Address," delivered before the General Assembly of Virginia and the City Council of Richmond (1 February 1912), *P P W W*, Vol. II, p. 377.

gross materialism, or less charitably, in terms of a sophisticated hypocrisy: "Beneath the layer of Christian moralism is the shrewdness of the
Puritan merchant. . . . "[7]

But Wilson's moralism was not simply a veneer "beneath" which
lurked supposedly amoral "commercialism." It was a genuine and basic
component of his ideological framework, though, it is submitted, no
more so than in that of William Howard Taft, Philander C. Knox, Theodore Roosevelt, or Huntington Wilson. Woodrow Wilson's "wrung
heart and wet hanky," we may be sure, were "real enough."[8] His
thought in matters of political economy embraced a body of moralistic
concepts, just as his moralism presumed certain principles of political
economy and corresponding social relations. Whether or not in human
thought and ideology the two have often failed to be inextricably interrelated, in Wilson they certainly were. A view of ideology that casts morality and ethics into one realm and political economy into another, that
sees history as a struggle between the "ethical" men and the "materialistic" men, between the lofty and the commercialistic, suffers from an
inverted economic determinism that overlooks the possibility that commitment to an economic way of life may go hand in hand with the most
intense and highly systematized morality; with respect to Wilson, it for-
gets that just as classical political economy, "despite its worldly and
wanton appearance – is a true moral science, the most moral of the
sciences,"[9] so Puritanism, as the works of R. H. Tawney and Max Weber
suggest, despite its heavenly concern, is a truly worldly doctrine.

For Wilson, like Burke, ideals and principles, to the extent that they
validly applied to society, arose from and satisfied, not rationally de-
duced abstract precepts, but practical experience with the concrete conditions of society drawn in the light of "the inviolable understandings of
precedent."[10] "Will you never learn this fact," he lectured Boston real
estate men in January 1912, "that you do not make governments by theories? You accommodate theories to the circumstances. Theories are
generalizations from the facts. The facts do not spring out of theories . . .
but the facts break in and ignore theories . . . and as our life is, as our

7. Richard W. Van Alstyne, "American Nationalism and Its Mythology," *Queens Quar-
    terly*, LXV, 3 (Autumn 1958), p. 436.
8. For this reference to Wilson by D. H. Lawrence, see his *Studies in Classic American
    Literature* (1922; New York: Anchor edition, 1951), pp. 32–33, which contains a
    valuable insight into the morality shared by Wilson in the chapters on Benjamin
    Franklin and Hector St. John de Crevecoeur, pp. 19–43.
9. Karl Marx, *Economic and Philosophic Manuscripts of 1844* (Moscow: Foreign Lan-
    guages Publishing House, n.d.), p. 119.
10. "The Ideals of America," *Atlantic Monthly*, XC (December, 1902), *P P W W*, Vol. I,
    p. 422; Baker, *Wilson, Life and Letters*, Vol. II, p. 104.

thought is, so will our Government be."[11] Accordingly, Wilson insisted upon the necessity of adjusting legal institutions to the changed circumstances of economics and politics:

> if you do not adjust your laws to the facts, so much the worse for the laws, not for the facts, because law trails after the facts . . . we must [adjust the laws to the facts]; there is no choice . . . because the law, unless I have studied amiss, is the expression of the facts in legal relationships. Laws have never altered the facts; laws have always necessarily expressed the facts; adjusted interests as they have arisen and have changed toward one another.[12]

It was the necessity, the "facts," which Wilson recognized that determined his world view.

Time and again Wilson emphasized that the facts of modern life to which adjustment was most urgent were economic in character. Indeed, Wilson viewed economic relations as basic to all other social relations. He analyzed conditions in the United States, its troubles and opportunities, as essentially the result of rapid industrialization aggravated by the passing of the continental frontier. He conceived the major issues of his time as "questions of economic policy chiefly," and defined in this manner not only the tariff, coinage and currency, trust, and immigration questions, but also, significantly, "foreign policy" and "our duty to our neighbors."[13] The life of the nation, he declared in 1911, was not what it was twenty, even ten, years before: Economic conditions had changed "from top to bottom," and with them "the organization of our life."[14] As New Jersey governor-elect Wilson noted: "The world of business [has

11. "Efficiency" (27 January 1912), *P P W W*, Vol, II, p. 361.
12. *The New Freedom* (New York, 1914), pp. 33, 34, 35; "Richmond Address" (1 February 1912), *P P W W*, Vol. II, p. 376. For an interesting comparison worth noting here, see Karl Marx, *The Poverty of Philosophy* (1847): "Indeed, an utter ignorance of history is necessary in order not to know that at all times sovereign rulers have had to submit to economic conditions and have never been able to dictate laws to them. Both political and civil legislation do no more than recognize and protocol the will of economic conditions. . . . Law is nothing but the recognition of fact." Translation is that found in Franz Mehring, *Karl Marx, the Story of His Life* (London, 1951), p. 123. (Cf. *The Poverty of Philosophy* [Moscow: Foreign Languages Publishing House, n.d.], p. 83). For a present-day view that regards law as subordinate to economic fact, specifically with respect to the rise of the corporation as the predominant form of business organization, cf. Edward S. Mason, ed., *The Corporation in Modern Society* (Cambridge, Mass.: Harvard University Press, 1959), p. I, where Mason, in his Introduction, states: "law in a major manifestation is simply a device for facilitating and registering the obvious and the inevitable. . . . "
13. "Leaderless Government," address before Virginia State Bar Association (4 August 1897), *P P W W*, Vol. I, p. 354.
14. "Issues of Freedom," address at banquet of Knife and Fork Club of Kansas City, Missouri (5 May 1911), *P P W W*, Vol. II, p. 285; *The New Freedom*, p. 3.

changed], and therefore the world of society and the world of politics. . . . A new economic society has sprung up, and we must effect a new set of adjustments. . . . " And as candidate for the Democratic presidential nomination in 1912, he declared: "business underlies every part of our lives; the foundation of our lives, of our spiritual lives included, is economic." Business, he emphasized, "is the foundation of every other relationship, particularly of the political relationship. . . . "[15]

Wilson's view of economic relations as basic to social, political, and spiritual life fits altogether consistently into his conservative-historicist, natural-law approach to society. Understood in these terms, Wilson's "idealism" arose, therefore, from his conception of practical experience, of "natural" social evolution, of the genius of evolved social institutions, custom, habit, and traditions, of "irresistible" social forces, and the laws of commerce. It was that mixture of classical nineteenth-century liberalism with conservative-historicism that made Wilson the Progressive he was: Rational adjustments, determined by enlightened men concerned with the general welfare, were to be made to irrational processes, that is, to processes not determined by men but evolving irresistibly in accordance with suprahuman natural law or predetermination.

Wilson's position on the "trust" question cannot be accurately understood apart from his firm conviction that law must correspond with the facts of economic life, must accommodate the people, their habits and institutions to, *and facilitate,* natural economic development, and in the process achieve the general welfare or national interest.

He defined the general welfare or national interest not in terms of abstract reasoning or visionary dreams, or from "pure" moral principles, but historically in terms of the "facts" of the existing economic structure and business organization. To Wilson, the "facts" were that the large corporation and large-scale industry had replaced the individual entrepreneur and small producing unit as the central and dominant feature of modern capitalism. Accordingly, the adjustments to be made, in Wilson's mind, involved not an attempt to restore the entrepreneurial competition of bygone days or the dissolution of large corporations, but, on the contrary, "the task of translating law and morals into terms of modern business. . . . "[16] More precisely, the problem to be defined was that "Our

15. Inaugural Address as governor-elect of New Jersey (17 January 1911), *P P W W,* Vol. II, p. 273; "Government in Relation to Business," address at Annual Banquet of the Economic Club, New York (23 May 1912), ibid., pp. 431, 432. In 1898 Wilson had observed: "For whatever we say of other motives, we must never forget that in the main the ordinary conduct of man is determined by economic motives." Quoted in Diamond, *Economic Thought of Wilson,* p. 52 n.
16. "Politics (1857–1907)," *Atlantic Monthly,* C (November 1907), *PPWW,* Vol. II, p. 19.

laws are still meant for business done by *individuals;* they have not been satisfactorily adjusted to business done by great *combinations,* and we have got to adjust them . . . there is no choice."[17] What was needed were "open efforts to accommodate law to the material development which has so strengthened the country in all that it has undertaken by supplying its extraordinary life with necessary physical foundations."[18]

Usually overlooked in discussions about the great "anti-trust" debates of the pre–World War I period is that the leading participants were concerned not so much with the abstract idea of "competition versus monopoly" as with the role of the corporation in the new industrial order and its relation to the state. This was as true of Wilson as it was of Roosevelt, Taft, George W. Perkins, Elbert H. Gary, and Herbert Croly. In his writings and speeches on the "trusts," Wilson placed particular emphasis upon "the extraordinary development of corporate organization and administration,"[19] as the dominant mode of modern capitalist enterprise, upon the corresponding decline of unrestricted competition and the growth of "cooperation," and furthermore, of particular importance, consistent with his overall view, upon the legitimacy of the process, the need to affirm and adjust to it. Large corporations were "indispensable to modern business enterprise"; "the combinations necessarily effected for the transaction of modern business"; "society's present means of effective life in the field of industry" and its "new way of massing its resources and its power of enterprise"; "organizations of a perfectly intelligible sort which the law has licensed for the convenience of extensive business," neither "hobgoblins" nor "unholy inventions of rascally rich men."[20]

As institutions that had developed "by operation of irresistible forces," large corporations could not be considered "immoral"; " . . . to suggest that the things that have happened to us must be reversed, and the scroll of time rolled back on itself," Wilson declared in 1912, " . . . would be futile and ridiculous. . . . "[21] On more than one occasion during the campaign of 1912, as he had in the past, Wilson declared:

> I am not one of those who think that competition can be established
> by law against the drift of a worldwide economic tendency; neither

17. "Richmond Address" (1 February 1912), ibid., p. 376.
18. *The New Freedom,* pp. 117–118.
19. "The Lawyer and the Community," annual address delivered before the American Bar Association, Chattanooga (31 August 1910), *P P W W,* Vol. II, p. 253.
20. Ibid., pp. 254–257, 262: "Bankers and Statesmanship," address before the New Jersey Bankers' Association, Atlantic City (6 May 1910), ibid., p. 229: *The New Freedom,* p. 5; Inaugural Address as governor-elect of New Jersey (17 January 1911), *P P W W,* Vol. II, p. 27.
21. "Richmond Address," ibid., pp. 376–377.

am I one of those who believe that business done upon a great scale by a single organization – call it corporation, or what you will – is necessarily dangerous to the liberties, even the economic liberties, of a great people like our own. . . . I am not afraid of anything that is normal. I dare say we shall never return to the old order of individual competition, and that the organization of business upon a great scale of cooperation is up to a certain point, itself normal and inevitable.[22]

Or, as he put it on another occasion, "nobody can fail to see that modern business is going to be done by corporations. . . . We will do business henceforth when we do it on a great and successful scale, by means of corporations. . . ."[23]

With respect to remedies in the matter of "trusts," the task according to Wilson was "not to disintegrate what we have been at such pains to piece together in the organization of modern industrial enterprise"; a program of dissolution of the large corporations would only calamitously derange the economy; it would "throw great undertakings out of gear"; it would "disorganize some important business altogether."[24] Rather, the task was to prevent the misuse of corporations by individuals, make guilt and punishment individual rather than corporate, prescribe in law those practices corporations might and might not undertake, prohibit unfair and coercive methods of competition, require reasonable competition among the large corporations, and assure that corporations operate in the public interest.[25]

Historians have argued over when it was that Wilson first declared in favor of commission regulation of business, as if this were of fundamen-

---

22. Address accepting Democratic party presidential nomination, 7 August 1912, *Official Report of the Proceedings of the Democratic National Convention*, 1912, p. 407. The "certain point" referred to by Wilson was the point of diminishing returns. The enterprise that made money in the market without recourse to coercive or "artificial" practices was normal, its size justified by its pecuniary success.

23. "The Tariff and the Trusts," address at Nashville, Tenn. (24 February 1912), *P P W W* Vol. II, pp. 410–411. In this connection, more than a decade before Theodore Roosevelt denounced the "rural tories" as reactionaries whose passion for unrestricted competition and small business units would turn back the clock of progress. Wilson, in December 1900 had applied the same criticism to Populists and Bryan-Democrats: "Most of our reformers are retro-reformers. They want to hale us back to an old chrysalis which we have broken; they want us to resume a shape which we have outgrown. . . . " "The Puritan," speech before the New England Society of New York City (22 December 1900), ibid., Vol. I, p. 365.

24. "The Lawyer and the Community" (31 August 1910), ibid., Vol. II, p. 254.

25. "You cannot establish competition by law, but you can take away the obstacles by law that stand in the way of competition, and while we may despair of setting up competition among individual persons there is good ground for setting up competition between these great combinations, and after we have got them competing with one another they will come to their senses in so many respects that we can afterwards hold conference with them without losing our self-respect." Wilson, Jackson Day Dinner Address (8 January 1912). ibid., p. 348.

tal importance to his overall view of the trust question.[26] To Wilson, however, the question of commission regulations did not involve that of laissez-faire versus "positive" government, or regulation of monopoly versus enforcement of competition. It involved instead, the question of whether the ground rules of the new corporate system were to be left to arbitrary decisions of executive officers, subject to change with each administration, and possibly productive of both interference with personal and property rights and irrational attacks upon corporations, or whether, as he advocated, they were to become institutionalized in law. As had the corporate leaders themselves who testified before congressional committees, what Wilson wanted was "the certainty of law." Within that context, he favored "as much power as you choose."[27]

Whether one examines Wilson's thought before or during his "New Freedom" years, it is evident that what is thought of as laissez-faire Jeffersonianism is not one of its characteristics. In 1908, for example, pointing to "the necessity for a firm and comprehensive regulation of business operations in the interest of fair dealing," Wilson stated: "No one now advocates the old *laissez-faire*. . . . "[28] As if to emphasize his conviction that the popular notion of Jeffersonianism bore little direct relevance to the problems of modern times, Wilson took the occasion of the Democratic party's Jefferson Day Banquet in 1912 to assert: "We live in a new and strange age and reckon with new affairs alike in economics and politics of which Jefferson knew nothing."[29] With respect to the government's role in particular, as William Diamond summarized the record: "Throughout his political life . . . [Wilson] was willing to use the government as a positive instrument in the economic life of the nation. . . . "[30]

In two most basic areas of policy and thought, then, that of the extent of government intervention in the economy and that of the "trust"

26. See e.g., John W. Davidson, ed., *A Crossroads of Freedom: The 1912 Campaign Speeches of Woodrow Wilson* (New Haven, Conn: Yale University Press, 1956), p. 80.
27. "The Vision of the Democratic Party," New Haven Address (25 September 1912), ibid., pp. 264–265. Davidson points out (see n. 26 above) that Wilson declared for commission regulation at his Buffalo speech of 2 September 1912, at least three weeks prior to the New Haven address, but the point Wilson made on these occasions was in no essential respect different from that which he made more than four years earlier, when insisting "everywhere upon definition, uniform, exact, enforceable," he stated (in criticism of the pending Hepburn amendments to the Sherman Act), "If there must be commissions, let them be, not executive instrumentalities having indefinite powers capable of domineering as well as regulating, but tribunals of easy and uniform process acting under precise terms of power in the enforcement of precise terms of regulations." "Law or Personal Power," address delivered to the National Democratic Club, New York (13 April 1908), *P P W W*, Vol. II, p. 28.
28. Ibid., p. 25.   29. "What Jefferson Would Do," ibid., p. 424.
30. Diamond, *Economic Thought of Wilson*, p. 130.

question, Wilson was no more a "Jeffersonian" than were Theodore Roosevelt, Edward D. White, Oliver Wendell Holmes, George W. Perkins, or Herbert Croly. If "Jeffersonian" is meant to connote a return to an agrarian yeoman republic, or to the regime of unrestricted competition among independent entrepreneurs or small business units, or a government policy of laissez-faire, then much as it obscures more than clarifies in applying the term to any leading twentieth-century figure in United States history, it certainly fails even allegorically to characterize, or provide much insight into, Wilson's thought or policy positions.

Accordingly, Wilson's New Freedom years, 1912–1914, may be more accurately comprehended not as a break with his past, just as his decision to make commission regulation the core of his trust program may be better understood not as a break with his New Freedom views. Before, during, and after 1914, Wilson's views on the trust question, like those of large corporate spokesmen within the Chicago Association of Commerce, National Civic Federation, and the United States Chamber of Commerce, and like those of Roosevelt and Bureau of Corporations chiefs James R. Garfield and Herbert K. Smith, embodied the common law – "rule of reason" doctrine ultimately handed down by the Supreme Court in its American Tobacco and Standard Oil decisions of 1911. Like the others, Wilson had opposed the Court's earlier decisions prohibiting both "reasonable" and "unreasonable" restraints of trade; like them his approach affirmed large-scale corporate organization, sought the institutional legitimization of reasonable restraints of trade and the prohibition of unreasonable restraints or "unfair" competition, as determined at common law and by judicial precedent, with the public interest as the central consideration.

Wilson's position on the trust question as of 1912–1914 may be looked upon as a synthesis of the positions of Taft and Roosevelt: on the one hand, acknowledgment of the demise of *individualist, entrepreneurial* competition, but the affirmation of and insistence upon reasonable *inter-corporate* competition; on the other hand, the prevention of "unfair competition" and affirmation of "reasonable" combination and intercorporate arrangements consistent with the "public interest" or "general welfare," under a government regulatory policy rooted in the settled precedents and practices of common and civil law jurisprudence, whether enforced by the courts or by an administrative commission or by a combination of both.

To cite the fact that Louis D. Brandeis exerted decisive influence in Wilson's acceptance of the trade commission bill as evidence of a basic alteration in Wilson's views on the trust question, is either to overlook Brandeis's public utterances at the time and the program he advocated, or to disregard Wilson's previous writings and statements. Brandeis's position avowedly embodied the Supreme Court's "rule of reason" decisions of 1911; he advocated "reasonable" restraints of trade (including limitations upon competition by trade associations) and the prohibition of "unfair practices."[31] The issue involved in Wilson's abandoning the Clayton bill was primarily the impracticality of specifying every unfair practice to be proscribed, and the severity with which, in its original form, it threatened to interfere with corporate practices. The "rule of reason" decision, on the other hand, provided the general term, "unfair competition," with a recognized meaning at common law as evolved over the past decades in court decisions. And after its establishment, when the Federal Trade Commission sought to define "unfair methods of competition," it began by cataloguing all practices that had been found by the courts to be unreasonable or unfair at common law.[32] The trade commission act, although not providing full certainty of law, as Wilson had wished, satisfied the basic elements of his position in removing regulatory powers from the arbitrary decisions of commissioners and grounding them in judicial precedent.

It should also be noted, within the context of the community of agreement on the trust question between Wilson and large corporate spokesmen, that the circumstances surrounding the writing of the bill bear no anomaly. As Arthur S. Link showed, Brandeis and George L. Rublee worked closely together and in consultation with Wilson in drafting the legislation; Rublee actually wrote the bill.[33] Generally unknown, however, is that at the time Rublee worked in Washington writing the measure, he was serving as a member of a special committee on trade commission legislation of the United States Chamber of Commerce. (Brandeis had been an initial member of the Chamber's committee, but retired in favor of Rublee under the press of other affairs.)[34]

31. See, e.g., Brandeis's testimony before House Committee on the Judiciary, *Trust Legislation* (Ser. No. 2) – *Patent Legislation* (Ser. No. 1), *Hearings on H. R. 11380, H. R. 11381, H. R. 15926, and H. R. 19959*, 26, 27 January and 19 February 1912, 62nd Cong., 2nd sess. (Washington, D.C., 1912), pp. 13–54 (Brandeis testified on 26 January 1912); and Brandeis, "The Solution of the Trust Problem," *Harper's Weekly*, LVIII, No. 2968 (8 November 1913), pp. 18–19.

32. *Memorandum on Unfair Competition at the Common Law* (printed for office use only by the Federal Trade Commission, 1915), cited and discussed in Thomas C. Blaisdell, Jr., *The Federal Trade Commission* (New York: Columbia University Press, 1932), pp. 21–23.

33. Link, *Wilson: The New Freedom* (Princeton, N.J.: Princeton University Press, 1956), pp. 436–438, 441 (hereafter cited as Link, *Wilson*, II). See also George Rublee, "The Original Plan and Early History of the Federal Trade Commission," *Proceedings of the Academy of Political Science*, XI, 4 (January 1926), pp. 114–120.

34. Senate Committee on Interstate Commerce, "Promotion of Export Trade," *Hearings on H. R. 17350*, 64th Cong., 2nd sess., January 1917 (Washington, D.C., 1917), pp. 10–13.

But all this is not to imply that Wilson "sold out," that he was obliged reluctantly to submit to "implacable" forces, or that his views or policies had undergone any basic change. Rather, it is to suggest that, viewed within the context of Wilson's overall thought and programmatic approach, the New Freedom years are not best understood as a distinctive period in his intellectual or political life, nor as "anti–big business" in nature or intent.

This view may be all the more forcefully substantiated if the interrelationship between the New Freedom legislation of 1913–1914 and promotion of U.S. economic expansion abroad is appreciated. Here again, it may be seen that, consistent with Wilson's previous and subsequent views, the New Freedom was not directed against large corporate development at home or abroad.[35]

That prior to 1912–1914 Wilson had been a firm advocate of U.S. economic expansion abroad is a matter of record upon which there is general agreement by historians. His views in this respect have been sufficiently observed and analyzed elsewhere.[36] The main elements of his thought may be briefly summarized here. As an early adherent of Turner's frontier thesis, Wilson defined the nation's natural political-economic development and its prosperity as a function of westward expansion. With the end of the continental frontier, expansion into world markets with the nation's surplus manufactured goods and capital was, in his view, indispensable to the stability and prosperity of the economy. It was also no more than a natural development in the life of any industrial nation, and, to him, in no way morally invidious, since, in his view, the nation's economic expansion was a civilizing force that carried with it principles of democracy and Christianity as well as bonds of international understanding and peace. Given the United States' superior

35. For a characteristic formulation of the conventional interpretation of the "New Freedom," particularly with respect to foreign relations, see Charles A. Beard, *The Idea of National Interest* (New York: Macmillan, 1934), pp. 121, 122, 464. In this valuable theoretical work designed to demonstrate that U.S. foreign policy has historically been based not upon abstract ideals, but upon the pursuit of national interest as defined by the realities of political economy, Beard felt obliged to classify Wilson as an exception to the rule. According to Beard, Wilson "turned a cold shoulder" to the great economic interests that had "on the whole, supported and benefited by dollar diplomacy." "From the turn of the century," Beard explained, "the practice of giving aggressive support to the interests of American citizens abroad grew until it appeared to attain almost world-wide range and received the authority of a positive official creed in the conception of dollar diplomacy. . . . After a brief setback during the Wilson regime, the pattern was restored again with the return to power of a Republican administration in 1921. . . . " But, "in the main, the policies of President Wilson, both domestic and foreign, ran counter to corporate development and commercial expansion under the impulse of dollar diplomacy, with their accompanying interpretations of national interest. . . . "
36. Diamond, *Economic Thought of Wilson*, pp. 131–161.

industrial efficiency she would assume supremacy in the world's markets, provided artificial barriers to her economic expansion were eliminated. Accordingly, Wilson admired and championed Hay's open-door policy and advocated vigorous government diplomacy and appropriate government measures to attain the ends in view.

Within this broad framework of thought, the application of the expanding-frontier image to economic expansion abroad assumed a significance more fundamental than the invocation of a romantic metaphor: The West had been developed by the extension of railroads, the opening of mines, the development of agriculture – in short by the extension of the sphere of enterprise and investment that resulted in the widening of the internal market and fed the growth of large-scale industry. Markets for manufactured goods were in this way actively *developed, created,* in the West, by the metropolitan industrial and finance capitalists, and not without the significant aid of the federal government. Similarly with such markets abroad: Foreign investments and industrial exports were seen by the corporate interests most heavily involved and by like-minded political leaders, such as Wilson, as going hand in hand, centered as their concern was on the needs of an industrial capitalist system in general and heavy industry in particular. Accordingly, the idea of "development" of agrarian areas in other parts of the world, and "release of energies," is prominent in Wilson's approach to economic expansion abroad.

Wilson's emphasis on exports of manufactures, his belief in their indispensability to the nation's prosperity, and his conception that the government should play a leading role in these matters, coincide in every essential respect with the views of the so-called Dollar Diplomatists, and of large corporate spokesmen within the United States Chamber of Commerce, the American Asiatic Association, the Pan-American Society, the American Manufacturers Export Association, and the National Foreign Trade Council. In like manner his advocacy of appropriate government measures to encourage an effective merchant marine and adequate international banking facilities flowed from this common concern for expanding the economic frontier; and his support of a low tariff was in large part informed by his belief that it was necessary to the nation's assumption of its proper role in world economic affairs.

But these were not merely the views of a supposedly "early" Wilson, later to be abandoned by the New Freedom Wilson; on the contrary, he carried them most emphatically, along with programmatic proposals, into his presidential campaign of 1912. Wilson's consistent theme, in this respect, during his bid for the presidency, is summarized in his address accepting the Democratic Party's presidential nomination: "Our

industries have expanded to such a point that they will burst their jackets
if they cannot find a free outlet to the markets of the world. . . . Our
domestic markets no longer suffice. We need foreign markets. . . . " The
alternative, as he had previously put it, was "a congestion that will operate calamitously upon the economic conditions of the country." The
economic imperatives, therefore, required institutional adjustments on
the governmental and private business levels to break an outmoded
"chrysalis," in order to "relieve the plethora," and "use the energy of the
[nation's] capital." They also pointed to "America's economic supremacy" (a phrase that Wilson shared with Brooks Adams): "if we are not
going to stifle economically, we have got to find our way out into the
great international exchanges of the world"; the nation's "irresistible energy . . . has got to be released for the commercial conquest of the
world," for "making ourselves supreme in the world from an economic
point of view." He stressed three major reforms to meet the new necessities of the time – the downward revision of the tariff, the development
of a strong merchant marine ("The nation that wants foreign commerce
must have the arms of commerce"), and laws permitting foreign branch
banking tied to a commercial-acceptance system ("this absolutely essential function of international trade . . . ").[37]

Wilson's concern for the promotion of foreign trade and investment
found expression in some of his key appointments upon assuming the
presidency. To China, for example, he sent Paul S. Reinsch, long a prominent spokesman for economic expansion abroad. He appointed his intimate friend, Walter H. Page, as ambassador to Great Britain; as editor
of *World's Work,* Page had published series of articles on such topics as
"the industrial conquest of the world," to which Reinsch contributed.[38]
Wilson's appointments of Edward N. Hurley and George L. Rublee to
the newly formed Federal Trade Commission proved decisive, in its first
few years, in making it a leading agency of foreign trade promotion, an
aspect of its activities that was not then widely anticipated nor since been
sufficiently appreciated.[39]

37. See in particular his speeches, "Efficiency" (27 January 1912), *P P W W*, Vol. II, pp.
     357–360, 372–375, 380; "The Tariff and the Trusts" (24 February 1912), ibid.,
     pp. 407–409; and "Speech of Acceptance" (7 August 1912), ibid., pp. 471–472.
38. See, e.g., Walter H. Page to Paul S. Reinsch, 13 August, 15 November, 10 December,
     28 December 1900, in *Paul S. Reinsch Papers, Correspondence, 1892–1908.* Col-
     lection owned by the State Historical Society of Wisconsin (Madison).
39. As a member of the Chamber of Commerce's special committee on trade commission
     legislation, Rublee played a leading role in the Chamber's campaign to authorize the
     Commission to investigate world trade conditions and make appropriate recommen-
     dations to Congress. Hurley was a prominent Illinois industrialist who had intro-
     duced the pneumatic tool industry to the United States, had been an active member
     and president of the Illinois Manufacturers Association, and, as an articulate advo-
     cate of economic expansion abroad, had played a leading role in the organization of

Wilson appointed William C. Redfield to head the Department of Commerce, which, with its Bureau of Foreign and Domestic Commerce, shared with the State Department the central responsibility within the federal government for promoting foreign economic expansion. It is a mistake to dismiss Redfield, as Link does with the remark that "perhaps his chief claim to fame was the fact that he was the last man in American public life to wear side whiskers. . . . "[40] For Redfield was a prominent member of the corporate community, enjoying the respect and confidence of corporate leaders. As a New York manufacturer of iron and steel products he spent many years abroad developing markets, and as a "business statesman" much of his time expounding the theme of expansion and downward revision of the tariff. Like Wilson he had been a gold-Democrat, and the views of the two men were strikingly similar in matters of trade expansion and the tariff. Indeed, Wilson, in January 1912, acknowledged: "I primed myself on Mr. Redfield's [tariff] speeches."[41] Of greater significance, indicating Redfield's prominence in the corporate community and the degree to which he represented corporate opinion, Redfield had been president of the American Manufacturers Export Association (organized in 1910), which, to use Robert A. Brady's terminology, was a peak association of large corporate interests. As Secretary of Commerce, with Wilson's support and approval, he immediately undertook to reorganize the Bureau of Foreign and Domestic Commerce for more efficient service in promoting foreign trade, and submitted a bill to Congress for the creation of a system of commercial attachés and agents, and trade commissioners, which Congress passed in 1914. Between the two of them, Redfield and Hurley, again with Wilson's approval, instituted many of the mechanisms of business – government cooperation in domestic and foreign trade, including the encouragement of trade associations, that are usually regarded as initially introduced by Herbert Hoover when he was Secretary of Commerce during the 1920s. Finally, it is important to note that although Wilson permitted Secretary of State William Jennings Bryan to make many

the National Foreign Trade Council. In 1913 he toured Latin America as an official trade commissioner for Wilson's Department of Commerce to investigate market and investment opportunities for U.S. industry and finance.

40. Link, *Wilson*, II, p. 139. It might also be noted that Link errs in stating (*Woodrow Wilson and the Progressive Era, 1910–1917* [New York: Harper & Bros., 1954], p. 74) that Rublee was prevented from serving on the Federal Trade Commission due to the Senate's refusal to confirm his nomination in deference to Senator Jacob H. Gallinger (R., N.H.), who declared Rublee "personally obnoxious." Actually, Rublee served, under a recess appointment by Wilson, for about eighteen months, from 16 March 1915, to 8 September 1916, before he was obliged to retire. See *Federal Trade Commission Decisions* (16 March 1915, to 30 June 1919), Washington, D.C., 1920, Vol. I, p. 4; and Rublee, "History of the Federal Trade Commission," p. 120.

41. "The Tariff" (3 January 1912), *P P W W*, Vol. II, p. 330.

ambassadorial appointments on the basis of patronage obligations, he refused to permit Bryan to disturb the consular service.

Against this background, the attitude of corporation leaders toward the three major pieces of New Freedom legislation of 1913–1914 (Underwood Tariff, Federal Reserve, and Federal Trade Commission acts), as well as the extent to which that legislation affected foreign trade expansion and to which, in turn, the nature of the legislation was determined by considerations relating to such expansion, may be more clearly understood.

Between 1910 and 1914, corporate leaders, particularly those connected with the large corporations and banking houses, were unusually active in organizing themselves for the promotion of their interests and programmatic objectives in domestic and foreign affairs. In 1910 industrial corporations organized the American Manufacturers Export Association (AMEA); in 1912 these corporations, along with other business organizations, such as the American Asiatic Association (AAA), established the United States Chamber of Commerce; and in 1914 the AMEA, the AAA, and the Pan-American Society joined together to form the National Foreign Trade Council (NFTC). These were all what might be called "peak associations" or large corporate interests; but the NFTC may be legitimately considered a peak association of peak associations. The officers and memberships of these associations interlocked as intricately as did the directors of the huge industrial corporations and finance houses of the time.

Of the more significant manifestations of the Wilson administration's concern for the promotion of foreign trade and of the community of agreement between large corporate interests and that administration, therefore, one was its endorsement of the purposes of the first National Foreign Trade Convention, convened in Washington, D.C., 27 May and 28 May 1914. The Convention, presided over by Alba B. Johnson, and the National Foreign Trade Council subsequently established, with James A. Farrell as its president, were led and dominated by men representing the nation's greatest industrial, mercantile, and financial corporations.[42] As Johnson related: "The Convention had its inception at a meeting in New York some time ago" with Secretary of Commerce Redfield. He gave the idea for such a convention "his most cordial approval, and, therefore, it is fair to say" that he "is in a sense the Father

42. *Official Report of the National Foreign Trade Convention* (1914), pp. 15, 16, 457–458. (Hereafter cited as NFTC, Proceedings.) Johnson was himself president of the Baldwin Locomotive Works, and Farrell the president of the United States Steel Corporation.

of this Convention. . . . "[43] Edward N. Hurley, the first Vice-Chairman and later Chairman of the Federal Trade Commission, also played a leading role in the organization of the Convention and in the Council's subsequent affairs.[44]

The Convention met in the afterglow of Secretary of State Bryan's appearance, in January 1914, as guest of honor at the annual dinner of the American Asiatic Association, of which Willard Straight was then president.[45] At that time, the Underwood Tariff and Federal Reserve act, measures most closely associated with the New Freedom, had been passed by Congress. The Association's expressed purpose for inviting Bryan to the dinner, which was attended by leaders of the corporate community, was to exchange views with him on, and have him clarify, the administration's foreign policy. Emphasizing that the "era upon which we are entering is not only that of the Pacific Ocean, it must be one of Pacific development as well," Straight cited the new tariff as a stimulant for "carrying the war into the enemies' camp and competing abroad with those who will now invade our own market. . . . " And to the cheers of the diners, he observed that with the Panama Canal and the opportunity provided by the reserve act for the extension of foreign banking and investment, "we are in a better position than at any time in our history aggressively to undertake the development of our export trade."[46] In response, Bryan pointed out that his duties as Secretary of State kept him "in touch with the expansion of American Commerce and the extension of American interests throughout the world," with which both he and the president were in "deep sympathy," and he assured the businessmen that the administration "will see that no industrial highwayman robs you. This government stands committed to the doctrine that these United States are entitled to the greatest possible industrial and commercial development." In this respect, like Straight, he singled out the tariff and reserve act as decisive instrumentalities for giving the doctrine practical effect.[47]

43. Ibid., pp. 203–204.   44. Ibid., pp. 15, 17, 457.

45. Straight had served as agent of the American Banking Group in China during the days of the Six-Power Consortium, was associated with the House of Morgan, and was a leading participant in the organization of the NFTC.

46. The reserve act, as Straight noted, permitted "the establishment of branches of American banking institutions abroad," and with its provision for a commercial-acceptance system promised to "free vast sums for use in an international discount market and for the purchase of desirable foreign securities." *Journal of the American Asiatic Association*, XIV, I (February 1914), p. 8 (hereafter cited as *AAA Journal*).

47. The reserve act, according to Bryan, as a law the nation "long needed," would stimulate foreign trade "not only in the Orient but also throughout South America"; the new tariff meant "a larger commerce between our nation and the world, and in this increase the Orient will have her share," to the advantage not only of the public in

The administration's endorsement of the National Foreign Trade Convention the following May assumed tangible forms. Secretary of Commerce Redfield delivered the opening address of the Convention on the morning of May 27 and he served as toastmaster at its banquet that night; Secretary of State Bryan delivered the main after-dinner speech at the banquet; and Wilson the next day received the delegates at the White House for a short interview.

As the Council later announced, the national importance of the Convention was

> attested by the fact that its purpose [to promote foreign trade and a coordinated national foreign trade policy based upon the cooperation of government and business] was cordially endorsed by the President of the United States, who received the delegates at the White House; by the Secretary of State, who delivered, at the banquet, an outline of the administration's policy toward American business abroad; and by the Secretary of Commerce, who opened the convention. . . . [48]

In his address to the delegates in the East Room of the White House, after having been introduced to them by Edward N. Hurley, Wilson declared his "wish to express . . . the feeling of encouragement that is given by the gathering of a body like this for such a purpose." For, he said: "There is nothing in which I am more interested than the fullest development of the trade of this country and its righteous conquest of foreign markets." Referring to Secretary Redfield's address of the previous day, Wilson confided: "I think that you will realize . . . that it is one of the things that we hold nearest to our heart that the government and you should cooperate in the most intimate manner in accomplishing our common object." He expressed the hope that this would be "only the first of a series of conferences of this sort with you gentlemen." In reply, Alba B. Johnson assured the president that as businessmen they realized "the deep interest which this government takes in promoting legitimate foreign trade. . . . "[49]

Bryan delivered two addresses at the banquet on the night of May 27, 1914, the first a short prepared statement for release to the press, the second a lengthier extemporaneous speech. In the prepared speech Bryan declared the administration "earnestly desirous of increasing American foreign commerce and of widening the field of American enterprise. . . ."

general, but "especially" of "those merchants and manufacturers now turning their eyes to the Far East." McKinley's advocacy of tariff reduction "as a means of extending . . . our exports," was "a prophetic utterance": we "must buy if we would sell." Ibid., pp. 12–13.

48. NFTC, *Proceedings* (1914), p. 8.   49. Ibid., pp. 392–393.

He reiterated its intention to cooperate with the business community to this end, and speaking for his own department he emphasized its "earnest purpose" to "obtain for Americans equality of opportunity in the development of the resources of foreign countries and in the markets of the world." Accordingly it was his "intention to employ every agency of the Department of State to extend and safeguard American commerce and legitimate American enterprises in foreign lands," consistent with the "sovereign rights of other governments."[50]

In his extemporaneous remarks, Bryan explained to the men of capital that his department's policy was Wilson's policy – what it "does in foreign affairs is but what the President desires." This meant, he said,

50. Ibid., pp. 206, 207. That this represented administration policy, not merely edifying rhetoric to win the favor of corporate interests, is corroborated, inter alia, by the exchange of notes during the summer of 1913 between Bryan and E. T. Williams (United States Chargeé d'Affaires at Peking). Williams requested instructions "as to the attitude to be taken by this Legation towards financial transactions between American capitalists and the Chinese Government," in view of President Wilson's statement of 18 March 1913, repudiating the Six-Power Consortium and the Reorganization Loan. Referring to the passages in that statement that the American people "wish to participate ... very generously, in the opening ... [of] the almost untouched and perhaps unrivaled resources of China," and that the U.S. government "is earnestly desirous of promoting the most extended and intimate trade relationship between this country and the Chinese Republic," Williams suggested as his understanding of the administration's policy that the State Department would support "industrial" loans and investments for the development of railways and mineral resources, secured upon the assets and earnings of such enterprises, but not "financial loans" to the Chinese provincial and central governments secured upon government revenues. Bryan replied that "the Legation is right in assuming that the Department is extremely interested in promoting, in every proper way, the legitimate enterprises of American citizens in China and in developing to the fullest extent the commercial relations between the two countries." He continued: "It may be stated, in general, that this Government expects that American enterprise should have opportunity everywhere abroad to compete for contractual favors on the same footing as any foreign competitors, and this implies also equal opportunity to an American competitor to make good his ability to execute the contract. . . . [This Government] stands ready, if wrong be done toward an American citizen in his business relations with a foreign government, to use all proper effort toward securing just treatment for its citizens. *This rule applies as well to financial contracts as to industrial engagements.*" (Emphasis added). Department of State, *Papers Relating to the Foreign Relations of the United States*, 1913, pp. 183–187, 170–171. It is essential to note that the conditions outlined by Bryan in this note and in one cited by himself from Secretary of State Richard Olney to Minister Charles Denby in 1896 (ibid., 1897, p. 56), delimiting the extent of government support for U.S. enterprise abroad (i.e., refusing special support for one U.S. firm to the exclusion of others, refusing to guarantee the execution of contracts or the success of an enterprise, and renouncing any commitment to intercede forcibly in the internal affairs of foreign nations on behalf of U.S. capitalists), were all well-established principles affirmed alike by the Dollar Diplomatists (such as Taft, Knox, Wilson, Calhoun, Straight) in their public statements and diplomatic notes, and by their predecessors. These delimiting principles were in no way peculiar to the Wilson Administration, and cannot be considered as distinguishing its policy from that of Taft and Knox.

"policies which will promote our industry abroad as well as at home";
already, in the short time of the administration's existence, it had taken
measures that would "tend directly and necessarily to promote commerce," such as the tariff and reserve act. But "more than that," Bryan
continued, the administration's efforts to win friends for the United
States, safeguard the peace, and conclude commercial treaties constituted a broad contribution to the stabilization and extension of foreign
economic expansion. "One sentence from President Wilson's Mobile
speech has done a great deal to encourage commerce." When he there
renounced territorial conquest as an object of U.S. policy in Latin America, "he opened the doors of all the weaker countries to an invasion of
American capital and American enterprise. (Applause.)"[51] As Bryan had

51. NFTC, *Proceedings* (1914), pp. 208–210. Along with the Mobile speech, the statement repudiating the Six-Power Consortium is most often cited to substantiate the
view that Wilson repudiated Dollar Diplomacy. If this is meant as a repudiation of
government support of corporate interests in expanding investments and exports
abroad, then as already indicated in the immediately preceding text and in note 50,
neither the Mobile speech nor the consortium statement is amenable to such interpretation. Wilson's consortium statement not only emphasized the government's intention to promote U.S. participation in the development of China and the closest of
commercial relations between the two countries, but also specifically declared: "The
present administration will urge and support the legislative measures necessary to
give American merchants, manufacturers, contractors, and engineers the banking
and other financial facilities which they now lack and without which they are at a
serious disadvantage as compared with their industrial and commercial rivals. This is
its duty. This is the main material interest of its citizens in the development of
China. . . . " *Foreign Relations*, 1913, p. 171. Cf. the version of and references to the
statement in George H. Blakeslee, ed., *Recent Developments in China* (New York:
G. E. Stechert & Co., 1913), pp. 159–160; John V. A. MacMurray, ed., *Treaties and
Agreements with and Concerning China, 1894–1919* (New York: Oxford, 1921),
Vol. II, p. 1025; Charles Vevier, *The United States and China, 1906–1913* (New
Brunswick, N.J.: Rutgers University Press, 1955), p. 210. All these versions include
the reference to banking and other financial facilities needed for effective competition
in Chinese markets. (These facilities were regarded as essential by corporate interests
to foreign economic expansion and were provided in 1913 by sections 13, 14, and 25
of the Federal Reserve Act, which permitted branch banking abroad and the establishment of a domestic discount market for foreign trade commercial acceptances.)
Unfortunately, in the widely used *Documents of American History*, edited by Henry
S. Commager, the consortium statement, there entitled "The Repudiation of 'Dollar
Diplomacy,' " is entirely reproduced, except for the passage referring to the banking
and other financial facilities (5th ed.; 1949, Doc. #390). For further evidence regarding the Wilson administration's intentions in repudiating the consortium, see Secretary of State Bryan's address before the Asiatic Association in January 1914, where
he explained: "The new administration in withdrawing approval from the Chinese
loan did not question the good faith or good intent of those who had seen in it a
means of increasing our influence, prestige and commercial power in China. The
President believed that a different policy was more consistent with the American position, and that it would in the long run be more advantageous to our commerce. . . ."
See also Willard Straight's remark on the same occasion that though many businessmen "have interpreted the announcement . . . to mean that the American Government would not extend to our bankers the support which those familiar with trade

put it at the Asiatic Association dinner: "The doctrine of universal brotherhood is not sentimentalism – it is practical philosophy. . . . " The government could not create trade, but it was its "duty" to "create an environment in which it can develop."[52] He looked forward with "great expectations" to the extension of United States trade and investment abroad; the Convention itself provided "evidence that we are going forward," and the statistics showing the increase in exports of manufactured goods left "no doubt" that the United States could compete successfully with the European industrial nations "in the newer countries that are awaiting complete development," and that the United States would thus become "an increasing factor in the development" of such countries.[53]

Bryan's approach to economic expansion exemplified a unified worldview, embracing "moralism" and "commercialism" as interdependent and mutually consistent elements, that was so common to the expansionists of the time; the underlying assumptions of the "Good Neighbor" policy of later administrations were not basically different; and like the policy of Wilson or Straight it emphasized not merely trade but also "development" of agrarian countries, and the government's responsibility to foster those operations.

Promising the complete support of his department for the extension of markets and investments abroad, and inviting the close cooperation between the businessmen and the State Department, Bryan told the corporate leaders: "I promise you that the State Department – every agency of it – will be back of every honest businessman in pushing legitimate enterprise in all parts of the world. (Applause.)" To emphasize the community of purpose between the State Department and the corporate interests, he continued by extending a colorful analogy:

> In Spanish-speaking countries hospitality is expressed by a phrase, "My house is your house." . . . I can say, not merely in courtesy – but as a fact – my Department is your department: the ambassa-

conditions in China consider necessary. . . . I personally feel assured, that this impression . . . is not justified. . . . " *AAA Journal*, XIV, I (February 1914), pp. 12, 8–9; cf. editorial ibid., p. 8. The present author examines this question in greater detail in his Master's thesis.

52. *AAA Journal*, XIV, I (February 1914), p. 13. Cf. Straight's remark: "The true armies of world peace . . . are the merchants engaged in international trade. In this army, the Secretary of State is a Chief of Staff, and the Ambassador a Corps Commander. We of this [Asiatic] Association are the rank and file. . . . " Ibid., p. 8. Also, that of M. A. Oudin, manager of the Foreign department of General Electric Company, that whereas the government could not create trade, it could "point the way to private enterprise." NFTC, *Proceedings* (1914), pp. 366, 367, 379–380.

53. Ibid., *Proceedings* (1914), pp. 207, 208.

dors, the ministers and the consuls are all yours. It is their business to look after your interests and to guard your rights.

If any of them failed to fulfill his responsibility, advised Bryan: "we shall be pleased to have you report them." For his part, the State Department would "endeavor to open all doors to you. We shall endeavor to make all people friendly to you. . . . "[54]

Given the general approach to expansion shared by men such as Wilson, Straight, Bryan, and corporate spokesmen, the question of "inner" motive is somewhat irrelevant. For example, what may be said of Straight's "inner" motive when he spoke of trade as the means to peace; or of the U.S. Steel Corporation's president, James A. Farrell, when he told the Convention: "there is no factor which is so much involved in . . . [the nation's] material prosperity as the export trade," and then proceeded to say that

> due to its great significance with respect to the economic conditions of our financial relations with the markets of the world, the export trade is likewise a vital factor in international affairs. . . . The contest today is for supremacy in the trade of the world's markets, because that country which is a commercial power is also a power in other respects."[55]

The important point is that they held in common the assumption that expansion of markets and investment abroad was indispensable to the stability and growth of the political economy. As Redfield had put it at the banquet when introducing Bryan as the next speaker, the mission of his fellow diners was "to make this land of ours one of continual increasing prosperity." For he continued:

> we have learned the lesson now, that our factories are so large that their output at full time is greater than America's market can continuously absorb. We know now that if we will run full time all the time, we must do it by reason of the orders we take from lands beyond the sea. To do less than that means homes in America in which the husbands are without work; to do that means factories that are shut down part of the time. And because the markets of the world are greater and steadier than the markets of any country can be, and because we are strong, we are going out, you and I, into the markets of the world to get our share. (Applause.)[56]

54. Ibid., pp. 210–211.   55. Ibid., pp. 35, 36.
56. Ibid., p. 205. For similar expressions on the indispensability of exports to the nation's prosperity by business and political leaders, see ibid., pp. 6, 7, 70, 74, 80, 86, 117, 140, 141, 214, 218, 230–231, 285.

The record leaves no reason to doubt that the knowledgeable corporate leaders understood and accepted as genuine the administration's policy statements.[57] The difficulty, in their view, lay not with the administration, but with the people. In this respect, upon closer examination, it is apparent that many of the pronouncements by businessmen in this period that have been interpreted as directed against the Wilson administration, were more often directed against an "unenlightened" public and/or hostile senators or congressmen. As one businessman put it, the public must realize "that government assistance to American shipping and the American export trade is not only a business but a patriotic policy, pertaining to national defense as well as to our industrial welfare."[58] Or as Willard Straight phrased it, under current conditions of public opinion, "any administration may be attacked if it utilizes the power of the Government for the profit of private interests, no matter what indirect advantage might accrue to the country as a whole." The problem was to educate the people to accept government support of private foreign investments as action not on behalf of a special, but of the national, interest.[59]

In the context of Wilson's approach to both foreign trade and the trust question, and of the community of views between large corporate interests and his administration in these areas, the significance for foreign trade of the Federal Trade Commission Act, as the legislative embodiment of the "rule of reason," may be better comprehended.

It was generally recognized in business circles that the large industrial corporations were most suited to successful export trade, and that the rapid rise in exports of manufacturers from the late 1890s to 1914 had been due largely to the operations of these corporations. The large corporations enjoyed low unit costs necessary for competition in world markets, particularly in the capital and durable goods industries. Their superior reserves and intimate connections with the great financial institutions enabled them to carry the expense of foreign sales promotion, offer attractive foreign credit facilities, and reap the benefits of foreign loans and concessions, all indispensable to an expanding and stable export trade. It was these corporations that were most intimately involved in the "development" of agrarian nations. Since the export of manufactured goods was considered primary in maintaining the nation's international exchanges, in liquidating foreign debts, and in guaranteeing domestic prosperity, the success of any business or governmental policy

---

57. See, e.g., the remark of M. A. Oudin of General Electric, ibid., pp. 366, 367, 379–380.
58. P. H. W. Ross, president of the National Marine League, ibid., p. 143.
59. Ibid., pp. 174–187.

looking to the promotion of export trade and the achievement of these related objectives appeared to stand or fall with the large corporation. A domestic policy, therefore, designed to atomize large corporations could only prove self-defeating.

These were the points emphasized by such prominent spokesmen for large corporate interests as John D. Ryan, president of the Amalgamated Copper Company, M. A. Oudin of General Electric, and Alba B. Johnson of the Baldwin Locomotive Works.[60] As Johnson put it: "To attack our business interests because by reason of intelligent management they have grown strong is to cripple them in the struggle for the world's trade.[61] But their views, insofar as they related to the maintenance of large business units, were in no essential respect different from those of Wilson, whose attitude, as already indicated, may be summed up by the declaration in his Acceptance Speech: "I am not afraid of anything that is normal."[62] It is important to note, therefore, that the criticisms of "antitrust" bills pending in Congress by speakers at the 1914 National Foreign Trade Convention were leveled not against Wilson and his administration, but against "radicals" in Congress and what was considered misguided and dangerous public opinion. They particularly applied to the policy of the previous Taft administration, which in its last year and a half had "mined the Sherman Act for all it was worth."[63] But Wilson's position on the trust question was clear to all who read or heard his speeches, at any rate by early 1914; indeed, in his special address on the trusts to Congress in January 1914, he had specifically declared: "no measures of sweeping or novel change are necessary . . . our object is *not* to unsettle business or anywhere seriously to break its established courses athwart."[64] Programmatically his position centered upon the legislative proposals advanced since the Hepburn amendments of 1908–1909, by large corporate interests through such organizations as the Chicago Association of Commerce, the National Civic Federation, and later the United States Chamber of Commerce. And by the end of 1914, large corporate interests found that they could look with satisfaction upon the status of the nation's antitrust laws.[65]

60. See their remarks in ibid., pp. 167, 168, 375–378, 327–328.
61. Ibid., pp. 327–328.   62. *P P W W*, Vol. II, p. 464; ibid.
63. Robert H. Wiebe, "The House of Morgan and the Executive, 1905–1913," *American Historical Review*, LXV, I (October 1959), p. 58. Cf. *The Federal Antitrust Law with Amendments, List of Cases Instituted by the United States, and Citations of Cases Decided Thereunder or Relating Thereto*, 1 January 1914, in Senate Committee on the Judiciary, *Hearings . . . Together with Briefs and Memoranda . . . Compiled for Use in Consideration of H. R. 15657*, 63rd Cong., 2nd sess. (Washington, D.C., 1914), pp. 164–183.
64. *P P W W*, Vol. III, pp. 82, 83. Emphasis in original.
65. See, e.g., the report of William L. Saunders to the second National Foreign Trade

The New Freedom legislation on trusts bore upon matters of foreign trade expansion in a more overt way. In February 1914 the Chamber of Commerce devoted its principal session, in which Secretary Redfield participated, to a discussion of the administration's trust program.[66] It was here that the Chamber appointed its special committee on trade commission legislation, of which William L. Saunders and Rublee were members. Other members included president of the Chamber R. G. Rhett, Professor Henry R. Seager of Columbia University, Charles R. Van Hise, president of the University of Wisconsin, and Guy E. Tripp, chairman of the board of directors of the Westinghouse Electric Manufacturing Company. One of the committee's recommendations, issued in the spring of 1914, urged that Congress "direct the Commission [when established] to investigate and report to Congress at the earliest practicable date on the advisability of amending the Sherman Act to allow a greater degree of cooperation" in the export trade. By a vote of 538 to 67 the Chamber's membership approved this specific recommendation (as did the National Foreign Trade Convention in May 1914), along with the broader one supporting a trade commission act.[67] Accordingly, in the drafting of the act, which Rublee wrote, it was this Chamber committee that inserted word for word section 6(h), which authorized the trade commission to investigate world trade conditions and submit appropriate recommendations to Congress.[68] With Rublee and Hurley appointed by Wilson as two of the agency's five commissioners, the FTC undertook and completed in its first year of operation four investigations, three of which dealt with foreign trade conditions.[69] One of these resulted in the two-volume *Report on Cooperation in American Export Trade,* which recommended that Congress pass what was to become the Export Trade

Convention in January 1915. Chairman of the board of the Ingersoll-Rand Company, Saunders was also a charter member of the National Foreign Trade Council, and had served with Rublee on the Chamber of Commerce's special committee that played a leading part in drafting the trade commission act. Saunders observed that the Sherman Act prohibited only those restraints of trade that were "unreasonable or contrary to the public welfare," and that there was "no likelihood" of its becoming "any more drastic." The Clayton Act "defines a monopoly and ... announces certain moral principles to which we all agree"; and the trade commission act "prevents unfair methods of competition," and as such "is the most wholesome legislation ... that has been passed recently" in the matter of trusts. Saunders criticized *opponents* of the trade commission act for not seeing that "cooperation among businessmen – cooperation and concentration – is wholesome business and a good economic condition." NFTC, *Proceedings* (1915), pp. 54, 56.
66. See *La Follette's Weekly,* VI, 8 (21 February 1914), pp. 1–2.
67. Senate Committee on Interstate Commerce, "Promotion of Export Trade," *Hearings,* 64th Cong., 2nd sess., p. II.
68. Ibid., pp. 10–12.
69. *Annual Report of the Federal Trade Commission for the Year Ended June 30, 1916,* p. 18.

(Webb–Pomerene) Act of 1918 permitting cartels in the export trade, a bill that Wilson strongly supported.

The requirements of foreign-trade promotion also influenced, in a negative way, the nature of the Clayton Act. As Oudin reported to the Foreign Trade Convention of May 1914:

> the Committee on the Judiciary of the House . . . has reported a bill containing strict prohibitions against discriminations in prices for exclusive agencies, but providing that such prohibitions shall apply only in respect to commodities sold within the jurisdiction of the United States. This emphatic recognition of the distinction between domestic and export commerce reflects the growing disposition of the Government to render sympathetic assistance to American exporters. . . . [70]

Just as the character of New Freedom legislation concerning the regulation of business related to the requirements of foreign-trade promotion and reflected a community of views between the corporate community and the Wilson administration, the same was true, as already indicated, of the two most important New Freedom laws passed in 1913, the Underwood Tariff and the Federal Reserve Act.

When Bryan, in his banquet address to the Foreign Trade Convention delegates, cited the tariff and the reserve act as measures taken by the administration for the promotion of foreign trade, he was not assuming the posture of protesting too much, nor was he merely waxing politically expedient to please his audience: The large corporate spokesmen among the delegates analyzed the two laws in precisely the same way. The two laws, it should be noted, were passed against the background of a trend among large industrial and financial interests, which had visibly emerged at least a decade before, toward tariff and banking structures oriented (inter alia) to their foreign trade and investment requirements. Bryan pointed to the elementary principle underlying the new tariff: "if we are to sell abroad, we must buy from people beyond our borders." The reserve act "will do more to promote trade in foreign lands than any other one thing that has been done in our history"; it had "set a nation free."[71] From no less a figure in large corporate circles than John E. Gardin, vice-president of the National City Bank of New York, came a similar view. Complaining of the nation's immaturity in matters of international finance, Gardin found encouragement in the tariff and the reserve act.

70. NFTC, *Proceedings*, (1914), p. 379; cf. House Committee on the Judiciary, *Hearings on Trust Legislation* (2 vols.), 63rd Cong., 2nd sess., Serial 7, 1914, pp. II, 1960–1963.
71. NFTC, *Proceedings* (1914), pp. 208–209.

The administration . . . certainly has given us two things of which
we might be proud: one, the reduction of the tariff . . . opening up
the markets of the world – if we want to sell we have got to buy; and
the other is the Federal Reserve Law, which relieves us from the
bondage

of an outmoded banking law, providing "relief just as important as the
emancipation of the slaves. . . . " In view of these laws, Gardin looked
forward to the projected program of the NFTC, as working "for the
benefit of all those who wish to partake . . . of the new freedom."[72]

Among those spokesmen of industrial and financial interests who
praised the Underwood Tariff, representatives of smaller interests were
conspicuously absent. It is a mistake to view the Underwood measure as
part of a New Freedom crusade against large corporations. It *was* part of
the New Freedom program; but the heathens were not necessarily the
large corporations. It was part of an attack on "special privilege" conceived to be in conflict with the national interest understood in terms of
the conditions of modern times; but it was the special privilege cherished
by smaller and by nonindustrial interests, no longer needed by the larger
interests as export trade became increasingly more important to them.

Aside from its immediate intent to stimulate export trade, the tariff,
consistent with Wilson's views, sought to enforce industrial efficiency by
inviting worldwide competition, which would result in making U.S. industry and finance a more formidable competitor in world markets. The
larger industrial interests could withstand, and expect to fatten on, such
competition, but not the smaller. Those items placed on the free list by
the tariff were, in the majority, articles of food, clothing, and raw materials, industries occupied by the "little man." Large corporations engaged in the capital and durable goods industries, and most heavily
involved in the export trade so far as manufactures were concerned,
could approve this provision, because should the tariff have the intended

72. Ibid., pp. 249, 250–251. See also the remarks of Fred Brown Whitney, chairman of
the board of directors of the Lake Torpedo Boat Co., Alba B. Johnson, Clarence J.
Owens, managing director of the Southern Commercial Congress (at whose convention in 1913 Wilson had delivered his Mobile address), Herbert S. P. Deans, manager
of the foreign exchange department of the Merchants Loan and Trust Company Bank
of Chicago, Edward N. Hurley, representing the Illinois Manufacturers Association,
ibid., pp. 251, 22–23, 90–91, 304, 291. Whitney: the reserve act represented the
people's "mandate – eternal and omnipotent – that the United States shall become a
World Power in international finance and trade. . . . " Johnson: the new tariff was
"part of the preparation . . . for this great forward movement in the world's market"; the reserve act "is designed particularly to facilitate exchange transactions with
other nations. . . . " Owens: along with the Panama Canal the reserve act "announced the beginning of a period of direct financial relations" with Latin American
markets, "giving America the chance, for the first time, to compete in this regard
with Great Britain and Germany."

effect, it would operate to keep wage levels down, reduce costs of materials, and in the process enable more effective competition in world markets, aside from increasing the profit rate. The issue was analogous to the great Corn Law debates in England during the previous century, where the industrialists sought to abolish import duties at the expense of producers of food and raw stuffs. Wilson, after all, had learned well from Cobden and Bright, the apostles of what has been aptly termed the "imperialism of free trade."[73]

At the same time, those items of heavy industry placed upon the free list, such as steel rails and agricultural machinery and implements, were already produced by the larger U.S. corporations with an efficiency and at a cost of production sufficient to permit not only successful competition in world markets in general, but within the national markets of the European industrial nations as well, a point Wilson frequently made. Of further aid to such competition, moreover, the Underwood Tariff granted drawbacks on exported items composed in part or in whole of imported materials subject to import duties.[74]

In effect, the Underwood Tariff strengthened the position of the larger corporations as against the smaller, and as against producers of agricultural materials. In this case, legal reform served the interest of those seeking to buttress the socioeconomic status quo, while adherence to established law and institutions rallied those whose interest lay in forestalling the onward rush of that status quo. Accordingly, the greatest danger to the Underwood bill's downward revisions while pending in Congress "came from a horde of lobbyists," among whom the "owners and managers of industries that produced the great bulk of American industrial products were unconcerned and took no part. . . . " As Link concluded, the Underwood duties assumed their greatest significance "in so far as they reflected a lessening of the pressure from the large industrial interests for a McKinley type of protection."[75] It is understandable, therefore, that among the congressional critics of the Underwood Tariff, as with the reserve act and the trade commission and Clayton acts, were "radical" and insurgent Democrats and Republicans claiming to represent the smaller and agrarian interests. Insofar as the tariff, perhaps

73. See John Gallagher and Ronald Robinson, "The Imperialism of Free Trade," *The Economic History Review*, IV, I, Second Series (August 1953), pp. 1–15. This is not meant to imply that the Underwood Tariff was a free-trade tariff; it was, in Taussig's terms, a "competitive tariff." F. W. Taussig, *The Tariff History of the United States* (8th ed.; New York: G. P. Putnam's Sons, 1937), pp. 418–422.

74. Federal Trade Commission, *Report on Cooperation in American Export Trade* (2 vols.), June 30, 1916, Vol. I, p. 162; Taussig, *Tariff History of the United States*, pp. 425–449.

75. Link, *Wilson*, II, pp. 186, 196. The lobbyists included representatives of such interests as wool, sugar, textile manufactures, citrus fruits.

more dramatically than other issues, brought into unified focus the elements of efficiency, bigness in business, foreign trade, and an expanding sphere of enterprise – the last holding out the promise of more room for the "little man" – it may be accurately described as one of the high points of Wilsonian reform.

It is not meant to imply that the corporate community had no criticisms of the Underwood Tariff or Federal Reserve Act; but large corporate interests in particular viewed the new tariff either as a worthwhile experiment or more positively as sound policy; and business opinion overwhelmingly viewed the reserve act as basically sound, in need of perfecting amendments, rather than as a measure directed against their interests. The conflict over the reserve-system bill during 1913 had not revolved so much around the provisions of the bill as around the question of how and by whom those provisions should be administered, except insofar as the "radical" and agrarian Republicans and Democrats insisted upon provisions that Wilson rejected. Otherwise, with respect to the manner of administering the system, the division lay not between Wilson and the "small" interests on the one side and "big business" on the other: the large corporate interests themselves were divided, particularly, the evidence indicates, along industrial and financial lines. As Link noted, the great mass of nonbanking business opinion approved the bill, and in October 1913, for example, both the Merchants Association of New York and the United States Chamber of Commerce (the latter by a vote of 306 to 17) endorsed it.[76]

The Federal Reserve Act may be interpreted, with respect to the issues raised here, in terms of a movement of large finance and corporate-industrial interests, extending back to and before the National Monetary Commission, for branch banking, a commercial-acceptance market for the facilitation of foreign trade and investment, and a reserve system that would protect the gold stock from foreign and domestic runs; a movement that, by expanding the credit structure, would reduce industrial corporations' dependence upon the money markets for investment capital, and insulate industrial operations from stock-market fluctuations and speculators; a movement that Wilson approved and responded to favorably without himself being in any way responsible for its initiation, just as in the case of the movement for the Federal Trade Commission Act.

Indeed, upon his election, Wilson had no well-defined specific program; he had a general approach, and even his "specific" proposals were couched in general terms. He had identified himself with, and then given

76. Link, *Wilson and the Progressive Era*, p. 51.

ideological and political leadership to, those movements with which his general approach corresponded, and which therefore corresponded with the concept of national interest embraced by that general approach. These movements – what are known as the Progressive reform movements (and they were reforms) – were movements led by and consisting of large corporate interests and political and intellectual leaders affirming the large corporate-industrial capitalist system, and convinced of the necessity of institutionalized reforms, legal and otherwise, to accommodate the nation's law and habits, and the people's thinking, to the new corporate business structure and its requirements, domestic and foreign. As Wilson had put it, laws "meant for business done by individuals" had to be "satisfactorily adjusted to business done by great combinations," requiring "open efforts to accommodate law to the material development which has so strengthened the country."

Wilson's careful and emphatic distinction between the large corporation and the trust may be cited as one of the more forceful illustrations substantiating this formulation. A corollary of his evolutionary historicism, this distinction, in terms of Wilson's programmatic proposals, was decisive to his approach to the trust question, just as it was to that of the Bureau of Corporations under Garfield and Smith, and to that of Roosevelt, Taft, Perkins, Gary, and Croly. The large corporation, in this view, and the restriction of competition by corresponding forms of "cooperation," were the inevitable product of natural economic development. The trust, however, was an artificial contrivance of predatory design, deliberately created by unscrupulous businessmen for undue ends. Accordingly, Wilson believed that although "the elaboration of business upon a great cooperative scale is characteristic of our time and has come about by the natural operation of western civilization," this was different from saying that the trusts were inevitable.

> Big business is no doubt to a large extent necessary and natural. The development of business upon a great scale, upon a great scale of cooperation, is inevitable, and . . . is probably desirable. But that is a very different matter from the development of trusts, because the trusts have not grown. They have been artificially created; they have been put together not by natural processes, but by the will, the deliberate planning will, of men who . . . wished to make their power secure against competition.

On the other hand, "any large corporation built up by the legitimate processes of business, by economy, by efficiency, is natural; and I am not afraid of it, no matter how big it grows . . . "[77]

77. *The New Freedom*, pp. 163–165, 166.

Conservative-historicism, with Edmund Burke as one of its more prominent spokesmen, regarded the politico-economic sphere of society "as a completely irrational one which cannot be fabricated by mechanical methods but which grows of its own accord. This outlook relates everything to the decisive dichotomy between 'construction according to calculated plan' and 'allowing things to grow.' . . . " "A mode of thought is thus created which conceives of history as the reign of pre- and superrational forces."[78] This mode of thought, transmitted to Wilson in particular from Burke, may be traced as a central thread winding not only through the early twentieth-century liberalism (Progressivism) of Theodore Roosevelt, Croly, et al., as well as Wilson, but also through the liberalism of such presently prominent bourgeois ideological leaders as Adolf A. Berle, Jr., who stated: "Unlike the socialist commissariat, the American corporation is not a product of doctrine and dogma; it is an organic growth. . . . "[79] With respect to the basic structure of society, modern liberalism regards as legitimate only those institutions that it conceives as emerging independently of and beyond the deliberate, conscious determination of men; the underlying principle is submission to natural law, as distinguished, for example, from Marxism, which demands the understanding of objective laws of social development operating independently of man's will precisely in order to subject social development to man's conscious will; and as distinguished also from French Enlightenment social thought, which assumed that man could determine his society in accordance with Reason.[80] Conscious determination by men assumes its legitimate and proper function, from the modern liberal standpoint, only in facilitating natural evolution (as manifested in the basic structure of society as it is), and in devising appropriate adjustments to it through parliamentary means (reforms).

78. Mannheim, *Ideology and Utopia*, pp. 120, 121.
79. In his Foreword to Mason, ed., *The Corporation in Modern Society* (Cambridge, Mass.: Harvard University Press, 1959), p. ix. In the same way, and characteristically, Wilson anticipated the downward revision of the tariff not "because men in this country have changed their theories," but because "the conditions of America are going to bust through [the high tariff]. . . . " "Efficiency" (27 January 1912), *P P W W*, Vol. V, p. 360.
80. In this connection, Wilson's conservative-historicism was reinforced by his adaptation of Darwin's theory of biological organic evolution to social evolution, though not in the form of survival-of-the-fittest "Social Darwinism" associated with Spencer, Sumner, and Fiske. See *Constitutional Government in the United States* (New York: Columbia University Press, 1908), pp. 56–57, 199–200, and *The New Freedom*, pp. 46, 47–48, where Wilson describes his view of government and social life as organic, Darwinian, as distinguished from the mechanistic, Newtonian conception of Montesquieu, the Enlightenment thinkers, and Jefferson. Cf. also, Diamond, *Economic Thought of Wilson*, pp. 39, 47, and Link, *Wilson*, I, pp. 21–22.

The sharp and protracted ideological and social conflicts of the late nineteenth and early twentieth century, revolving around the corporate reorganization of the economy and erupting in the great antitrust debates of that period, suggest that the growth of the corporation was not so "organic" as modern U.S. liberals insist; that capitalists and like-minded political and intellectual leaders fought hard and consciously, with "doctrine and dogma" and with economic, political, and legal strategem, to establish the large corporation, in a historically short period of time, as the dominant mode of business enterprise, and to attain popular acceptance of that development. Nevertheless, the "allowing-things-to-grow" doctrine achieves a triumphant renaissance, as the unifying conception, in twentieth-century U.S. liberalism, which may be accurately referred to as corporate liberalism (though now Burke is left neglected backstage and Croly given the curtain calls). It is the fundamental element that makes modern U.S. liberalism the bourgeois Yankee cousin of modern European and English social democracy.[81]

Within this essentially natural-law framework, while consistently holding that the large industrial corporations were natural and beneficent products of social evolution, Wilson attributed much of the evils with which they were popularly associated to financiers, *dei ex machina*, manipulating corporate securities and practices for speculative profit and creating artificial corporate structures for monopolistic advantage.[82] At the same time, by tying credit and currency mechanisms to the "natural laws" of commerce, that is, by basing the banking system upon commercial paper rather than upon government bonds, and building up a reserve system, measures long sought by large financial and corporate-industrial interests, the Federal Reserve Act corresponded with Wilson's view that trade and investment should be set "free" to pursue their "natural" course, unhindered by the arbitrary will of a few financiers; in theory, it would encourage greater competition (through greater opportunities for investment borrowing), and permit "little men" to obtain credit with which to start or maintain a business enterprise of their own, though no longer in the central areas of production, transportation, or communication. *Mutatis mutandis*, Wilson's position on the tariff flowed from similar considerations: the government's role was

81. Herbert Marcuse, *Reason and Revolution* (2nd ed.; New York: Humanities Press, 1954), pp. 398–401. Since completing this essay the author's attention has been drawn to Arnold A. Rogow's "Edmund Burke and the American Liberal Tradition," *The Antioch Review* (Summer 1957), pp. 255–265, which analyzes the decisive relevance of Burke to Wilsonian liberalism in particular and modern U.S. liberalism in general.

82. See, e.g., "Law or Personal Power" (13 April 1908), *P P W W*, Vol. II, p. 29.

to provide business with the "environment" best suited to the assertion of its "natural" course.

Wilson held no dogmatic views on the question of the extent of government intervention in economic affairs – he had long believed that the state should intervene so far as "experience permits or the times demand" – and with respect to the reserve act, he had by June 1913, firmly decided upon government control of the central board, in the face of stiff banker opposition. The compromise that resulted constituted a concession to the large banking interests. After the bill's passage, and the announcement of Wilson's appointments to the central reserve board, the large banks' spokesmen, as well as spokesmen for large industrial corporations, expressed widespread satisfaction,[83] just as they had in the case of the Underwood Tariff and Federal Trade Commission Act.

In this way, Wilson emerged as a foremost ideological and political leader of a social movement affirming corporate-industrial capitalism, and as the preeminent personality in the nation's public life, acting as a bridge of communication between that movement and the public (or, the electorate to which the movement appealed), popularizing the movement's ideology and program, and making them understandable and acceptable to the people in terms of the nation's traditions, evolutionary development, and "destiny." The ideology embraced a neo-Comtean positivism that (in European terms) Wilson, the conservative-historicist and modified Manchestrian liberal, was eminently qualified to serve. Wilson's position was not that of a representative of the "little man," or the "middle class," *against* "big business"; but that of one who, affirming the large corporate-industrial capitalist system, was concerned with establishing the legal and institutional environment most conducive to the system's stability and growth, while preserving some place within the system for the little man. His formula was fair competition and impartial

83. See annual address of American Bankers' Association president Arthur Reynolds at the 1914 convention, and his later remarks at the same convention. *Proceedings of the Fortieth Annual Convention of the American Bankers' Association*, Richmond, Va., 12–16 October 1914, pp. 57–68, 312–315. See also letters expressing approval of the Federal Reserve Act from George M. Reynolds, president of Continental and Commercial National Bank of Chicago, A. Barton Hepburn, chairman of the board, Chase National Bank, and A. J. Hemphill, president of Guaranty Trust Company of New York, to F. H. Goff (president of Cleveland Trust), president of Bankers' Association's Trust Company Section, dated 23 September, 9 October, 5 October 1914, respectively, ibid., pp. 305–308. Cf. *La Follette's Weekly*, VI, 4 (24 January 1914), p. 3, where Jacob H. Schiff of Kuhn, Loeb & Company is quoted praising the reserve law as "legislation highly pleasing to me." La Follette, who opposed the measure, remarked, "The published reports that Wall Street banking interests were fighting the Administration's currency bill tooth and nail now appear somewhat pale in the light of the enthusiastic approval Wall Street is bestowing upon this law." See also, Link, *Wilson*, II, pp. 451–452, 454–455.

access to credit at home, and expansion of the economic frontier abroad, upon the assumption that the wider the market and the more impersonal its conditions, the more room and opportunity for the little man to co-exist side by side with the big. The very conditions of industrial production and of foreign economic expansion, however, made the little man, as an independent entrepreneur, increasingly irrelevant to the national economy, except in peripheral spheres of services and distribution. Theodore Roosevelt sought to meet this disturbing reality by acknowledging it and insisting upon equal opportunity for every young man to rise within the established corporate structures. Although similarly insisting upon such equality, Wilson refused to concede the irrelevance of the little man; but his refusal was not a matter of sentimentality: it stemmed from his fear that given a growing irrelevance of little men in the nation's economy, fewer and fewer people would retain a stake in the capitalist system, and more and more would lose hope for betterment under capitalism and turn toward socialism or other forms of radicalism.[84] As such, the Wilsonian and Rooseveltian variants of Progressivism signified, if not the birth, then the coming of age, of twentieth-century U.S. liber-

84. As Wilson advised leading businessmen in his address at the Annual Banquet of the Economic Club in New York (23 May 1912) *P P W W*, Vol, II, pp. 446, 449–451: "How would it suit the prosperity of the United States, how would it suit the success of business, to have a people that went every day sadly or sullenly to their work? How would the future look to you if you felt that the aspiration has gone out of most men, the confidence of success, the hope that they might change their condition, if there was everywhere the feeling that there was somewhere covert dictation, private arrangement as to who should be in the inner circle of privilege and who should not, a more of less systematic and conscious attempt to dictate and dominate the economic life of the country? Do you not see that just as soon as the old self-confidence of America . . . as her old boasted advantages of individual liberty and opportunity are taken away, all the energy of her people begins to subside, to slacken, to grow loose and pulpy, without fibre, and men simply cast around to see that the day does not end disastrously with them."

   "What is the alternative, gentlemen? You have heard the rising tide of socialism. . . . Socialism is not growing in influence in this country as a programme. It is merely that the ranks of protestants are being recruited. . . . . If it becomes a programme, then we shall have to be very careful how we propose a competing programme . . . the programme of socialism would not work; but there is no use saying what will not work unless you can say what will work. . . .

   "If you want to oust socialism you have got to propose something better. It is a case, if you will allow me to fall into the language of the vulgar, of 'put up or shut up.' . . . It is by constructive purpose that you are going to govern and save the United States. . . .

   "Very well, then, let us get together and form a constructive programme [that posterity will say that after America had passed through a simple age] . . . when the forces of society had come into hot contact . . . there were men of serene enough intelligence . . . of will and purpose to stand up once again . . . [and who found out] how to translate power into freedom, how to make men glad that they were rich, how to take the envy out of men's hearts that others were rich and they for a little while poor, by opening the gates of opportunity to every man. . . . "

alism, whose present-day fundamentals, converging upon large-scale corporate capitalism at home and economic expansion abroad, remain genetically true to the components of Wilson's world-view, their immediate parental source.

According to the generally accepted interpretation offered by Arthur S. Link, Wilsonian Progressivism, as applied and developed during Wilson's two terms as president, from 1913 to 1921, can be divided into two periods: the first, the period of the New Freedom, characterized by government attempts to regulate and stand in hostile posture apart from big business, and directed at restoring some semblance of a laissez-faire, free-competition social order; the second, characterized by a government policy of cooperation with big business and active regulatory intervention in the economy. The divide, according to this view, lay somewhere around November 1914 (though at points the divide is rolled back to early 1914, as a response to the continuing depression, leaving scarcely a year to the New Freedom phase). Thus, it is argued, the New Freedom was capable of serving the cause of Progressivism for only a short time; Progressivism gained new life after November 1914, through the abandonment of the New Freedom and the move toward Herbert Croly's and Theodore Roosevelt's "New Nationalism."

If Wilson is properly understood in terms of the widely current evolutionary-positivistic world view that he shared alike with leading industrial and finance capitalists and with prominent politicians and intellectuals within the bipartisan Progressive movement, and if the approaches taken by his administration to both foreign and domestic affairs are viewed as basically interrelated, rather than compartmentalized, as affecting each other, rather than operating in isolated spheres, then it is of greater analytical value to view the attitude assumed by Wilson and his administration toward "business" before and after November 1914, as undergoing consistent development, rather than fundamental change. That attitude corresponded with a world-view that affirmed large-scale corporate-industrial capitalism as the natural and inevitable product of social evolution, and that regarded foreign investments and exports, defined in terms of the needs of industrial and finance capital, as indispensable to the nation's prosperity and social well-being. Beneficence at home and abroad, in this view, was a function of necessity. Large corporate production appeared as the vehicle of domestic material progress; foreign economic expansion, considered a decisive condition of such production, promised to carry "civilization," bourgeois-liberal ideas and institutions, and a better way of life to the agrarian areas of the world, particularly as "development" of natural resources in those areas was considered essential to such expansion.

It no more occurred to such liberals as Wilson than it did to the so-called Dollar Diplomatists before him, or than it does today to the "internationalist" liberals, that investment in, and ownership of, other nations' resources, railroads, and industry, by U.S. capitalists, constituted imperialism or exploitation. Imperialism to them meant British- and European-style colonialism or exclusive spheres of interest; exploitation meant unscrupulous gouging, exorbitantly profitable concessions gained by undue influence with corrupt government officials, and the like, in short, "unfair practices" analogous to those characteristics that distinguished the trust from the large corporation in domestic affairs. Open-door expansion, on the other hand, appeared to them as simply the implementation of the natural international division of labor between the industrialized and agrarian nations; it meant mutually beneficial (and beneficent) business relationships and trade; it meant the assumption by the United States of its natural place in the world economy vis-à-vis the other industrial nations, by the elimination of "artificial" impediments to the operation of the laws of competitive commerce; it meant "free trade."[85]

In the Wilsonian manner, former president Truman recently remarked: "The Open Door policy is not imperialism; it is free trade." Unfortunately, the bourgeois-liberal mind seems unable to understand how any transaction that involves the exchange of equivalent for equivalent can carry with it any quality of injustice or exploitation. In the economic realm, morality and justice are defined as exchange at value, so long as it is devoid of any element of extrapecuniary coercion; in more sophisticated ideological terms, morality and justice correspond with natural law. But it is precisely in the relationship defined by natural law, precisely in the exchange of equivalent for equivalent (assuming the free and competitive exchange of equivalents in the first place, though this is often not

85. See, e.g., Wilson's "Be Worthy of the Men of 1776" (4 July 1914), *P P W W*, Vol. III, pp. 142–143: "The Department of State . . . is constantly called upon to back up the commercial . . . and the industrial enterprises of the United States in foreign countries, and it at one time went so far in that direction that all its diplomacy came to be designated as 'dollar diplomacy.' . . . But there ought to be a limit to that. There is no man who is more interested than I am in carrying the enterprise of American businessmen to every quarter of the globe. I was interested in it long before I was suspected of being a politician. I have been preaching it year after year as the great thing that lay in the future for the United States, to show her wit and skill and enterprise and influence in every country in the world. . . . [But if] American enterprise in foreign countries, particularly in those . . . which are not strong enough to resist us, takes the shape of imposing upon and exploiting the mass of the people . . . it ought to be checked and not encouraged. I am willing to get anything for an American that money and enterprise can obtain except the suppression of the rights of other men. I will not help any man buy a power which he ought not to exercise over his fellow-beings."

the case), that the exploitation, the injustice, the immorality, from the point of view of the agrarian peoples, resides. For, whereas the relationship is reified by the liberal mind as purely an exchange of goods, a confrontation of things, of private properties, what is really involved is a relationship between human beings. Concern for the nicely balanced exchange of things according to their market value – "a fair field and no favor" – blinds the liberal mind to the real relationship between people, of which the exchange of goods is but a consequence, and to the resulting conditions of life (the "human relations" and "individual dignity" with which the liberal is so articulately preoccupied).[86] Hence, the innocent shock consistently evinced by liberals at anti-Americanism and resentment in the agrarian areas of the world regardless of whether U.S. foreign policy is of the Dollar Diplomacy or the Good Neighbor variety.

For, the essence of open-door expansion involved an international system of economy identical to that established by England and the European industrial nations with their colonies and other agrarian areas. The latter were to become increasingly familiar with modern relations of capital and labor, but with capital appearing in the form of the foreigner and labor in the form of the indigenous population; they were assigned the role of suppliers of raw materials and markets for industrial goods and capital investment; and, of particular importance, control over, and investment decisions affecting, decisive sectors of their economies were to be transferred from their determination to that of capitalists in the United States. Those sectors of their economies were to become "complementary" to, and integrated with, the U.S. corporate economy, each an *imperium in imperio* within its respective nation, with all the implications of economic dislocation, political instability, and restriction of national economic and political independence. To Wilson, such implications were no necessary part of open-door expansion, but rather of imperialism and exploitation as he narrowly conceived them; as for the

86. "We are told that free trade would create an international division of labor, and thereby give to each country the production which is most in harmony with its natural advantages. You believe perhaps, gentlemen, that the production of coffee and sugar is the natural destiny of the West Indies. Two centuries ago, nature, which does not trouble herself about commerce, had planted neither sugar-cane nor coffee trees there." "If the free-traders cannot understand how one nation can grow rich at the expense of another, we need not wonder, since these same gentlemen also refuse to understand how within one country one class can enrich itself at the expense of another." ". . . the protectionist system is nothing but a means of establishing large-scale industry in any given country, . . . of making it dependent upon the world market, and from . . . [that] moment . . . there is already more or less dependence upon free trade. . . ." Marx, "On the Question of Free Trade," public speech delivered before the Democratic Association of Brussels, 9 January 1848, in *The Poverty of Philosophy* (Moscow: Foreign Languages Publishing House, n.d.), pp. 222–223, 224.

rest, it all appeared as only natural in relations between "capital surplus" and "capital deficient" nations, and as the mode of progress in international affairs.[87]

It was the part of statesmanship to make law the expression of the necessities and facts of the time: to institutionalize the ground rules of the
corporate economy at home and the mechanisms of economic expansion
abroad, so that day-to-day business, the laws of commerce, and the government's role with respect to them, might flow smoothly along settled
paths, rather than by the fits and starts of fire-brigade policy or executive
fiat. As Wilson had put it in 1907: "an institution is merely an established practice, an habitual method of dealing with the circumstances of

87. See, e.g., the report of Edward E. Pratt, chief of the Bureau of Foreign and Domestic
   Commerce under Wilson, for the fiscal year 1 July 1914, to 30 June 1915: "we can
   never hope to realize the really big prizes in foreign trade until we are prepared to
   loan capital to foreign nations and to foreign enterprise. The big prizes . . . are the
   public and private developments of large proportions . . . the building of railroads,
   the construction of public-service plants, the improvement of harbors and docks . . .
   and many others which demand capital in large amounts. New countries are generally poor. They look to older and richer countries to supply them with the capital to
   make their improvements and to develop their resources. The country which furnishes
   the capital usually sells the materials and does the work . . . there is no doubt that the
   loans of one nation to another form the strongest kind of economic bond between
   the two. It is commonly said that trade follows the flag. It is much more truly said
   that trade follows the investment or the loan." " . . . A foreign commercial policy . . .
   is gradually taking shape under a wise and careful administration. American investments abroad are being encouraged. The fact that investment must precede
   trade and that investments abroad must be safeguarded is fully recognized." *Reports of the Department of Commerce,* 30 October 1915 (Washington, D.C., 1916),
   pp. 247, 249. Cf. the more recent statement of the prominent liberal spokesman,
   Dean Acheson: "in the nineteenth century an international system of sorts not only
   kept the peace for a century but also provided highly successful economic working agreements. It brought about the industrialization of Europe and of many other
   parts of the world – our own country, for one. It stimulated production of raw
   materials and led to a great, though unevenly distributed, rise in the standard of
   living. This was accomplished by the export of capital, primarily by Great Britain,
   but also by all of Western Europe." " . . . a system for the export of capital, much
   greater than our present . . . efforts, is necessary. The system has been destroyed
   which expanded the power of Western Europe. . . . One to replace it will be devised, managed, and largely (but not wholly) financed by the United States; otherwise, it is likely to be provided by the Soviet Union, under circumstances destructive
   of our own power. . . . " "Foreign investment can provide wider opportunity for
   use of national energies. This can well enhance pride in national achievement
   and relieve frustrations among members of the populace now denied opportunity
   to use their full capabilities and training. This should tend to lessen xenophobia,
   strengthen social fabric and political stability, and bring new meaning to national
   independence. . . . " Acheson, *Power and Diplomacy* (Cambridge, Mass.: Harvard University Press, 1958), pp. 18, 19–20, 22. The first chapter of the book
   includes a subsection entitled, "The Collapse of a World Order," referring to the dis-
   integration of the imperial system of the nineteenth century, and argues the necessity
   of replacing it with one similar to it, in its economic aspects, led by the United States.
   Acheson prefaces the chapter with lines of verse from Alfred Noyes: "When his hundred years expire / Then he'll set hisself a-fire /And another from his ashes rise most
   beautiful to see!"

life or the business of government. . . . "[88] In Wilson's view, it was this, with respect to modern circumstances of the modern industrial order, that the legislation of 1913–1914 promised to do.

Historians who have studied Wilson appear to harbor guilt feelings about capitalism: A policy based upon considerations of the economic imperatives of capitalism is sordid, immoral, or amoral; a policy based upon noneconomic principle is moralistic. The corporate and political policymakers of the United States, Wilson included, have had no such guilt feelings or compulsion to make such a division in their thinking. To them there was (and is) nothing immoral about capitalism; it embraces the highest morality. The strength and spread of morality appear as the function of the strength and spread of capitalism. Historians, however, disregarding the imperatives of modern capitalism, while assuming its existence all the same, seem to have created an ideal construct of what liberalism ought to be, arbitrarily imputing to it certain characteristics of a transcendent nature and withholding from it others, particularly those relating to the affairs of political economy. It is an academic, idealized liberalism, not the responsible political liberalism as it operates as a functional ideology outside the university walls; it is a liberalism from which historians have written history in the manner of advice, consent, and dissent, rather than history that analyzes the nature of liberal ideology as it operates and appears in the hurly-burly of political economy. Accordingly, historians have tended to appraise the nature of the Wilsonian liberal (or Progressive) movement by deduction from, and in comparison with, the supposed nature of its ideology, instead of basing their analyses on an empirical study of the movement and comprehending the ideology of its leaders as emerging from and interacting with that movement and its adversaries. The latter approach is particularly essential to an analysis of Wilson, to whom the great issues of his day turned upon concrete economic interests and questions.

Finding that Wilson's thought and policies often deviated from the ideal model, many historians have concluded superficially that Wilson was a "hypocrite" or a conservative in liberal's clothing. The point raised here, however, is not a quarrel about whether Wilson was in fact a liberal or a Progressive; on the contrary, it is submitted that a successful, comprehensive effort at analyzing precisely what Wilsonian liberalism or Progressivism was (and modern U.S. liberalism in general) has yet to be made.

It would be conducive to a more impartial and comprehensive understanding of Wilson and Wilsonianism to discard as a tool of analysis both the New Freedom–New Nationalism formula and the "moralism" versus "commercialism" presumption. This approach sees behind the

88. Wilson, *Constitutional Government*, p. 14.

New Freedom the shadow of a misconstrued Brandeis, who is taken inaccurately to symbolize an anti–big business program for the restoration of some sort of laissez-faire, free-competition society; more accurately, it sees behind the New Nationalism the shadow of Croly as represented in his book, *The Promise of American Life*. At the outset, and only at the outset, it may be more pertinent and analytically suggestive to a reevaluation of Wilson and Wilsonianism, to see instead the shadow of Croly-the-adolescent behind the earlier years of Wilson's presidency, Croly-the-strapping-young-man behind the later (and lingering into the 1920s), with Croly-the-nearly-mature biding his time until the advent of the New Deal. In view of the present "national purpose" campaign of corporate spokesmen, liberal political and intellectual leaders, the Luce publications and *The New York Times,* short of a basic reordering of U.S. society, Croly-the-mature may yet arrive, and then the nation will surely be in need of a new freedom.

V

Some political and cultural consequences of the disaccumulation of capital: Origins of postindustrial development in the 1920s

1. Historical consciousness: The archetypal and the social

For the most part, modern U.S. intellectuals, and particularly those of us who most claim to be critically conscious, to be rigorously and steadily engaged in developing our understanding, are devoid of a serious conception of human destiny. To put it more precisely, we are devoid of a conception of a nature peculiar to humanity as an historical self-producing species. With respect to the possibility of our living – that is, behaving and acting as well as thinking – in accordance with our ostensible principles, ideals, and hopes, this quality is our chief characteristic. It is, indeed, the quality that chiefly characterizes our mode of feeling and thought about the world, our mode of acting in our day-to-day public lives.

Several different abstract definitions of humanity have been in the recent past, and some still are, current among U.S. intellectuals and in the public discourse, definitions associated with such terms as Industrial Man, Postindustrial Man, Political Man, Psychological Man, Religious Man, Secular Man, Linear Man, Media Man, Technical Man, Global-Village Man, One-Dimensional Man. All these modestly state the denial

This essay was originally published as "On the Proletarian Revolution and the End of Political-Economic Society," *Radical America*, III:3 (May-June 1969). It is republished here with the consent of *Radical America*, with editorial corrections and revisions.

The essay sought to view U.S. history in terms of world history, and U.S. political-economic development in terms of general capitalist development, the latter specifically in accordance with basic concepts of Marx, and in those terms, to see the United States as having arrived at a further stage of development than other industrial capitalist societies.

The essay was also an attempt to induce "radicals" of the Left in the United States to see *themselves* historically, precisely by seeing their *society* historically, and to counter their or nonconceptualization of a human-rooted destiny as a dimension of historical reality. The denial of or aversion to a concept of human destiny in terms of a historical human nature, is the way modern U.S. intellectuals acknowledge the renunciation of history as the study of a necessary process of human development, as a science of laws of social development, our inability or unwillingness to conceptualize history as such a science of laws and act upon that conceptualization. It is the way in which we withdraw purpose from history, which itself is only a conception of history held by those who withdraw themselves from creating, affirming, and laboring to actualize a purpose in history, who acquiesce in acquiring a prescribed purpose rather than fashion a purpose for themselves. It is a characteristic of the consciousness of more or less solidly functioning people, whose apparent purposeful functioning is an unacknowledged mode of their primarily living out a purpose which they have not created and chosen for themselves but which others, from the past and in the present, have created and chosen for them.

Variously, we complain of, or detachedly comment upon, the anomie and malaise of modern society and modern life, yearn abstractly for Community, identify purposefulness with totalitarianism, or celebrate the obsolescence of ideology, in the spirit of feeling relieved of the burden of a self-purpose. Particularly, those of us most avowedly critical and most rigorously and steadily engaged in developing our understanding, if not our reason, those most vociferous in denouncing mindless acts and

tendency to view themselves as "outside" of history, or "outside" their society, and hence their tendency to fall either into an ahistorical estrangement or despair, if not nihilism, or into a *volkisch* romanticism. In the more immediate intellectual situation at that time, it was intended in part, as a criticism of Herbert Marcuse's "One-Dimensional Man" concept, which seemed to me an ironic ahistorical acquiescence in the positivism Marcuse ostensibly opposed, especially ironic because it struck me as the ultimate "Americanization" even of Marcuse – the great holdout against the American ahistorical ("escape from history") mentality, and the author of the previous seminal works, *Reason and Revolution* and *Eros and Civilization,* which had helped me, and many other U.S. intellectuals, to see U.S. history in broader perspectives of world history and human development. Hence, the idea toward the end of this essay, that Americans should acknowledge and transform rather than seek to evade or "erase" their history, that is, move through and in their own history, not as if "outside" it.

The "end of political-economic society" meant the end of times when classical and neoclassical political-economic and economic theory alone could adequately describe the modern mode of production and its dynamics. This idea, I believe, has been substantiated by the work of the "Chandler School" (Alfred D. Chandler, Jr.) and others in analyzing modern corporations' operations, and by the recognition of such economists as Herbert Stein that modern society invites the need for theory that interrelates the workings of the "private" and "public" sectors. As for the "proletarian revolution," it may be considered that modern U.S. development has been the scene not of a "triumph of the *middle class,*" but increasingly of the working class. What else is "instant gratification" and "consumerism" (Gompers's "more, more now")? Consumption is the quintessential proletarian principle. Would Marx have agreed? Maybe – in the sense of "triumph," but not "revolutionary transcendence."

demonstrative disruptions by the youth, for the most part neither exercise control over the dominant institutions of society, no less the immediate institutions within which we labor, nor place ourselves in active opposition, rebellion, or insurrection against them. An overtly unteleological, sophisticated, and up-to-date state of thought tends to express a purposeless mode of life, that is, a prescriptively purposeful mode of life. Blind fate, alias predetermination by "objective conditions," has replaced a historical human destiny.

More specifically, those educated individuals who feel deeply disaffected from modern U.S. society, by and large, neither comprehend a transhistorical destiny nor feel at home in their own world, in their own society. They feel no homogeneity with the society of their own times and retreat into a pseudo-privatization or into suprahistorical, formally rationalistic abstractions or mystifications. They can neither identify their estrangement or disaffection with a future rooted in a revolutionary comprehension of, and action transforming, the past society in its present stage, nor revolutionize society with their estrangement or disaffection. Their disaffection, no less than the accommodation of their more conventional counterparts, stands as the hallmark of their loss of control over their own social life, and hence also over their own personal lives to some large degree. It stands, that is, as the hallmark of their alienation from others and from themselves, to use a word commonly in favor among them. They glorify their alienation, while despising it, just as they glorify a circumscribed social–political role in outward contrivances (dress, personal appearance, idiom and phrasemaking), because they can neither dispel their alienation nor comprehend, shape, and control their social relations and themselves. They are acquiescing in their reduction to an object of "social forces," or "objective conditions." In some cases, they may seek a false escape from purposelessness by serving those who have power and who exercise it purposively – in corporations, the state, policy-forming groups: the modern stoic resigned to objective reality, to serving Caesar, or, less ambitiously, to serving time.

The modern educated individuals in the United States – accommodated and disaffected alike – shocking or flattering as it may seem to them, stand as the positive denouement of the outlook of those who long ago expressed and personified revolutionary bourgeois liberty willfully disrupting established social relations in the name of republicanism, democracy, freedom, equality, and fraternity. For what our modern intellectuals would regard as metaphysics, namely, "destiny," is the consciousness of an essential human quality, that of being a self-producing species elaborating myriad potentialities in a developmental process of becoming, a consciousness that resided centrally though not adequately formed within bourgeois liberty in its revolutionary phase and from which it faded away as bourgeois society developed.

For bourgeois liberty in its revolutionary phase, the meaning of humanity coincided, not with a supramundane conception, nor with a historical conception, but with "natural law" validating a particular societal conception, or a conception of a particular type of society. This conception itself abstractly expressed, in ahistorical thought, and from the standpoint of the early bourgeoisie, the social relations of capitalism emerging from, and breaking up, the soil of the medieval world. The society it affirmed purported to validate the self-controlling, self-determining, self-mastering individual – self-dependent for the means of life in economic activity, which in turn guaranteed the free expression of the individual's personality as producer and appropriator of the material world and as participating citizen vigilantly safeguarding the eternal existence of the conceived societal type.

The revolutionary bourgeoisie, in other words, brought the archetypal freedom concept out of the realm of literary myth and theological mystery, into the mundane world of social life: The Greek Prometheus and the Protestantized Christian god-man became the bourgeois citizen in the conceptualized bourgeois society. It was this intersecting of the archetypal and the social that powerfully inspired the Puritan, the French, and the American bourgeois revolutionaries with the purposiveness, or sense of destiny, with which they reshaped their societies. But that intersecting no more proved durable than did the reshaping they found themselves engaged in correspond with their expectations and intentions.

Bourgeois liberty itself both in theory and in fact constituted an all too historically constricted, and hence altogether inadequate, form of the self-mastering person; while at the same time, the societal conception corresponding with revolutionary bourgeois liberty comprehended less and less of concrete historical reality the more bourgeois society developed along the lines of capitalist industrialization. First, ostensibly, the societal conception affirmed a mode of production (petty proprietorship) and a political system (republic or parliamentary monarchy) as the means of the realization of the self-mastering personality. But the self-mastering personality itself resided, in this case, in the narrow confines of the bourgeois work-property system, wherein individuality and personality became virtually synonymous with wealth accumulation and appropriation. So that in the very essence of bourgeois liberty, the end and the means continuously underwent inversion, until that inversion became irreversible: that is, from a certain kind of individual or personality as the end, validated by a particular mode of production and societal type as the means, to a mode of production of wealth and a society conforming to it as the end, and the individual as the means. The inversion constantly erupted at the outset and can be observed in what appears as the inconsistencies or "realistic" opportunism in the writings and political actions of, for example, Locke and Jefferson. It found much less equivocal expression in the classical political-economic thought of the mercantilists, the physiocrats, Smith, and Ricardo: from the health of man, to the wealth of nations.

Second, with the development of bourgeois liberty in real history, the condition of self-mastery for some became of necessity the condition of proletarianization for the many, who become reduced to the position of dependent "factors" of production, employed as means by others, the capitalists; and even the self-employed entrepreneur found that one's self-directed activity resulted in social and economic consequences that did not remain the object of one's own control, but reacted upon and conditioned that activity as external forces estranged from the person's effective understanding, intentions, and will.

The more bourgeois society developed, the more the archetypal image, expressing more or less clearly humanity's essential nature as an historically developing species, expressing a purpose or "destiny," split off from social theoretical thought, just as in bourgeois reality, capital and the means of production split off from labor, and individuals became a means subordinate to the production of wealth as the end. The archetypal image increasingly receded to the realm of unactualized thought, especially to the sphere of aesthetics, divorced from effective social theory and practice, at best reproaching and denouncing the historical world. Social theory, on the other hand, became increasingly abstract and uncomprehending of real historical society in so far as it sought to portray capitalist society as validating the archetypal image. Or, where social theory purported to be "realistic," it surrendered the archetypal image altogether; it made "objective society," or "objective spirit," the subject of history, evolving "naturally" in its fixed capitalist form according to "laws" of technicoeconomic development, the imperatives of which determined social and individual behavior like unalterable laws of nature. The meaning of humanity underwent a reduction to correspond with *functions* made necessary by and accommodated to the specific structure of capitalist society, now made synonymous with history and indeed displacing humanity as the transhistorical being – functions such as nation (and race), vocational specialization, consumption, divisions of production, mental and manual labor, etc., or romantically, as transcendent poet, rebellious mystic, "free-floating" or critical intellectual, these too regarding people in terms of special function rather than as whole human beings and citizens.

Bourgeois social theory denatured humanity and naturalized capitalist society, losing all sense of history as the development of self-producing human beings. This was the essence of positivism as it became the predominant current of social thought by the latter part of the nineteenth century and extending into the twentieth to the present time. Comte's "Religion of Man" quickly fell away as the husk it was, revealing the weed beneath – the adulation of wealth in its abstract money form, technology, and national power alias "advanced civilization," spreading to every corner of the world in imperialist domination.

The chief characteristic, referred to earlier, of the modern U.S. intellectuals is rooted in the demoralization, the dehumanization of social theory, attending the divorce of historical consciousness from archetypal consciousness, that is, most especially from aesthetic consciousness, of social theory from ethical theory of human creativity and self-determination (freedom), which sets in and fully develops with the evolution of capitalist industrial society. Lincoln Steffens once reported the traction magnate Patrick J. Calhoun to have remarked that U.S. workers were not working-class conscious but ruling-class numbed; insofar as this has been true, it only remains to observe that the numbness has never stopped with the industrial worker but has always spread to, and to a large extent from, the professionals, the sophisticated scholars and intellectuals, and sad to say many of the self-proclaimed socialists and Marxists themselves.

In a sense, then, we have come to a full, though unclosed, circle: from ahistorical rationalism of the eighteenth century to ahistorical positivism (or structural functionalism) of the twentieth century – to the positive denouement of revolutionary bourgeois liberty in the shape of the generality of modern U.S. intellectuals, who stand, as it were, in a limbo of consciousness, neither sacred (archetypal) nor humanly profane.

But wherever the archetypal intersects with the social in a sustained unity, rather than a temporary rendezvous, the numbness wears off and historical consciousness rooted in the human being as self-determining, self-controlling, self-mastering doer and thinker floods in. Understood properly, this is the meaning of the archetypal – it "eternally recurs" because humanity is transhistorical while social systems are historically specific and ephemeral forms of human development. As Marx put it, when "peeled away," the "narrow bourgeois form" of wealth, the production and accumulation of which appears as the end to which the individual is subordinated as a means, reveals itself as "the universality of needs, capacities, enjoyments, productive powers, etc., of individuals, produced in universal exchange . . . the full development of human control over the forces of nature – those of his own nature as well as those of so-called 'nature' . . . the absolute elaboration of his creative dispositions, without any preconditions other than antecedent historical evolution which makes the totality of this evolution – i.e. the evolution of all human powers as such, unmeasured by any *previously established* yardstick – an end in itself . . . where man . . . produces his totality . . . [and] does not seek to remain something formed by the past, but is in the absolute movement of becoming . . . this complete elaboration of what lies within man," which in capitalist society "appears as the total alienation and . . . as the sacrifice of the end in itself to a wholly external compulsion."[1]

Once the bourgeoisie brought the archetypal back into the social world, the positive denouement in predominant bourgeois positivist thought inexorably followed, but equally so the negative denouement in Marxian thought, that is, in historical consciousness rooted in the nature of humanity as the species capable of conscious self-production, self-control, self-mastery. It is this negative outcome that fills the gap of the unclosed circle of bourgeois consciousness, and that is swelling ever larger in the present era as the aesthetic consciousness once again increasingly begins to intersect with social consciousness, and as social theory begins to return to history centered upon the transhistorical. Here, unlike predominant U.S. social theory and historiography, we want to begin to reconceptualize and comprehend the modern era from the standpoint of such historical consciousness – that is, as Charles S. Peirce might have put it, from the standpoint of human purpose, or "destiny," as the effective dimension of historical reality.

2. The essence of corporate-capitalism: From accumulation to disaccumulation and the crisis of political-economic society

World history has involved more than the contours of politics and economy and state power. But throughout the history of civilization, that is, throughout the history of society based on labor exploitation, politics and economy and state power have imposed their contours upon and commanded everything else. We want to transform our political, economic, and state system, not merely acquiesce in its ongoing change proceeding without reference to *our* particular activity or inactivity. We want, that is, to give our command to politics and economy, and the

1. Marx, *Pre-Capitalist Economic Formations*, ed., E. J. Hobsbawm (London: Lawrence & Wishart, 1964).

state, so that the "everything else," that is, man purposively creating and recreating his social existence, can come into his own concretely as the shaper of history, and before which political economy itself, as a system of man's domination and exploitation of man expressed in class division and conflict, may be retired to the peripheries of harmless memory and of arcane studies in social pathology.

The question is, Is this possible? and, In our time?

What we are also asking, at another level, is, Can we change our social existence deliberately and in accord with our conceived intentions? To affirm that we can assumes that we can satisfactorily conceptualize the object of our attempt (ourselves, our society) in such a way as to reveal the possible changes its nature allows as well as the changes its nature requires. It also assumes that among the possible and required changes immanent in the nature of the "thing" (in this case, present-day people as the subjects of the historical social process), some correspond with our intentions. If none do, then (1) we may resign ourselves to frustration and suffering, or (2) we may pragmatically recast our intentions and proceed afresh, or (3) we may simply reconceptualize our object to make its nature seem to encompass possibilities corresponding with our intentions. All these courses express alienated forms of surrendering the struggle to reunify the transhistorically human (archetypal) and the social. The first of the three alternatives is what most people in most times ultimately do (otherwise known variously as "growing up," "maturing," "accepting responsibilities," "adjustment," "joining the rat race," "acculturation" or "socialization," "thanking god for his blessings, – or small favors," etc.). The second is the usual course of reformers and conservatives; the third that of utopians and visionaries and mystics. In practical life the devotees of the second and third can be found, albeit unwittingly, shuttling back and forth from one standpoint to the other. The *blending* of the second and third, however, into an entirely different world-outlook, in the struggle against the frustration and suffering inhering in the first alternative, is the way of revolutionaries – it is their art, their science, which expresses their comprehension of the dialectic of historical and transhistorical existence, their comprehension of the interpenetration of permanence and change, of freedom and necessity, of desire and restraint, of subject and object, of thought and instinct, of reason and history.

As revolutionaries, engaged upon the struggle of transforming our social existence and conforming it to our intended conception of the human, we must state our conception of that social existence in its concrete historical reality, objectify it in language that we and all people may critically regard it, and in so doing deny or affirm or modify it. At the same time, and in the course of this, we will also engage in reappraising, and denying, affirming, or modifying, our conception of the human in its present historical form. As the physicist begins by defining the object in terms appropriate to it, such as energy and mass, the revolutionary begins by defining the object in appropriate terms, which object, being human, is historical in essence and rooted in the real production and reproduction of material and social human life; and this means, in terms of the past mode of this production as it has emerged in its present form, and the future it embraces, that is, in terms of historical human development identified as *epoch*.

This is the starting point from which we must begin: To conceptualize our epoch is to come to grips broadly with what we conceive our social existence to be, what we conceive humanity, historically, to be in a developmental way, at the specific historical juncture of our own times, and what humanity is about to become. It is the basis of self-critically appraising our intentions, our conception of the human, and it is the mark of taking our intentions seriously enough to hazard their affirmation, denial, or modification in the deliberate attempt at achieving their realization.

The exceptional and the universal

U.S. historians have invariably been able to view the relation of the United States to world history from the particular standpoint of the United States as they have understood it, but seldom have they been able to view the United States from the standpoint of general world history. With this in mind, Louis Hartz has made the judgment – and he is right in this respect – that "the American historian at practically every stage has functioned quite inside the nation: he has tended to be an erudite reflection of the limited social perspectives of the average American himself"; with the result that "our current historical categories reflect but they do not analyze the American political tradition": our historians, on the left no less than those in the middle and on the right, "have not produced a study of American political thought: they have produced a replica of it."[2] That was written in 1955. It is still accurate today, and applies not only to U.S. political history and thought but to all phases of U.S. history. The historians, in short, have only *replicated* the United States in different ways; the task remains to comprehend it. And to comprehend it means, as Marx observed, to change it in an intended way – from the standpoint of an historical consciousness unifying the

2. Louis Hartz, *The Liberal Tradition in America* (New York: Harvest Books, 1955), pp. 29, 101, 174.

transhistorical with the social theoretical. It is precisely this standpoint of which our historians, like most other U.S. intellectuals, are totally devoid – with a rare exception here and there such as William A. Williams, but becoming less and less rare in present times.[3]

U.S. historians accordingly, by and large view U.S. history as a "thing in itself," as "fact speaking for itself" as it were, whose relevance to world history is essentially a matter of contingencies such as the accidents of geography and transportation, or of specific economic "interests" or political "moralists," or of "vacuums" in other parts of the world sucking flustered Yankee statesmen in, along with armies, taxpayers' money, missionaries, businessmen, and the like. By the same token, they view the relevance of U.S. history to humanity's transhistorical nature as really not worthy of professional notice – but as belonging to the metaphysical realm of poets, novelists, philosophers, speculative anthropologists, psychologists, existentialists, mystics, and weirdos, and at the outside, of that strange inelegant breed of "intellectual historians." (Hence sophisticated historians assure themselves that Williams's work is essentially "religious," not professional history – good for Sunday reading but not for the seminar and "serious" business.) The U.S. historians' characteristic method amounts, on the one hand, to a high-grade though often secondhand, journalism, as they periodize and conceptualize U.S. history in terms of the current headlines and notions that the newspapers, magazines, and the people of the time in question entertained and purveyed about themselves and events. Hence, we get categories expressed in such rubrics as Liberal, Conservative, Radical, New Freedom, New Deal, Normalcy, Age of Jackson, Cold War, Progressive Era, etc., parading about as analytical or explanatory terms that, however, though "replicating" perhaps everything, analyze and explain nothing. On the other hand, and especially in more recent times, their method has "expanded" to an eclectic – and revealing – appropriation from the social sciences, of positivistic categories expressing an ahistorical view of society and social relations as "objective" mechanisms or systems engulfing, shaping or shaking people, who are viewed as either

3. Williams's works stand as a monumental achievement in bringing into U.S. historical writings, so far as I know for the first time, the revolutionary consciousness uniting the transhistorical (archetypal) and the social theoretical. He is a giant among historians, given the parochial state of the historical profession especially in the 1950s and early 1960s. And this, regardless of the differences many younger radicals may otherwise have with him. Those differences should not deter revolutionaries from reading, studying, and reading and studying again, his works – reading, studying, discussing, and learning from his works, and learning also their disagreements with his works as well as their agreements. Keep their disagreements with him as they may, the point is for them to "dig" his works – deeply, just as, not accidentally, he dug deeply the works of Marx.

passively adjusting and submitting to the objective process or risking the fall into irrationality and even the forfeit of survival.

The one approach U.S. historians characteristically have not systematically applied in their study of U.S. social development, is precisely that which comprehends U.S. history as involving a particular mode of social production and reproduction in its bourgeois, capitalist-industrial phase, and conforming therefore, like other nations undergoing a similar bourgeois phase of development, to certain common general laws of socioeconomic metamorphosis integrally related to developments in the political, cultural, and intellectual spheres. Again, it is an approach that at the same time comprehends the capitalist-industrial epoch as a certain point in humanity's transhistorical development, that is, man as a self-producing being capable of self-determination and self-mastery. In this respect, our historians no less than most Americans, are like the lost souls in the Open Theater's play, *The Serpent*, who are in "the middle" and can neither remember humanity's beginning nor imagine humanity's future end.

It is this neglected approach with which, here, we seek to comprehend the epoch the people of the United States are presently passing through. Insofar as we discover about the United States something new or "exceptional," we find it *in* the universally human-historical, not as with most U.S. historians who tend to translate real or imagined American peculiarities into something universal.

Accumulation and disaccumulation of capital

We start from Marx's theory of capitalist development in general as it flows from his theory of value and surplus value. Understood properly, far from being "obsolete" or no longer "relevant," it is indispensable to the comprehension of the modern epoch, because it is directed at understanding society, not from the standpoint of an abstract or external Nature, technology, money, price-system, etc., etc., but from that of *human activity* in the production and reproduction of material and social life – its attributes, metamorphoses, and development at a specific stage of human history.

More particularly, we start from Marx's theory of the capital accumulation process, and its outcome in the disaccumulation process, which is implicit in Marx's stated theory, and which at points in *Capital, III, Theories of Surplus Value,* and the *Grundrisse,* Marx explicitly anticipated. At the same time, and again more concretely, we start from Marx's accumulation theory because, from the class standpoint of the proletariat struggling to realize for its members their human essence as self-determining associated individuals, it expresses the comprehension of the capitalist-industrial epoch as the social-historical form par excellence of human immersion in the development of the material means of production. But this is still only part of it. Marx's theory of capital accumulation simultaneously comprehends that process as corresponding with the highest, that is, last, historical stage of human immersion in the immediate goods-production process, in the sense that the outcome of that process is increasing release of labor from engagement in the immediate production and reproduction of the material means of life, and the emergence of society whose basis can no longer comprise relations of people in the goods-production process as the directly effective determinant of general social relations. This comprehension, embraced by Marx's theory, underlay his diagnosis that capitalism represented the last of social forms resting upon antagonistic relations of production, upon labor exploitation, and his prognosis that as such it must, short of self-destruction or decay, give birth to a society where people, no longer necessarily preoccupied with and immersed in the immediate goods-production process, could realize the more fully human course of directly engaging in the self-conscious production and reproduction, the shaping and reshaping, of their sociocultural reality. In other words, capitalism constituted the emergence and development of the political-economic society, which by the very nature of its development results in the end of political-economic society, the demise ultimately finding expression in the proletariat's revolutionary struggle to establish socialism in place of capitalism, as the basis for further evolution toward communism.

Here, I do not propose to present the theory of accumulation and disaccumulation as it flows out of Marx's value theory, nor the application of the theory to the concrete development of historical events. I merely want to indicate the central relevance of capitalism's transition from accumulation to disaccumulation, to the comprehension of the modern epoch. In the following pages, therefore, I propose to present a general description of the broader trend involved and some of its revolutionary implications for our times, and then to offer preliminary empirical evidence of ways in which this trend concretely expressed itself in the social relations and consciousness of Americans, including, on the one hand, evidence concerning those Americans expressing the standpoint of the capitalist ruling class, and, on the other, those expressing the standpoint of anticapitalist intellectuals.

In the process of capitalist industrialization, *capital accumulation* denotes a certain relationship among people in the production process, involving the ratio between the labor-time represented by those exercising labor-power, and the social labor-time embodied in the means of production – or between living labor and past, "dead" labor. Without referring now to the capitalists' appropriating role within the process, which must always be understood as integral to it, the relationship is one of capital accumulation so long as an increased production and operation of means of production require an increased employment of living human labor-power measured in hours of socially necessary labor. For example, in a society undergoing capital accumulation in the course of industrialization, the expansion of manufactured goods-production entails the expansion of the labor force in the production and operation of the means of production in manufacturing. At the point where there is no such increased employment of labor-power in the production and operation of the means of production, that is, where the production and operation of the means of production results in expanding production of goods without the expansion of such employment of labor-power, capital accumulation has entered the process of transformation to disaccumulation. In other words, disaccumulation means that the expansion of goods-production capacity proceeds *as a function of* the sustained decline of required, and possible, labor-time employment in goods-production.

Properly understood, therefore, the terms "accumulation" and "disaccumulation" refer not to concentration of production facilities in itself, though this is involved, nor to quantity of money values in itself, but to the relation of present living labor to past-produced means and materials of goods production, and to the consequent social relations of people in the production of society's goods. By implication, the period of the passage from the accumulation phase of capitalist industrialization of goods-production, to the disaccumulation phase, coincides with the partial and progressing extrication of human labor from the immediate goods-production process. This is as true of agriculture as it is of industrial manufacturing. In consequence, and increasingly, human labor (that is, the exercise of living labor-power) recedes from the condition of serving as a "factor" of goods production, and by the same token, the mode of goods-production progressively undergoes reversion to a condition comparable to a gratuitous "force of nature": Energy, harnessed and directed through technically sophisticated machinery, produces goods, as trees produce fruit, without the involvement of, or need for, human labor-time in the immediate production process itself. Living labor-power in goods-production devolves upon the quantitatively declining role of watching, regulating, and superintending. With the passing of the production process into the disaccumulation phase, the hitherto necessary contradiction, in the absolute sense, of the necessity of deferring immediate consumption as the condition of expanded production capacity,

156 The United States as a developing country

falls away. In profound contrast with the condition of industrialization in the accumulation phase (for example, in Western Europe, Britain, the United States, Japan, in the nineteenth and early twentieth centuries), expansion of production capacity and the decline, in a direct proportion, of immediate consumption-deferral, may thenceforth go hand in hand, and, short of the malfunctioning or underutilization and perverted utilization of production capacity, *must* go hand in hand.[4] As it turns out historically, given capitalism as the socioeconomic system within which this technical-labor phase of the production process transpires, though the contradiction, in the absolute sense, between production-expansion and immediate consumption deferral no longer pertains, the class-determined contradiction between private appropriation and social productive forces sustains and reinforces the former contradiction in practical social reality, resulting precisely in the malfunctioning, underutilization, and perverted utilization of production capacity.

Let us consider the same process from a somewhat different approach. In the accumulation phase, the expansion of goods-production capacity requires the allocation of an absolutely increasing quantity of aggregate social labor-time to the production and operation of the means of production. Expanded reproduction therefore entails restriction of immediate consumption in two senses: (1) The added labor force in the means-of-production sector must be supplied with consumer goods that thereby comprise a deduction of consumer goods available to the labor force in the consumption-goods sector. (2) Income revenues (whether profits, interest, rent, or, with savings banks and secondary exploitation through the price and tax system, wages too) must be withheld from circulation as immediate consumer demand and directed instead into the purchase of producer goods over and above those required for replacement of depreciated, worn-out, or obsolete producer goods.

In the disaccumulation phase, on the other hand, expansion of production capacity proceeds as a function of, in effect, simple reproduction and increasingly of negative reproduction (or, replacement), rather than through net additions of aggregate labor-time to the production and operation of the means of production. To say that the previous contradiction, in the absolute sense, between immediate consumption deferral and

4. For related statistical and theoretical material available in more conventional economic writings, which acknowledge and attempt to come to grips, though not adequately, with the process indicated here, see, most conveniently, Anatol Murad, "Net Investment and Industrial Progress," and Martin Bronfenbrenner, "Some Neglected Implications of Secular Inflation," in Kenneth Kurihara, ed., *Post-Keynesian Economics* (New Brunswick, N.J.: Rutgers University Press, 1954), pp. 227–250, and 31–58, respectively. Also, T. C. Cochran, *The American Business System* (New York: Harper Torchbooks, 1962).

expansion of production capacity drops away, means in essence that surplus-value loses its "investment" function in the expansion of goods-production capacity – though, as already indicated, as long as capitalism persists, the capitalist class retains its social function of appropriating surplus-value both as its source of income and as the relation essential to sustaining its domination of the labor force and labor system.

Shorn of its capitalist integument, the process that appears under capitalism as disaccumulation means the ongoing net release of labor-power, measured in aggregate social labor-time, from goods-production. In particular, it means that less and less labor-power is required for the production of the goods necessary for sustaining and reproducing physical and social life. The people are increasingly freed to apply their labor, or life-time, to other pursuits and fields of endeavor.

This process, however, is not to be understood in terms of "scarcity" and "abundance," which comprise an all too abstract and essentially false approach to the social reality in question. "Scarcity" itself is a bourgeois ideological concept applied to economic apologetics for profit on the one side and deprivation and poverty on the other. "Abundance" is an entirely relative category that depends for concretization as much on prevailing conceptions and customary habits of living standards and on the simple matter of an area's resource endowment as on technology and social relations of production. The real question involved here is the extent to which technicoeconomic development has brought society beyond relations of goods-production as the necessary focus and direct determinant of social organization for the mass of the people; and, related to this, the extent of the people's conscious control of their own life-activity in those fields of work involving the production of the very social relations and forms of social consciousness themselves, as well as in the traditional goods-production and related areas of work – the extent to which this social self-control as life-activity is progressively extricated from engagement in the immediate goods-production process.

In this connection, it is fundamentally false, and probably demagogic, to hold that disaccumulation plus socialism would put an end to *necessary* work: There will always be necessary work in the human interchange with the natural environment, and in satisfying the imperatives of sustaining, reproducing, and transforming the existing system of social relations. The objective of socialism is a society where people increasingly express their freedom – recognize, realize, transmute, their talents and capacities – in dealing with necessity, and where they open greater and greater areas for discretionary, voluntary life-activity; a society, moreover, where no people are doomed to narrow specialization as a class or subsection of a class to one particular function or restricted set of functions, where the social organization for executing society's necessary tasks and for developing discretionary pursuits is not that in which one class organizes, dominates, exploits, the labor of another class, but that in which the people discharge that execution and development as freely associating equals, and in which every person is increasingly educated for universal competence in the broad range of society's activities.

Finally, the question of "abundance" versus "scarcity" resolves itself essentially into this, that insofar as social labor-time is not significantly required for goods-production, such goods acquire no value (materialized labor-time), and the conditions are established for severing work as such from income, or (what is the same thing) from access to a share of society's goods, so that work may increasingly become an activity valued and pursued for itself, however necessary or discretionary, instead of a *means* to a portion of the material means of life – a means to a means that tends to become transmogrified into a prescribed end in itself. Nevertheless, though the market-money-income system may be eliminated as the principle governing the distribution of goods (and services, which themselves are analyzable into goods-components), some governing principle will be necessary. Marx's theory is, essentially, that a social-ethical principle will supplant the bourgeois economic principle; that an actualized conception of needs (both "natural" and "artificial", material and sociocultural) will supplant the system determined by labor abstracted into a commodity and bought and sold at its exchange value. To put it another way, under the economic scheme of things, quantitative measurements, proportions, standards, dictate the "quality of life"; under a genuine communist social-ethical scheme of things, qualitative standards will dictate to quantitative distribution, proportions, measurements, standards.

It is from this standpoint seeking to unite the transhistorical with the specifically historical social reality that we may begin to reassert a critical comprehension of the modern epoch. In these terms we may understand the current epoch of U.S. history to comprise the emergence, development, and decomposition of the imperialist corporate-capitalist order, *as* the historical mode of the United States' passage from accumulationist industrialization *to* industrialized disaccumulation as the condition of production-expansion; and on the basis of this, and to the extent that the emerging revolutionary movement succeeds, the historical mode of passage *from* society organized around and dominated by relations of goods-production *to* society gone beyond relations of goods-production as determining and dominating social relations; *from* society imposing work as a means of subsistence and comfort *to* society redefining work as self-determining expression of life.

We can begin to comprehend "corporate liberalism" as the response of the bourgeoisie in general, and of high industrial and finance capital in particular, to the disaccumulation process – a response suited to sustaining the existence and power of a profit-appropriating social class where such appropriation no longer bears a necessary relation to expansion of production capacity, and increasingly devolves upon a parasitic engrossment of social wealth – a response expressed in the following decisive ways:

1. The extension of the employer-employee, enterprise-for-profit system beyond the sphere of goods-production, finance, distribution, and exchange, to all other social spheres, or the subordination of other social spheres to the imperatives of that system; this extension being necessary to sustain capitalist class domination of the labor system and labor force as a whole, thereby extending the proletarianization of labor to virtually all other spheres of work, and preempting the possibility of those spheres expropriating for their own respective uses the capitalists' surplus-value appropriated in the goods-production sphere.

2. The capitalist class's intercession against the uninhibited operation of the disaccumulationist tendency through action in the production-investment system, the price-system, and the state's tax and fiscal system, involving monopolistic control of production, price, and investment schedules, coercive establishment of markets for superfluous goods through taxation and imperialism, and expressed in secular inflation, consumer-debt financing, subsidization of production-inefficiency, underderutilization of production capacity, and chronically rising unemployment except in time of sufficiently large-scale war. Accordingly, what appears as a blundering imposition of "artificial scarcity" comprises in essence the capitalistically planned allocation of production capacity and goods to uses outside the domestic civilian market – most crucially in production of the means of destruction and in aggressive imperialist expansion of the sphere of capitalist enterprise (both of these undergoing their most dramatic, remarkable, and inextricably interrelated increases since about 1940–1945, dwarfing all previous records).

3. The indispensable role of the state, and its control by the corporate-capitalist class, in enforcing this "capitalization of inefficiency" (Veblen), this system of labor domination, this system of restricted and perverted production.

Historically, the transition from accumulation to disaccumulation in the United States occurred in the period about 1907–1929, and disaccumulation first asserted itself forcefully and in a sustained way from about 1919 to 1929, resulting, in the immediate case, in the great collapse of 1929–1940.[5] What Marxists have called "the general crisis of capitalism" since World War I, and what Keynesians have referred to as "stagnation" or "the stationary state," centers in capitalism's passage from accumulation to disaccumulation. Similarly, what everyone refers to as the "welfare state" (or "welfare-warfare state"), and what the New Left now refers to as corporate liberalism, comprises in general the corporate bourgeoisie's class-determined response to disaccumulation.

3. The 1920s: The swing period

The unitary character of the post-1900 era

Although the period from about 1907 to about 1929 as a whole registered the first signs of impact of the disaccumulation process upon the political economy, upon the policy considerations, and upon the intellectual life of the United States, this impact was muted by the First World War. It was not until the 1920s, therefore, that it may first be observed as having registered its effects in a sustained and indelible manner. Hence, although peculiarly discerning historians have characterized the 1920s as an "Age of Normalcy," leading figures in business, labor, political, and intellectual circles of the 1920s saw their own period as a "New Era," and felt about it an exhilaration and expectancy auguring a break with old ways and a leap into an unprecedented future fulfilling the dreams of what had previously been regarded as utopian fancy. With profound differences regarding the conclusions and implications to be drawn from it, this broad feeling, nevertheless, was common to a wide diversity of people, from corporate liberals such as Herbert Hoover and Samuel Gompers, Gerard Swope and Owen D. Young, to such anticapitalist Young Intellectuals as Randolph Bourne, Van Wyck Brooks, Harold Stearns, Waldo Frank, and Lewis Mumford.

Corresponding with the substantial force of the impact referred to here, a wide range of characteristic political, economic, social, and ethical questions assumed a prominent place in the public discourse of the decade and impinged significantly upon the attention and active concern of policymakers and intellectuals alike. Briefly, these questions included

unemployment in the midst of "prosperity";
the conquest of scarcity and the challenge of abundance;
"pockets" of poverty;
wage and price stabilization;

5. This was the United States' first and so far only disaccumulationist depression; as such the depression of 1929–1940 differed significantly from the previous capitalist accumulationist depressions of the nineteenth and early twentieth centuries.

controlling the business cycle to ensure full employment;

the need to increase effective market demand to meet the nation's prodigious productive capacity;

technological disemployment;

the stabilization or decline of the labor force in the goods-production
sector of the economy, in the midst of substantial rises in productivity and production;

the sharply rising labor force in the services sector;

the shift of investment funds from production- to consumer-financing,
attended by installment selling, market research, and advertising;

the shape of the cities and urban planning;

the "quality of life";

social cooperation and national interest versus narrow self-interest;

the people's right to participate in the shaping of their own destiny (or
social reality);

the need for a "vision" as a standard by which people might fashion
their existence rather than confining their vision to the extant shape
of their existence.

The economic collapse of 1929, issuing in the prolonged depression of
the 1930s, and the Second World War and its aftermath with their colossal destruction, and equally colossal reconstruction, of productive
forces in Europe and Asia, submerged, obscured, or rendered apparently
irrelevant all of these questions either entirely, or in the particular form
they had assumed in the 1920s. But it is only a matter of easy observance
that after the depression, the war, and the war's aftermath had run their
course, all of these questions reemerged as central matters of policy and
intellectual inquiry, to a certain extent in the late 1950s, and in full force
in the 1960s. Seen in this way, there is a fundamental bond of continuity
and kinship between the 1920s and 1960s, as well as between the 1920s
and the previous years of the twentieth century.

Viewed from this perspective, the period from the turn of the century
through the 1920s (and up to the present time) possesses a unitary
character, not merely in an abstract sense of impersonal "objective conditions," but also in the sense that central developments in the sociopolitical history and in the cultural and intellectual history of the nation,
were significantly related to the emerging phase of disaccumulation.
Such developments may be fruitfully viewed in terms of the responses
and adjustments of people, and more particularly in terms of the responses and adjustments of the different social classes comprising capitalist society, to conditions characterizing that society's passage from the
phase of industrializing accumulation to the phase of industrialized

disaccumulation, taking social relations into the "postindustrial" era and into the maturing crisis of political-economic society.

The political-economic and the literary writings of the period 1915–1930 offer evidence at two essential levels: (1) They offer direct empirical evidence of the changes in production processes and social relations connected with the declining requirement of human labor-power in the production of goods. (2) They offer evidence of the *ways* in which people were perceiving and responding to those changes, as well as evidence *that* they were perceiving and responding to those changes. With respect to the political-economic sphere, a very brief indication of the nature and the availability of such evidence, follows.

Herbert Hoover's conferences and reports

The President's Conference on Unemployment, which convened at Washington, D.C., in 1921, under Warren G. Harding's auspices and the initiative of Secretary of Commerce Herbert Clark Hoover, established several continuing research committees. Among them, the Committee on Recent Economic Changes, with Hoover as chairmen, conducted an examination of the national economy in cooperation with the National Bureau of Economic Research, and published its final two-volume report in 1929. The significance of the Report lies on several levels: its very conception at the *outset* of the decade; the scope and depth of its inquiry and findings; the businessmen, political leaders, farm organization and trade union officers, and scholars involved in its preparation[6]; the valuable information about and analysis of the trends of the national economy and their implications; and the general orientation of its framers toward subjecting a more fully understood economy to certain kinds of effective controls and rationalized management.

It is of particular significance that although the Report displayed no lack of awareness of the remarkable economic and technical developments of the 1920s, it characterized them not so much as new or dra-

6. *Recent Economic Changes in the United States,* Report of the Committee on Recent Economic Changes, of the President's Conference on Unemployment, Herbert Hoover, Chairman, 2 vols., published for the National Bureau of Economic Research, by McGraw-Hill, (New York: 1929). The Committee's members were Herbert Hoover, chairman, Walter F. Brown, Renick W. Dunlap, William Green, Julius Klein, John S. Lawrence, Max Mason, George McFadden, Adolph C. Miller, Lewis E. Pierson, John J. Raskob, Arch W. Shaw, Louis J. Taber, Daniel Willard, Clarence M. Woolley, Owen D. Young, Edward Eyre Hunt. The NBER's Directors-at-Large were Matthew Woll, Harry W. Laidler, George O. May, Elwood Mead, Thomas W. Lamont, George Soule, N. I. Stone. The NBER's research staff members were Edwin F. Gay, Director, Wesley C. Mitchell, Director, Willford I. King, Leo Wolman, Frederick C. Mills, Willard L. Thorp, Harry Jerome, Simon Kuznets, Frederick R. Macauley, Walter F. Willcox.

matic departures, but as accelerations and culminations of trends already established at the turn of the century, and as representing a continuity, rather than a break, with developments of the recent, pre–World War I, past.[7] These developments included the increased supply and wider uses of electric power in industry, on the farm, and in the home; "the multiplication by man of his strength and skill through machinery"; and the division and organization of work in mines and factories, on the farms, and in the trades, "so that production per man hour of effort has risen to new heights."[8]

Among the consequences of these trends, the Committee specified the growing production capacity of the nation's economic plant with less labor, and accordingly the shift of labor from goods production to services; the problem of technological unemployment; the adjustments necessary to sustain a pace of market demand commensurate with the growth of production; and the release afforded by production technique from the living patterns, anxieties, and constraints of the traditional "scarcity" regimen dictated by previous production technique.[9]

By comparison with over-all growth rates in gross production in the past, the Committee observed, those of the 1920s were not in themselves remarkable. But no past period had "shown such a striking increase in productivity per man-hour." Reductions of hours of labor proceeded steadily in the 1920s, while per capita productivity by 1929 exceeded by 60 percent that at the close of the nineteenth century. In manufacturing, a 60 percent increase in horsepower from about 22.3 million in 1914 to about 35.8 million in 1925, and from 3.3 to 4.3 per worker in that period, matched a 35 percent increase in per capita productivity in the four-year period of 1922–1925 alone.[10] In agriculture, "the productivity of farm workers has increased at a rate never before equaled." With

7. "Acceleration rather than structural change is the key to an understanding of our recent economic developments. . . . the distinctive character of the years from 1922 to 1929 owes less to fundamental change than to intensified activity . . . the novelty of the period . . . rested chiefly in the fact that developments such as formerly affected our old industries have been recurring in our new industries. The changes have not been in structure but in speed and spread. . . . But the breadth and scale and 'tempo' of recent developments give them new importance." Ibid., I, p. ix.

8. Ibid., pp. ix–x.

9. The term, "technique," is used here in the broad sense as well as in the more specific application to the modern industrial apparatus, following Jacques Ellul's definition in *The Technological Society* (New York: A. A. Knopf, 1965); see ch. 1. In effect, the Committee utilizes essentially the same concept, since it stresses organization as well as machine technology in characterizing the trends in question.

10. *Recent Economic Changes*, I, pp. xv, 87, 91. In different terms, the value of output per worker in manufacturing increased from $1,600 in 1900 to $7,500 in 1919, the increment remaining substantial after allowing for price inflation. The ratio of the value of products to capital investment rose about 35 percent from 1.04 in 1890 to 1.4 in 1919. Ibid., p. 88.

1919, a good crop year, representing the index number of 100, physical crop production rose to 102 in 1922, 104 in 1925, and 106 in 1927. On a per capita basis, "the rates of increase would be decidedly greater," for "the smaller numbers of workers left on the farms, cultivating less land," were responsible for these increases.[11] As these comments indicate, the rising productive capacity rested "largely upon the fact that our productive machinery is not only *time saving* in character but *labor saving* also"; so that the general tendency was to "reduce the number of employees producing the same, or an increased quantity of production."[12] The developments in manufacturing and agriculture ran along similar lines, those in agriculture being considerably more dramatic. "So far as reduction in number of workers goes, there is a close parallel between the record of farming and manufacturing."[13] In the seven-year period, 1920–1926, the cumulative loss in farm population amounted to over 3 million people. In manufacturing, between 1919 and 1925, among the traditional industrial states, the New England area recorded a decline in the number of manufacturing establishments of 11.7 percent and a decline of wage-earners in manufacturing of 16.7 percent; the corresponding figures for the mid-Atlantic area were 17.5 percent and 13 percent.[14] In the country as a whole, the absolute number of factory wage-earners reached its peak in 1919–1920, at about 9 million, and steadily declined during the 1920s in the midst of rising production, to an average annual figure of about 8.5 million for the three-year period 1927–1929.[15]

Concerning the long-term trend, President Hoover's Committee on Recent Social Trends observed that while in 1870, 77 percent of the gainfully employed persons in the United States were "engaged in transforming the resources of nature into the objects of usable form through manufacturing, mining, and agriculture," in 1930 only 52 percent were

11. Ibid., I, xv; II, 881.   12. Ibid., I, 91, 92.
13. Ibid., I, 471. The net decrease in farm population in 1922 alone was estimated at 460,000, in 1923 at an unspecified larger number, in 1924 at 182,000, in 1926 at 479,000. Ibid., II, 880.
14. Ibid., I, 591.
15. *Recent Social Trends in the United States*, Report of the President's Research Committee on Social Trends, with a Foreword by Herbert Hoover (New York: McGraw-Hill, 1933), one-volume edition; from Table 11, p. 312. With 1920 representing the index number 100, the average annual index number of factory wage-earners for 1927–1929 stood at 93.4. The figures for the number of steam railroad wage-earners are similar: They stood at a peak of about 2 million in 1920, and at an average annual number of 1.7 million in 1927–1929; the index number, with 1920 as 100, stood at about 85 for 1927–1929. (In the autumn of 1929, President Hoover appointed Wesley C. Mitchell to undertake and supervise the study. The members of the Research Committee were Mitchell, chairman, Charles E. Merriam, vice-chairman, Shelby M. Harrison, secy-treasurer, Alice Hamilton, Howard W. Odum, and William F. Ogburn.)

so engaged. With respect to the second and third decades of the twentieth century more specifically, the Committee noted that "until 1910 the decline of agricultural employment was relative only, owing to the more rapid growth of other industries, but since 1910 the numbers engaged in farming have decreased absolutely as well as relatively." In manufacturing occupations, the number of persons "has declined relative to the total gainfully occupied population between 1920 and 1930." During the 1920s, "the trend of actual employment in manufacturing industry was downward for the first time in our history. This was likewise true of steam railroads." The failure of factory and railroad employment to advance, the Committee noted, was "especially significant," since the gainfully employed population increased in those years from 42.6 million to 48.8 million (or by about 14.5 percent).[16]

The Report on recent economic changes assumed it to be "a sign of progress when a given economic result can be achieved with fewer workers." But accordingly, the "constant accompaniment of progress in modern industry" consisted in the shifting of labor "called technological unemployment,"[17] or what the Committee on Recent Social Trends subsequently referred to as "the terror of unemployment."[18] Describing the process of technological unemployment, the Report noted that "the output per man constantly increases and this, coupled with the changes due to the introduction of time-saving apparatus, tends to unemployment without reference to good or bad times." In this sense, technological unemployment was not only "as old as the present industrial system," and "nothing new," but it was "inherent in the system." But in the 1920s the phenomenon had been increasing in magnitude, so that it had become a new social problem in kind. Unemployment remained steadily high during the 1920s not only when compared with the buoyant prosperity of the era, but also when compared with previous periods. The supply of new jobs "has not been equal to the number of workers plus the old workers displaced," with the result that there "has been a net increase of unemployment, between 1920 and 1927, which exceeds 650,000 people."[19] Accordingly, while cyclical unemployment had not been prominent in the 1920s, the Committee noted, " it has become evident

16. Ibid., pp. xxvii, 283, 311–312.
17. *Recent Economic Changes*, II, p. 594, and I, p. 95.
18. *Recent Social Trends*, p. xxxvi.
19. *Recent Economic Changes*, I, 92, II, 878–879. The unemployment figures, in percentages, for 1920–1927, from II, Table 8, p. 879, are: 1920, 5.1%; 1921, 15.3%; 1922, 12.1%; 1923, 5.2%; 1924, 7.7%; 1925, 5.7%; 1926, 5.2%; 1927, 6.3%. The Report emphasizes that due to hidden and unreported unemployment, these figures underestimate the real extent of unemployment, and if anything "minimize the seriousness of unemployment."

that unemployment can arise as a result of industrial efficiency as well as of inefficiency." Inefficiency produces "seasonal or intermittent unemployment"; efficiency produces "what has come to be known as 'technological' unemployment resulting from the introduction of new machinery and processes." The Committee's findings indicated, therefore, "that the time has come to devote continuing attention not only to the problems of cyclical unemployment but also to this newer problem of 'technological' unemployment if we are to forestall hardship and uncertainty in the lives of the workers." The absorption of workers in "the newly expanded service industries which create and serve leisure" has prevented "much more serious unemployment" from the effects of "the acceleration of technological shifts in production and consumption."[20]

In spite of persistent unemployment, considerable poverty, and unprosperous conditions in agriculture, coal mining, and many light industries, the Report concluded from its data on productivity and production advances that "as a people we have become steadily less concerned about the primary needs – food, clothing, and shelter," as the economic system moved from the age-old condition of relative scarcity to a new one of general abundance. "We have long since lost all fear concerning our food supply, and so we no longer look on food as a luxury or as a primary source of pleasure . . . and the slogan of the 'full dinner pail' is obsolete. . . . Our wants have ranged more widely and we now demand a broad list of goods and services which come under the category of 'optional purchases'." Not itself new, the expansion of consumer wants had been "going on since the beginning of the Industrial Revolution," and was not, except in degree, a phenomenon of the postwar period. "But it is this degree of economic activity, this almost insatiable appetite for goods and services, this abounding production of all things which almost any man can want which is so striking a characteristic of the period covered by the survey."[21]

Insatiable as the appetite for goods and services may have become, however, effective consumer purchasing power proved persistently insufficient to satisfy it, and at any rate, production capacity continuously outran effective market demand. Since at least the 1890s, a reverse Malthusian doctrine of production "naturally" outrunning population pervaded the business mind, and in large part the political also, in the United States. Imperialist expansion emerged as one response to this situation. In the 1920s, modern advertising and consumer financing through installment debt, took their place along with imperialism as another response. As the Committee on Recent Social Trends put it, "manufacturers and merchants had to teach masses of men and women new

20.   Ibid., I, p. xvi.   21.   Ibid., I, p. xv.

tastes and ways," resulting in "an enormous increase in the thought and money lavished upon selling, and an enormous intensification of the attack upon the consumer's attention."[22] If in earlier times, occasional aggressions and catastrophes helped to keep demand from pressing too closely upon supply, in modern times an enormous and sustained aggressiveness was required to keep supply from spurting too far ahead of demand.

Nevertheless, advertising, sales organization, and consumer financing, not to mention imperialism, failed to allay the difficulty of using to optimal extent the growing production capacity afforded by advancing technique in the fabric of the capitalist investment system. The inability to market all that was produced, no less all that could be produced, had appeared as a major and constant industrial problem in the United States since the late nineteenth century, and it relates in a crucial way to the disparity between the relatively less rapid rate of advance of *actual production* than of *productivity*. Even during World War I, when it might be assumed that the war stimulus primed the pump of national production, in reality physical production, in the midst of substantial increases in production capacity and rising prices, remained about the same or declined during the years of America's participation in the war, with output in key basic industries (including in agriculture) *lower* in 1918 than in 1916.[23] Similarly, less than optimal capacity utilization of productive plant remained a serious problem throughout the 1920s.[24]

In the late nineteenth century, relatively high levels of net investment in new plant and equipment accompanied underutilization of plant. After about 1907, however, the secular trend toward declining net investment as a percentage of total national income set in to aggravate employment and market dislocations. In the boom of the 1920s, average annual net investment as a percentage of national income remained lower than that in the previous twentieth-century period, which in turn had dropped from the levels of the *depression* years of the 1890s. In the 1930s, net investment virtually disappeared, with "negative investment" (net capital consumption) actually the case in some sectors of industry.[25] In more concrete terms, declining net investment meant the employment

22. *Recent Social Trends*, p. xxxvii.
23. *Recent Economic Changes*, II, Table 1, p. 851; see also George Soule, *Prosperity Decade: From War to Depression, 1917–1929* (New York: Rinehart, 1947), pp. 54–56.
24. See Donald Streever, "Capacity Utilization and Business Investment," *University of Illinois Bulletin*, 57, No. 55 (March 1960), p. 64; E. G. Nourse, et al., *America's Capacity to Produce* (Washington, D.C., Brookings Institution, 1934); and Paul Baran and Paul Sweezy, *Monopoly Capital* (New York: Monthly Review Press, 1965), pp. 237, 242; Murad, "Net Investment and Industrial Progress," p. 242.
25. See Cochran, *The American Business System*, pp. 25–33, 49–50. Citing Simon Kuznets, *National Income*, NBER, 1946, p. 53, Cochran notes (p. 25) that the per-

of less labor in the production of new plant and equipment, as it also expressed the declining labor *requirement* in the production of new plant and equipment and of more goods generally, both in agriculture, and, especially as electrochemical processes increasingly displaced mechanical processes, in industry. Net investment therefore came not only to mobilize less labor, but also to result in the further increase of production capacity with less labor required for its production and operation, resulting generally in dislocating previous employment-investment relationships and employment patterns, and further exacerbating the imbalance between the capital-goods and consumer-goods sectors of production, and between production capacity and effective demand.

This general process, involving declining net investment and the increasing extrication of living labor-power from goods-production both relatively and absolutely – this process of disaccumulation – operated forcefully upon the American sociopolitical scene in the early twentieth century, and with particularly powerful impact in the 1920s, reaching a first culmination, as it were, with the collapse of 1929 and the subsequent long depression. The movement in the American political economy toward increasing corporate reorganization of the industrial and banking system, and toward increasing government intervention in the economy, the movement identified at least in the latter respect in popular discourse and in predominant American historiography alike, with modern liberalism, comprised in essential respects the response of the corporate bourgeoisie to the process of disaccumulation. Without at this point going into the details of this response, suffice to say that in the private sector, trade associations, agricultural cartel arrangements (cooperatives), and corporate consolidation, and in the public sector, government intervention with credit and subsidies to agriculture and transportation, export financing and promotion, public works, and money and credit management, all tracing back to the Wilson period, were continued and elaborated further in the Harding, Coolidge, and Hoover administrations. As Secretary of Commerce and President, Hoover, along with prominent executives from large industrial, commercial, and financial corporations such as Charles G. Dawes, Owen D. Young, Dwight W. Morrow, Julius Rosenwald, Howard E. Coffin, Gerard Swope, Theodore N. Vail, and Daniel Willard, warmly supported and worked for the adoption of measures along these lines. They viewed it a government responsibility to ameliorate unemployment with public works, to facilitate

centage of national income going into net capital formation declined from an average of 12.6 percent in the period 1899–1908, to 10.2 percent in 1919–1928, and that the rate of net capital formation declined by 20 percent comparing 1900–1910 with 1920–1930. See also Murad, "Net Investment and Industrial Progress," p. 242, and p. 239 n. 36.

and protect imperialist corporate enterprise abroad, and to stabilize the investment cycle by appropriate subsidy, price-support and credit measures designed to encourage the advance of productivity and hence profitable investment opportunities, while *restricting the volume of products* thrown onto the domestic market. They spoke glowingly of the era of "abundance," but warned and took action against *too much of it,* which in their view would disastrously derange the private market economy and throw the whole system of employment-for-income and private discretionary investment into hopeless disarray. Their approach amounted to government-fostered production *restriction,* secular inflation, and aggressive imperialist expansion, to sustain the flow of profitable investment and the capitalist domination of the labor force within the framework of the corporate-industrial system.[26]

It is important to understand Hoover and such like-minded business leaders as mentioned above in this sense, rather than as representing some sort of recidivistic laissez-faire individualism and free-market conservatism, for a more accurate comprehension of the political-economic development of the 1920s.[27] Political leaders like Hoover, and large corporation executives whose policy outlook corresponded with his,

26. See William A. Williams, *The Contours of American History* (New York: World, 1961), pp. 425–438; Murray N. Rothbard, *America's Great Depression,* (Princeton, N.J.: D. Van Nostrand, 1963), ch. 8, pp. 194–211 for government agricultural policies, and chs. 7, 9–12, pp. 167–185, 212–295 for detailed materials on Hoover and other like-minded political and business leaders; Joseph Brandes, *Herbert Hoover and Economic Diplomacy: Department of Commerce, 1921–1928* (Pittsburgh: University of Pittsburgh Press, 1962), esp. chs. 1–3, pp. 3–60; Gerald Nash, "Herbert Hoover and the Origins of the Reconstruction Finance Corporation," *Mississippi Valley Historical Review,* XLVI (1959), pp. 455–468. See also Herbert Hoover, *The New Day: Campaign Speeches of Herbert Hoover, 1928* (Stanford, Calif: Stanford University Press, 1929).

27. Recent studies of political-economic trends in the 1920s have already pointed toward a reevaluation of Hoover and business developments along these lines. As one historian put it, "Behind the bright facade of 'normalcy' some perplexed Americans were awakening to a realization that normalcy would not return. Indeed, the term was peculiarly ill-fitted to years so characterized by sweeping economic and social change." He goes on to observe that studies of the age of Franklin D. Roosevelt "have shown how much its origins, its philosophy and its measures derive from the period presided over by Harding, Coolidge and Hoover." Historians, he writes, are coming to view the 1920s "not alone as an era of rampant materialism, reaction and individualism but as a troubled decade in which old and new were inextricably intermingled and confronted. It was a time of deep uncertainty and conflict: of faltering efforts to face – or sometimes to avoid – the fact of change. It was an age, as we have come to understand, not so very different from our own." Morell Heald, "Business Thought in the Twenties: Social Responsibility," *American Quarterly,* XIII:2, Pt. 1 (Summer 1961), pp. 126–139. See also the works cited in the previous footnote, above. The standard view of the business outlook in the 1920s is expressed in James Warren Prothro, *The Dollar Decade: Business Ideas in the 1920s* (Baton Rouge: Louisiana State University Press, 1954). The basic defect of Prothro's account is that he presents as the business view ideas associated with the NAM, that is, generally, middle-range and

represented what today is, and what at that time was, identified as liberalism in national politics, as against the "conservatism" particularly of smaller businessmen (but not excluding other large-business leaders) and their political and ideological compatriots. The Young Intellectuals rejected and acutely criticized this liberalism no less than they did laissez-faire and individualistic conservatism.

The emergence of a nonacademic intelligentsia

With the disaccumulation of capital comes the accelerated accumulation of intellectuals and other mental workers. During the accumulation phase of industrialization, the ranks of professional and intellectual occupations increase, but with the disaccumulation phase their quantitative increase becomes such as to result in a qualitative change within the social system. At that phase, Education becomes not only a significant social formation within society, but a necessary component of the productive and socioeconomic system. Education becomes an industry. Secondary schools and institutions of higher learning become the place of training and work for rising numbers of men and women and youth whose labor is no longer immediately required in the production system at large. Educational institutions also become a growing outlet for investment of money-capital, as the requirements for capital and the opportunities for its profitable investment in the sphere of production decline. Colleges and universities proliferate and grow. They turn out "capital goods" in the form of more teachers for the expanding industry, who work up, fashion, and refine the increasing flow of raw materials in the form of information and students. They turn out other finished products – books and study materials, technicians, professionals, and intellectuals – in demand by other sectors of society and the economy such as manufacturing and commerce, government agencies and civil service, advertising and publishing. At this point, it begins to become possible to speak of an academic community as a significant social formation in society by virtue of its size and function, without regard to "intrinsic" or ethical value: an academic community with progressively expanding claims upon the loyalties, good will, and revenues, of businessmen and corporations, politicians and government, professionals and intellectuals.

In the process, however, the number of college-produced intellectuals who want to be writers and artists, but prefer neither to return to education as teachers nor to offer themselves to the demand of other indus-

small business. Given this approach he does not look for basic ideological differences among business leaders, and accordingly does not find them.

tries as professional employees, begins to rise. To their number may be added youths who, entering neither college nor the labor market, also aspire to be writers and artists, as well as those who may be in the labor market but view writing and art as their true vocation. Just as the academic community emerges, so too, in sustained and increasing flow, the nonacademic intelligentsia – the free-lancers, the detached artists and writers, the professional critics, radicals, and revolutionaries, the "superfluous men," and the "men without qualities," the men and women without a productive or market function traditional to economic society. They emerge over and above, and functionally distinct from, professionals performing services long recognized as auxiliary to the socioeconomic society, such as lawyers, clergy, teachers, engineers, doctors, although the number of such latter professionals grows also. They are neither leisured wealthy aristocrats or bourgeoisie spending free time in writing and the arts, nor singular artists or men of letters attached to men of wealth in a patronage relationship, nor, typically, so exceptional as to become independently wealthy from the consumption of their works by a mass readership; nor are they footloose, uneducated destitute peasants or proletarians finding apostacy as wandering bards or such. They are by and large from families deriving their income from small or moderate business enterprise, or the professions, though they include individuals from every social stratum, and increasingly (though in relatively smaller numbers) from the working class and farmers. Above all, they must make a living from their writing and art if they are to practice it as a full-time vocation, and if they do not they resent their having to engage in other labor or accept family handouts or other charity. They characteristically think in terms of jealously guarding the integrity of their writing and art. But they must sell their work on a market to individual and corporate buyers or publishers who may require compromises of or deviations from their own standards and values. On the whole, seeking other occupations than in traditional market and professional functions, in effect they comprise a "middle" stratum continuously caught, like farmers and small businessmen of late nineteenth- and early twentieth-century America, between resisting proletarianization and falling into the condition of proletarians. They are in the nation, but also outside it. They present themselves as the nation's conscience, as humanity's conscience, or as the conscience of the singular individual against the herd.[28]

It was in the late nineteenth century, but more especially in the first two decades of the twentieth century, when growing numbers of youth

28. Cf. Henry F. May, *The End of American Innocence*, pp. 303–304; Frederick J. Hoffman, "Philistine and Puritan in the 1920s," p. 253.

were entering college instead of the market, and when this nonacademic intelligentsia emerged in the proportions suggested here, that also appeared "democratizing" college reforms and social work agencies; that appeared a growing Socialist party and press, and big business in daily newspapers; mass circulation magazines, and muckraking journalism; bohemian neighborhoods, and the "little" magazines. Just as in industry, large-scale production requires not only a mass market, the means of distribution, and a regularly frequent turnover of capital, but also in the first place an assured and sufficiently large supply of materials and labor, so in publishing, production on a large business scale of daily newspapers and weekly and monthly magazines, and even production on a smaller scale of regularly published journals, require not only a mass readership but also an assured and sufficiently large supply of writers and artists and the materials they deliver.

Some specific quantitative data may help to visualize more concretely the developments referred to here. Between 1875 and 1900, the number of college students in the United States more than doubled, compared with a doubling of total population. But in the period 1890 to 1924, the number of college students increased 352 percent (more than quadrupled) compared with a 79 percent increase of total population. Between 1900 and 1930, the number of college students multiplied fivefold, while population rose by only 62 percent.[29]

It was not until the last quarter of the nineteenth century that graduate schools and graduate students became established social phenomena in the United States. Their appearance accompanied the rise of state universities and colleges and the change in American colleges from their traditional religious to their modern secular founding and orientation. In 1871–1872, there were only 198 graduate students in America; by 1890 there were 2,382, and by 1900, 5,832. The number doubled in each decade from 1890 to 1920, and it tripled in the decade 1920 to 1930, reaching 47,255.[30]

Indicative of the trend away from traditional market occupations and toward the professions, of 18,936 recipients of Bachelor's degrees at the University of Chicago from 1893 to 1930, 62 percent went into professional occupations, and 32 percent into business, commercial, and proprietary occupations, though 24 percent of the recipients' fathers were professionals, and 40 percent were businessmen.[31] With respect to the trend toward the professions, for further example, the first school of

29. C. Wright Mills, *Sociology and Pragmatism: The Higher Learning In America* (New York: Paine-Whitman, 1964), pp. 51–52; *Recent Social Trends*, p. xlvii.
30. Mills, *Sociology and Pragmatism* 41, 44, 69.   31. Ibid., 59–60.

journalism was established in 1908, and by the period 1915–1920, journalism schools were graduating on the average of 1,000 students per year.[32]

Corresponding with the rise in college attendance, from 1900 to 1930, there occurred an eightfold increase in high school enrollments, which brought to 50 percent the proportion of high school age students actually attending high school.[33]

In the meantime, the numbers of teachers and professors also rose sharply. While throughout the period 1870–1930, the rate of increase of total population, and the rate of increase in total gainfully employed, rose at relatively similar paces, the rate of increase in the number of teachers and professors was dissimilarly, and substantially, higher. From 1870 to 1900, the number of teachers and professors rose by 251 percent (more than tripled), from 127,000 to 464,000, while population and the gainfully employed each about doubled. From 1900 to 1930, the number of teachers and professors rose by 152 percent (more than doubled), from 464,000 to 1,125,000; while population increased by 62 percent, from about 76 million to about 123 million, and the total gainfully employed rose by about 78 percent, from about 27 million to about 48 million. In the decade of 1920 to 1930 alone, the number of teachers and professors rose by 41.5 percent, while the total gainfully employed rose by 18 percent, and total population by 16 percent. Accordingly, for every one teacher or professor in 1870 there were ten in 1930; compared with four gainfully employed persons in 1930 for every one such person in 1870. Similarly, for every one newspaper journalist in 1870, there were ten in 1930. The number of artists recorded by the Census rose from 4,000 in 1870, to 25,000 in 1900, and to 57,000 in 1930. As was the case with journalists, the 1920s witnessed an especially large rise in the recorded number of artists, from 35,000 to 57,000. As the Committee on Recent Social Trends reported, with reference to the 1920s, "artists of various kinds are increasing more rapidly than the general population"; and it noted "the enlistment of art and artists by commerce and industry as an aid to sales."[34]

Concerning the nonacademic writers and artists of the early twentieth century, and their social psychology, a note should be made about the rise of the "little" magazines. Their appearance was a post-1910 phenomenon, the term "little" with reference to magazines first coming into

32. Ibid., 47.   33. *Recent Social Trends*, p. xlvi.
34. Ibid., Table 6, pp. 281–282, and p. liii; for the population figures, Morison and Commager, *The Growth of the American Republic* (New York: Oxford University Press, 1955), vol. I, p. 899.

general usage during the World War I years.[35] Though there had been "little" magazines in the nineteenth century, neither in number nor in literary significance did they compare with the flood of such magazines and the role they played from about 1912 onward. In this respect, "The first decade of the twentieth century seemed as barren as any decade of the nineteenth."[36] But from 1912 to the mid-1940s, the little magazines, as against the commercial publishing houses and journals, "introduced and sponsored every noteworthy literary movement or school" in the United States, and they first published about 80 percent of America's leading critics, novelists, poets, and storytellers, and of poets about 95 percent.[37] Characterizing the social psychology of the typical little magazine editor and writer, Hoffman notes:

> Such a man is stimulated by some form of discontent – whether with the constraints of his work or the negligence of publishers, at any rate with something he considers unjust, boring, or ridiculous. He views the world of publishers and popularizers with disdain, sometimes with despair. If he is a contributor and wishes to be published, he may have to abandon certain unorthodox aesthetic or moral beliefs. Often he is rebellious against the doctrines of popular taste and sincerely believes that our attitudes toward literature need to be reformed or at least made more liberal. More than that, he generally insists that publication should not depend upon the whimsy of conventional tastes and choices.
>
> Certainly one of the great values of the little magazine for us, who are anxious to know more about the cultural history of our time, lies in its spirit of conscientious revolt against the guardians of public taste. . . . In summary . . . little magazines have been founded for two reasons: rebellion against traditional modes of expression and the wish to experiment with novel (and sometimes unintelligible) forms; and a desire to overcome the commercial or material difficulties which are caused by the introduction of any writing whose commercial merits have not been proved.
>
> When there is money for contributors, promises of payment are made triumphantly, always as though such payment is to be made in spite of, rather than because of, the bourgeois system of values.[38]

The little magazines, and the social psychology to which they gave expression, comprised an important part of the Young Intellectuals' milieu. Brooks, Bourne, Mumford, Frank, and Stearns edited or contributed to,

35.   Frederick J. Hoffman et al., *The Little Magazine: A History and a Bibliography* (Princeton, N.J.: Princeton University Press, 1946), pp. 1, 3, 7.
36.   Ibid., 7.   37.   Ibid., 1–2, 7–10.   38.   Ibid., 3–5, 2.

and significantly participated in defining and articulating the general outlook and specific concerns of, such magazines. The role and significance of the little magazines and the writers and artists connected with them, when taken together with the other foregoing observations, permit the positing of certain generalizations regarding traits widely common to the class of nonacademic intelligentsia of the early twentieth century, whatever the other many differences among them. They came from the increasing numbers of college-educated (sometimes self-educated), articulate, and creative men and women who were seeking to forge life-patterns apart from the market relations of production and distribution of goods, and apart from the characteristic employment relations of the market. They viewed their work as carrying a value in itself and as not to be measured by money or market considerations, and as not to be pursued as primarily a means to making money in order to subsist. As will become apparent in the discussion to follow, their style of life and their values suggested to them the desirability of a society characterized by the involvement of all the people in the kind of work that could have value in itself, and incited their disdain for, or outrage at, the market-dominated society. The high regard they held for their own endeavors contrasted in a humiliating manner with the low esteem accorded them by the predominant market-oriented mentality of most other persons in their society, and especially by most of those persons among the dominant class in their society, the capitalists. To the extent that, in order to pursue their chosen work *and also* earn a living, they found themselves obliged to assume an employee condition, serving an external authority and other people's purposes, or act as merchants of their wares, their critical distaste for the society grew and deepened.

In nineteenth-century America, only a comparative handful of such professional, artistic, and literary people appeared; in the first decades of the twentieth century their numbers swelled, issuing in a multifarious intellectual movement of social criticism, political dissent, and literary disaffection, expressed by a new social formation of nonacademic intelligentsia who institutionalized, as it were, their particular style of life and its expression in communities and publications of their own,[39] a

39. "Intellectuals have existed in all literate societies, but they have only recently come to constitute a kind of subculture. In fact, the word 'intellectual' does not seem to have found its way into American usage much before the turn of the century. Before that, most intellectuals belonged to the middle class, and though they may sometimes have felt themselves at odds with the rest of the community, they did not yet conceive of themselves as a class apart . . . " Christopher Lasch, *The New Radicalism in America, 1889–1963: The Intellectual as a Social Type* (New York: A. A. Knopf, 1965), p. x. Lasch observes that "the intellectual class," composed of intellectuals with a "class-consciousness" of themselves as intellectuals, "is a distinctively modern phenomenon, the product of the cultural fragmentation that seems to characterize industrial and

176   *The United States as a developing country*

movement that expressed the writers' and artists' response to their condition, to their relation to their society, and to the society that they viewed as having produced and necessitated that condition and that relation.

Many of the characteristics attributed here to these intellectuals, with respect to their surrounding circumstances and their attitudes, were not entirely new to them: They bring to mind the German and French romantics, and the Russian intellectuals, or the late eighteenth and early and mid-nineteenth century, as well as other intellectuals in Europe and the United States throughout the nineteenth century. Indeed, these early twentieth-century American writers and artists strongly identified with their past European counterparts. But what was new, or different, was the particular circumstances out of which these intellectuals emerged in early twentieth-century America – circumstances related to the disaccumulation phase of capitalist industrialization – or what was referred to earlier as the tail end of the age of work. For while the thought of these intellectuals shared important similarities with that of their predecessors, it also departed from the previous thought in significant ways corresponding with the particular conditions prevailing in America at the time and with the transformation of those conditions then being wrought by the disaccumulation process.

4. The Young Intellectuals contra the American Ideology

The aesthetic voice of despair:

> In the last analysis, what is the significance of life? If we divide mankind into two great classes, we may say that one works for a living, the other does not need to. But working for a living cannot be the meaning of life, since it would be a contradiction to say that the perpetual production of the conditions for subsistence is an answer to the questions about its significance. . . .
>
> Kierkegaard, Either/Or, I

post-industrial societies." As such, he places its emergence "in the first couple of decades of the present century." Ibid., pp. x, xi. Lasch's identification of "the intellectual class" as "a distinctively modern phenomenon," belonging in its origins to the early twentieth century, is sound, but his explanation is questionable. First of all, to regard them as an intellectual class is only to replicate their own view of themselves and their own confusion of function with class. Second, the cultural fragmentation he refers to predated the early twentieth century by many decades at least. Even if it be granted that the emergence of "the intellectual class" were a delayed product of such cultural fragmentation (itself a rather vague and imprecise term), it still remains to identify and describe the more immediate precipitating circumstances; and here the disaccumulation process is crucially pertinent.

The aesthetic voice of defiance:

> To be, to feel oneself, a "victim" is not in itself to be an artist, for it is the nature of the artist to live, not in the world of which he is an effect, but in the world of which he is the cause, the world of his own creation.
>
> Van Wyck Brooks, 1922

Sometime between 1915 and 1922, D. H. Lawrence wrote that "the true myth of America" was: "She starts old, old, wrinkled and writhing in an old skin. And there is a gradual sloughing of the old skin, towards a new youth."[40] R. W. B. Lewis refers to this as the American Adamic Myth, which saw "life and history as just beginning," a new order of things in a new world, "a divinely granted second chance for the human race, after the first chance had been so disastrously fumbled in the darkening Old World." America represented life and society liberated from "a long historical process," separated from the past and connected only with the future.[41] However mythic, this view of America as the scene and occasion of human liberation from the past ran deeply through American ideological reality, from Puritanism, to Jeffersonianism, to frontierism (as symbolic metaphor and as the mentality of a tangible life-style), to Populist and Progressive reformism.[42] Americans could thrive and prosper in the present, secure that the future would fulfill a present progres-

40. D. H. Lawrence, *Studies in Classic American Literature* (Garden City, N.J.: Doubleday Anchor Books, n.d. (195?)), p. 64. Lawrence began writing this work in 1915; it was first published in 1922. These years coincide with the period in which most of the formative works of the Young Intellectuals first appeared: Van Wyck Brooks, *America's Coming-of-Age* (New York: B. W. Huebsch, 1918); Harold E. Stearns, *Liberalism in America* (New York: Boni and Liveright, 1919), *America and the Young Intellectual* (New York: George H. Doran, 1921) (comprising essays first published in *The Dial*, 1918, and *The Freeman*, 1920, 1921), and Stearns, ed., *Civilization in the United States* New York: Harcourt, Brace, 1922); Waldo Frank, *Our America* (New York: Boni and Liveright, 1919); virtually all of Bourne's essays (1915–1918). By the first years of the 1920s, the outlook associated with the Young Intellectuals had been formed and articulated; their subsequent works through the 1920s represented the replication, application, and elaboration of the viewpoint essentially forged in the period 1915–1922.

41. R. W. B. Lewis, *The American Adam* (Chicago: University of Chicago Press (1955), Third Impression, 1961), pp. 4–5.

42. Cf. Henry Nash Smith, *Virgin Land: The American West as Symbol and Myth* (New York: Vintage Books, 1961), passim, and especially pp. 3–13, 16–37, 138–164, 220–226, 291–305; Roland Van Zandt, *The Metaphysical Foundations of American History* ('S-Gravenhage, The Hague: Mouton, 1959); William A. Williams, "The Frontier Thesis and American Foreign Policy," *Pacific Historical Review*, XXIV (November 1955), pp. 379–395, and *The Great Evasion* (Chicago: Quadrangle, 1965); and David W. Noble, *Historians against History: The Frontier Thesis and the National Covenant in American Historical Writing since 1838* (Minneapolis: University of Minnesota Press, 1965).

sively improving, by applying their practical reason, naturally bestowed by a beneficent Maker, to their specific tasks and concrete enjoyments; and this precisely because, being Americans and being in America, they were free of "metaphysical" ideas and hindering institutions of all the historical past.

So deeply has this mythic self-conception moved through the American consciousness that, in its various manifestations, it may be uniformly identified and referred to as The American Ideology. In the nineteenth century, it not only powerfully shaped political ideology, but also served as the richest native source upon which leading American poets, novelists, and writers drew for "a fresh definition of experience and a fresh contribution to the culture."[43] Insofar, however, as its content and historical tenacity represented "repeated efforts to revert to a lost childhood and a vanished Eden," the myth of the American Adam represented "a kind of resistance in America to the painful process of growing up." But where, on the contrary, it entered the writer's consciousness as an "awareness of the American habit of resistance to maturity," the writer's effort invariably evidenced a tendency toward "cultural maturity."[44] Such an awareness definitively shaped the outlook of the intellectuals under discussion here. America, for them, had not escaped history but had only replicated a particularly deformed version of history; America had never in reality offered humanity the hope of a fruitful new beginning, whatever its ideal pretensions; and America had yet to grow to maturity, culturally or otherwise, by mustering the strength to acknowledge the difference between its mythic pretensions and its historical reality. What historians refer to as "the end of American innocence," which marks the second decade of the twentieth century as the intellectual beginning of our own times,[45] involved at its core the articulation of this historically conscious critique of America by a relatively larger number of writers exerting a greater and more lasting intellectual impact than ever before in America in a comparable span of time. The Young Intellectuals acted, in effect, as a vanguard in the formulation and relentless expression of this critical perspective on American life.

The historical dimension assumed a central place in the outlook of these intellectuals. It, though not it alone, distinguished their thought from that of eighteenth-century rationalistic naturalism as well as from the evolutionary positivism and pragmatic instrumentalism of their own time. They neither believed in the ahistorical rationalist doctrine of natural rights, nor valued or credited the theory of suprarational evolution

43. Lewis, *The American Adam*, p. 129.   44. Ibid.
45. Henry F. May, *The End of American Innocence: A Study of the First Years of Our Own Time, 1912–1917* (Chicago: Quadrangle, 1964).

of existing institutions and its corollary of expert adjustments of those institutions or of people within them.[46] They saw themselves as living within an historical continuum, but affirmed the imminence of, or their hope for, its disruption. To translate this hope into an actionable intention, to actualize an historical imminence, it was necessary, in their view, to become conscious of, and understand, the historical continuum in which they found their lives unwillingly caught; it was necessary to know of what the existing continuum consisted, and why they were estranged from it and opposed to it, as the condition of their disrupting it and reconstructing a new continuum in accordance with their will. They viewed their research into the American past, therefore, as integral to the process of discovering and therein creating the future America. In formulating and defining their own consciousness – their own world outlook, their own personal view – they saw themselves as embarking upon the rediscovery and reconstruction of America. The merging of their biography with America's future history offered the condition for ending the situation where their biography appeared to them sundered from the history of the American past and present. But that meant projecting their biography, their style of life, their outlook, their aspirations and desires, onto the nation's historical reality, and making the two coterminous and identical. It was from this perspective that they rejected dualistic modes of thought that posed fact against value, intellect against desire, reality against ideals, actuality against dreams. Their approach, they believed, embraced an historical and ethically responsible realism, while all those approaches that acquiesced wittingly or unwittingly in existing reality, as they perceived it, devolved upon an ethically irresponsible and barren idealism. Against affirming and idealizing the real, they raised the slogan: Realize the Ideal.

In this outlook lay the general basis for declarations of revolt sounded over and over again by younger intellectuals in these years. "We are in revolt," Waldo Frank proclaimed in 1919, "against the academies and

46. For a delineation of the doctrine of natural rights and natural liberties, and its decisive role in shaping American social thought and jurisprudence, see Thorstein Veblen, *The Theory of Business Enterprise* (New York: Mentor, 1958), pp. 128–143. Though it is not essential to the present purpose, it may be noted that Veblen published many of his essays in the same magazines as those in which these young intellectuals published theirs, and that it is reasonable to assume that these intellectuals were acquainted with Veblen's views in this matter as well as in others (the work cited above being originally published in 1904). For a delineation of scientific and evolutionary positivism as referred to here, see H. Stuart Hughes, *Consciousness and Society* (New York: Vintage, 1961), ch. 2: "The Decade of the 1890s: The Revolt against Positivism," pp. 33–66; Karl Mannheim, *Ideology and Utopia* (New York: Harvest Books, n.d.), pp. 120–121; Herbert Marcuse, *Reason and Revolution* (New York: Humanities Press, 1954), pp. 323–388. As for pragmatic instrumentalism, the ensuing discussion will make plain its meaning as understood by these intellectuals.

institutions which would whittle America down to a few stale realities current fifty years ago. . . . But we are in revolt as well against that organized anarchy today expressed in Industrialism which would deny to America ʾny life – hence any unity at all – beyond the ties of traffic and the arter.ᵤₛ of trade. . . . "⁴⁷ Or, more succinctly: "the younger generation . . . is in revolt . . . [against] the type of people dominant in our present civilization, the people who actually 'run things'. . . . "⁴⁸

The Young Intellectuals, then, wanted and anticipated a new beginning. This was very American. It resembles the Adamic mythos. But the resemblance should not obscure the essence. The desire for a new beginning, for a disruption of the historical continuum, and for a future different from and negating the past, is not in itself identical with the escape-from-history Adamic mythos, and the two should no more be confused for their similarities than should eighteenth-century rationalism with Marx. It makes all the difference, what kind of a new beginning, what kind of an historical disruption, and what kind of a future, their protagonists desire and conceptualize. The new beginning that these young intellectuals wanted, and the way of achieving it that they prescribed, represented a break with, and so distinguished their outlook from, the American Adamic tradition. This is also to say that their outlook represented at the same time a break with and departure from traditional, prevalent American conceptions of progress, of the relationship between consciousness and reality, of political economy, of work and character, of freedom and individualism, and of America's world significance. In short, their outlook embraced a critique of, and break with, The American Ideology.

Whereas older liberal reformers during and after World War I, such as John Haynes Holmes and Frederick C. Howe, found to their disillusionment that America was like Europe after all,⁴⁹ the younger intel-

47. *Our America, pp.* 8–9.
48. Harold E. Stearns, *America and the Young Intellectuals* (1921) pp. 11–12.
49. John Haynes Holmes, "Where Are the Pre-War Radicals?" *The Survey,* 55 (1 February 1926), pp. 564–565. Holmes recalled that the older liberal reformers like himself had "believed passionately in America as a country unique among the nations of the earth. . . . Then came the War – and America was seen to be just like every other country! The America we loved was gone, and in its place, was just one more cruel imperialism. This discovery ended a movement which had for its purpose the protection and vindication of an ideal America. . . . But America will follow where we once hoped that she would lead, and thus find her place at last in the commonwealth of man." Cf. Frederick C. Howe's recollection: The war "all but destroyed my picture of America. It does not come to life again. . . . I felt a moral obligation for our personal and political liberties. . . . Liberty was as dear to me as another kind of patriotism was dear to other hundred per cent Americans. And when I saw liberty laid prostrate by those from whom I had expected protection, when I found my kind of Americanism under suspicion, if not denounced as criminal, when I saw my government using its power in a hysteria of fear to crush civil and political liberties, when

lectuals, not so much found as they took for matter of fact, that America combined the worst features of being like Europe with the worst features of being unlike Europe and a world unto itself – a view much like the theory of combined underdevelopment applied by Trotsky to prerevolutionary Russia; a conception that in both cases animated its advocates to a comprehensive critique and rejection of their respective existing societies, and to a sense of unbounded possibilities for the future. America combined classic European capitalism and imperialism, an unvarnished and stupendous material exploitation and human wastage, with the virtual absence of classical or any other nonbourgeois sources of culture, philosophy, and ideas. A nonbourgeois culture, in their view, lay in the future; but for its unfolding, the dominant American past, as rendered by the scholars and historians, provided no source. They had one immediate native source at their disposal for the conceptualization and construction of the future, themselves: their own desires and creative capacities, and, drawing upon those desires and capacities, their own reconstruction of the American past through which, by the possible rediscovery of elements overlooked and suppressed by the conventional scholars and historians, they might supply themselves with a modicum of sustenance abiding in their native soil. In this twofold resort to consciousness – artistic consciousness and historical consciousness – they made themselves their own source; they conceived themselves the future in embryo. Their emphasis upon the reexamination of American history, upon the search for a "usable past," distinguishes their outlook from traditional American outlooks defining the future in terms of a present divorced from the past. They did not ignore, or repudiate, history: They sought to come to terms with American history. They repudiated that American history, and that scholarly replication and celebration of it, which represented America as a nation acting and thinking as if it had itself escaped from history. Their repudiation proclaimed an escape from an escape: a reimmersion in history and the forging of an historical consciousness.[50] Their creative capacities and desires, they believed, could take root and bear fruit only upon a sufficiently fertile historical ground, without which those capacities and desires would remain mere compensatory

I saw these things, much of my belief in men, in the political state and in my own America all but died. I think it died for millions of others. . . . " F. C. Howe, "Where Are the Pre-War Radicals? A Rejoinder," *The Survey*, 56, 1 (April 1926), p. 50.

50. Cf. Warren I. Susman, "The Useless Past: American Intellectuals and the Frontier Thesis: 1910–1930," *Bucknell Review*, XI:2 (March 1963), pp. 1–2, where, referring to Brooks, Frank, Mumford, and others, he notes as a "striking fact," "this fascination with the American past," and "the enormous interest shown by intellectuals – not themselves professional historians or even professors – in the study of American history."

dreams and fantasies contorted into nightmares of stillborn conceptions never to grow into living social organisms.

The belief in the interconnection of art and history, or perhaps more precisely, the belief in the intersecting of art and science upon the creation of historical consciousness and the construction of an intended and desired historical reality, lay at the heart of the Young Intellectuals' outlook. If their thought places them among the executioners of the American age of innocence and the procreators of our own times, then we must understand that by "our own times" we mean the throbbing in our consciousness of those conceptions flowing from the heart of the Young Intellectuals' outlook. But there is for us the glaring incongruity, that "our own times" is no longer ours, if it ever was. The expression of experience in America, says R. W. B. Lewis, "has been clearest and most rewarding" when it has evoked the dialectic between past and future involving the Adamic myth. "Only recently has the dialogue tended to die away. For only recently has the old conviction of the new historical beginning seemed to vanish altogether, and with it the enlivening sense of possibility."[51]

The Young Intellectuals' "dream" and "promise" of a new historical beginning and their enlivening sense of possibility appear to us today defunct, unredeemed, or beyond redemption, like Czarist bonds or Imperial Chinese treasury notes. "Our own times" seems already an antiquity, and each yesterday appears to have been long ago. Each today seems so much another unwanted future, every tomorrow so much a replication upon replication of the same old "new beginnings," that the sense of possibility, the anticipation of a future, to which our own consciousness and desires make a difference, appears preempted and benumbed and futile before the onward rush of the past in its present form. If we say, then, that the Young Intellectuals were the procreators of "our own times," it must be understood provisionally if it is to be understood at all with a meaning that rings true. For "our own times" is something since them but not yet, or sometime since us and yet to be retrieved, or somewhere within and among us and yet to be articulated and achieved. To say this, however, is to occupy a frame of mind, which though somewhat different from, is yet closely intimate with, that of the Young Intellectuals.

As the medium of dialogue between past and future, the Young Intellectuals supplanted the Adamic mythos with artistic and historical consciousness. To take liberties with a now familiar maxim, their present was the medium, their present developing consciousness reevaluating the past and projecting into the future. With it, the younger intellectuals demystified and detheodicized America as well as the American veneration

51. Lewis, *The American Adam*, pp. 8–9.

of scientific-rationalist manipulation of environment in the service of capitalism, otherwise known as Yankee practicality. If, in this project they recognized only themselves as an immediate native source, they nevertheless enjoyed access to numerous contemporary and bygone foreign sources. They had at their disposal, drew upon, and in varying degrees identified their own thinking with, the broad and vigorous movement of European thought reacting against abstract rationalism and scientific and evolutionary positivism, including the works of a whole range of diverse philosophers, artists, poets, and political theorists from Hegel, Kierkegaard and Nietzsche, to Dostoevsky, Proust, and Cezanne, to Bergson, Simmel, and Sorel. The Americans were also able to, and did, draw upon, Marx, for his critique of the capitalist political economy, and Freud, for his critique of bourgeois morality.

If social history unfolds, as positivism seemed to prescribe, according to objective processes of evolution independent of human will, then people can not intercede against, interdict, or supplant those processes, but merely learn what they are, and adjust, accordingly, to their necessity. In effect, the social system becomes, in this view, the historical subject, and humanity the object, the one the seat of rationality, the other the fount of irrationality unless firmly held to a "scientific method" of faithfully reflecting and registering the indefeasible processes of development. Against this, a multitude of European thinkers who in other respects differed widely, reasserted the indispensable role of human consciousness and will in shaping personal and social existence. They reasserted humanity as the creating subject, and social existence as the moldable object. They argued that people come to know their world not simply by passive perception (or mirror reflection), which turns out to be only the current dominant conceptions and deceptions, but by seeking consciously, deliberately, and intentionally to change or fashion it: People learn about their existing reality in the process of mastering and creating a new reality. Within this perspective avant-garde art and revolutionary politics converged upon the attack against positivism and the affirmation of the creative, responsible, transforming, and willful human subject as the agent of human and historical destiny.

Within this mainstem of thought, however, the Europeans formed themselves into two subsidiary branches, sometimes at first mutually complementary and congenial, later increasingly antagonistic. The one insisted that people should affirm and actualize their desires, place their reason, intellect, and way of life at the service of desire, and fashion thereby, in their personal life-activity or in discrete subcommunities, a counterreality to the existing society. The other emphasized the role of consciousness in transforming the existing society in such a way as to actualize its immanent possibilities: Consciousness discovers the historically possible and actively proceeds to transform it into the actual. In Europe, the House of Consciousness Resurrected divided. Revolutionary art and revolutionary politics embarked upon a parting of ways: The spires of art and aesthetics on the one side, the fortresses of politics and history on the other, glowered at one another across a spiritual abyss in a mutual stand-off.

The outlook of the Young Intellectuals in America represented a particular expression of the larger mainstem of thought that had emerged so forcefully and subdivided in Europe in the late nineteenth and early twentieth century. But the Young Intellectuals did not draw upon this general body of European thought in the manner of intellectual and spiritual expatriates, or brokers of imported notions. "The importation of radical ideas and the ferment of [imported] radical ideas," as Brooks wrote, " . . . scarcely touch . . . the center of the American problem. So far as we are concerned, the sea-crossing, to begin with, has a very dampening effect on the gunpowder contained in them. Transplanted they have at once the pleasing remoteness of literature and the stir of an only half-appreciated actuality; they become admirably safe, they become even delightful." In America, Nietzsche and A. C. Benson, "the lion and the lamb," lay down "quite peacefully together, chewing the cud of culture." The more "arduous" and "inspiriting" task was to "get civilization out of the Yankee stock." The signs that this was possible and already in process appeared "anything but obvious," but if one kept "quite still" and held his "ear close to the ground," he might hear "the sap stirring and the little half-inconsequential voices that whisper and breathe in the intervals of bombast and business."[52] The emergent America was like Huck Finn on the Mississippi: "the unceasing elemental march of a vast life, cutting a continent, feeding its soil. And upon the heaving surface of this flood, a human child: ignorant, joyous, and courageous. The American soul like a midge upon the tide of a world."[53]

In other words, European ideas might bring aid and comfort, but for defining and attaining their objectives, the Young Intellectuals regarded the American historical reality, in its actuality and potentiality, and their own consciousness, as fundamental. Taking this view, these Americans brought into momentary synthesis the branches of thought that in Europe tended to diverge into mutually antagonistic world-outlooks. A

52. *America's Coming-of-Age*, pp. 162–163. Cf. Waldo Frank, *Our America*, pp. 4–5: "The problem is not to force America to speech. Such forced speech must be what most of ours has been: the parroting of foreign phrases, lip service to the maturity of England and of France – or worse, expression of the one formed and conscious entity in American life, the world of commerce."
53. Frank, *Our America*, pp. 39–40.

dualistic opposition of desire and reason, of ideals and reality, or art and social relations, was precisely the condition they defined as the pathology of American thought and society, the sickness they set themselves to heal. For them, desire was integral to consciousness, and consciousness to historical reality; the separation of desire from the historical existent meant a default upon the active exercise of consciousness and a submission to the domination of the past; it meant that people had let themselves become crippled, fragmented specimens of human being. If historical society represented necessity, necessity nevertheless included consciousness, and in translating their consciousness into historically existent social relations and styles of life, people could thereby transform desire into necessity. Necessity could become the fulfillment of desire, rather than its nemesis. If, therefore, freedom meant the recognition of necessity, understood in this way, it meant nothing else than humanity's recognition of itself, writ whole, in the world of historical reality. Everyman therefore, given the fulfillment of this outlook, was involved in the creation of the historical world and of oneself; if everyman was the whole person as artist; each artist was everyman as a whole person. America, then, could become a scene of the emergence of universal man. As yet, the turmoiled giant's eyes "wander about the clouds: his feet are sunk in the quicksands of racial and material passion. One hand grasps the mountains, and the other falls bruised and limp upon the lowlands of the world." But his "need" was great "and what moves across his eyes is universal."[54]

If the Adamic outlook presented the American as the negation of the European, the Young Intellectuals' outlook brought the Adamic to a new level of meaning, transforming by transcending it, a negation of the negation, projecting the American as potentially the universal man, the portent of another new beginning, not by a supposed escape or departure from culture and historical society, but through the integration of art and history. As noted earlier: an escape from an escape.

The bourgeoisie, in the Young Intellectuals' view, constituted the nation; so the history of the nation recorded the various stages of development of the American bourgeoisie: The bourgeois as Puritan had become the bourgeois as pioneer, and he in turn had become the captain of industry and the plutocrat. Puritan, pioneer, and plutocrat, encapsulated one within the other, comprised the three-layer psyche and life-style of the twentieth-century American bourgeoisie, who presented themselves culturally as philistines. Puritan, pioneer, plutocrat, philistine were for the Young Intellectuals as much interchangeable terms describing the various types, often interbred, of the one species bourgeois, as each

54. Ibid., p. 4.

bourgeois was essentially interchangeable with every other. The society of uniformity and interchangeable parts was the society the bourgeoisie had only naturally made in its own image. It really misses the point to berate the Young Intellectuals for having misrepresented the true character of the Puritans of seventeenth-century America,[55] for their concern was not a characterization of the Puritans as such, but a critique of, and justification of their antipathy to, bourgeois America. Sometimes deliberately, sometimes unawares, they utilized terms such as puritan and pioneer in effect as metaphorical and analogical references to the traits of the bourgeoisie they opposed, and they did so creatively, effectively, and within that frame of understanding, validly.[56]

Had the Young Intellectuals' view of the national history gone no further than an apprehension such as this, it is unlikely that their outlook would have been different from the prevailing European dualism of art versus history. But their own experience so informed their historical understanding as to bring the latter to an emphasis upon another aspect of the social relations inhering in national development under bourgeois auspices, which inscribed upon their consciousness a dimension that decisively shaped their outlook. They were aware that if America were indeed the most thoroughly bourgeois of all nations, this had left the bourgeois political economy virtually free of social hindrance to bring its productive forces to so advanced a stage of development, with so prodigious an output capacity, as to set in motion the processes of the bourgeoisie's own obsolescence. The bourgeoisie had brought industrialization from its accumulation to its disaccumulation phase, or, as the Young Intellectuals perceived the situation, it had brought the human economy from the phase of "scarcity," which had characterized all previous history, to the historically new phase of "abundance." While there may have been, during the frontier era and the earlier phases of material development, an ethical and social justification for the bourgeoisie's, and hence the entire nation's, absorption in material produc-

55. See, e.g., Frederick J. Hoffman, "Philistine and Puritan in the 1920s," *American Quarterly,* I:3, Fall 1949, p. 247, et passim, pp. 247–263; and Hoffman's *The Twenties,* New York: The Free Press, 1965 (orig. copyright 1949), pp. 355–368; on the other hand, Hoffman recognizes the use by intellectuals in the 1920s of "the Midwest" as a metaphor, pp. 369–377.

56. Indeed, many of the Puritan divines themselves might have agreed with parts of the Young Intellectuals' critique, at least so far as it applied to their own lay brethren and to some wayward among their own colleagues. More than that, the Young Intellectuals' view of the Puritan epistemology and work ethic enjoyed considerable substantiation in contemporary, and even more recent, historical scholarship. See Perry Miller, *The New England Mind: The Seventeenth Century* (Boston: Beacon Press, 1965, orig. pub. 1939), ch. XVI: "God's Controversy with New England," 463–491, and ch. I: "The Practice of Piety," pp. 35–63, esp. pp. 42–44, and ch. V: "The Instrument of Reason," pp. 111–153.

tion, and for exploitation for profit as the incentive for such absorption, everyone now knew that the age of the frontier was gone, and that intrepid capitalist enterprise had turned the nation, if not into a land flowing with milk and honey for all to drink as they pleased, then at any rate into a veritable corporate cornucopia of abundant goods available beyond effective demand and otherwise glutting the warehouses or overflowing to foreign markets.

The bourgeois system of production had developed to the point, moreover, where in its normal course of operation, more and more goods could be, and by the 1920s, visibly were being, produced with less and less labor, relatively and absolutely. This meant that less and less were men and women required as either laborers, or as entrepreneurs or capitalists, in the production process proper, a trend accelerated and made all the more irrevocable by the concentration of the production process in ever larger units and their ownership and control by fewer corporate entities. It also meant, and the Young Intellectuals themselves were living empirical evidence for their own apprehension of this, that the labor of increasing numbers of young men and women was no longer required in the production process, nor claimed by market demand, and that accordingly rising numbers of people found themselves released from the sheer necessities of producing the primary material means of life, to choose and try to fashion other kinds of careers and life-styles. But more than this, it meant that the old bourgeois ethic and regimen of work for production's sake, of production for the sake of more production, of production as the aim of man instead of man as the aim of production, of withholding from engagement in immediately gratifying and self-expressing activity for the sake of earning the means of subsistence and ease, of deferring desire to necessity and the present to the future, appeared to increasing numbers of young men and women, no longer to represent a self-evident, natural way of life; no longer appeared, and no longer was, an unalterable necessity. On the contrary, with the release of what would ultimately become the great mass of the people from relations of production, the life of desire could, and properly should, become the life of necessity.

As the Young Intellectuals perceived it, however, the bourgeoisie sustained its domination of the American society by turning all these trends to their perversion, by constricting them within the limitations of its own ethical and sociopolitical regimen, instead of bringing these trends to their conversion into a new society. Given its particular values, and its inability, no less than its unwillingness, to depart from and leave behind its social system and way of life, which was suited if at all to the "frontier" and "scarcity," or accumulation, phase of industrialization, the bourgeoisie could respond in only one way to the consequences of its own material success: by extending into all areas of endeavor outside the area of material production and exchange, the same relations and ethic, of work, employment, enterprise for profit, accumulation, and deferral that had nurtured it, and within which it flourished, in the sphere of relations of production and exchange. The bourgeoisie appeared furthermore determined to extend its sway over all the other spheres of life to protect the way of life its members enjoyed in the sphere of production and commerce, from the threat of rivalry by a growing and attractive alternative mode of life, and to assure thereby the conformity of the entire nation to the only pattern of life with which they felt familiar, in which they felt themselves confident and at home, and over which they felt themselves and in reality were the masters. The bourgeoisie could not be expected to react and do otherwise; all the more reason that the Young Intellectuals and increasing myriads like them should not be expected to confine their own growth, potentialities, and imaginative horizons to the stunted, atavistic, and obsolescent life-style and psychic boundaries of the bourgeoisie.

It was precisely this monochromatic, and at the same time, this genetic, view of the nation they were in but not of, that inspired the Young Intellectuals to project themselves as the emergent counternation in embryo, to interrelate art and aesthetics with history and politics, to discover in the historical continuum the conditions of its disruption and renewed resumption, to reintrude their biography upon the nation's history. Their declaration of revolt was accordingly systemic, not partial, in essence and reach. Directed against the bourgeoisie and the nation interchangeably, it encompassed an opposition to the whole of the dominant past and present social reality, and to each of its parts from top to bottom, ranging from the general organization of the political economy, to the academies, to the middle class family and the "restricted reality of their fathers."

Since the Young Intellectuals themselves, and their outlook, had emerged as the outcome of the successful workings of the bourgeois system, they could regard themselves as representing the historically legitimate alternative to the bourgeois system, and as therefore the rightful heirs to leadership over the entire nation. They could view their aesthetic ethic as coinciding with historical possibility, capable of translation into principles defining the basic relationships of the future historical society. By conceiving the current social reality in terms of a clear bipolarization between the bourgeoisie and themselves, they could view their opponent as representing a now "useless" past and a decrepit present, and themselves and their consciousness as representing the young, dynamic, and

indubitable future. Their monochromatic view of the society they opposed nourished their equally monochromatic view of themselves as representing the future society, and this in turn facilitated identifying their
own outlook, not with an exclusive minority or elite in society, superior
to, standing above, and aloof from, a benighted masses, but with, potentially, the entire American people. In breaking with the bourgeois
past, the Young Intellectuals were also, then, keeping faith with, and re-
juvenating, the traditional American democratic professions; they could
regard themselves as redeeming the democracy from its abasement and
mockery at the hands of a plutocratic domination enthroned by the
bourgeois system of economics and politics. The Young Intellectuals presented themselves, therefore, as aesthetic democrats, not as aesthetic aristocrats, elitists, or snobs, and this all the more reinforced their view that
their outlook and the nation's historical development were interrelated
and must ultimately merge to become the dominant America.

In still another way, their emergence from a bourgeois historical reality
tended to reinforce their view. They affirmed a work ethic, and in their
rhetoric used terms common to bourgeois social relations, but they endowed that ethic and filled those terms with different meanings. No less
than bourgeois moralists, they deprecated idleness and voluntary unemployment. But they insisted upon the right of all persons to engage in
directly self-expressing and self-fulfilling work, and upon the principle
that work, properly, constituted not a means to life, but one of the more
important expressions of life. They argued that the bourgeoisie, however, was not in the market for such work, and left those who sought it
involuntarily unemployed. The only effective alternative, therefore, was
the abolition of the bourgeoisie as society's arbiter of work opportunities, and its displacement by nothing less than civilization itself. The
Young Intellectuals, accordingly, projected the transformation of the employer from what was now a specific class in society, with its own limited
interests, to the society as a whole. But in that case, the values and interests of society, as employer, must necessarily coincide with the values
and interests championed by the Young Intellectuals.

In this way, art and history would converge upon the reconciliation of
the individual and society, of the particular will and the general will, of
desire and necessity. Rousseau, Blake, Hegel, Marx, Freud, and other
such kindred souls might then walk the land as fellow countrymen along
with the American everyman in the new world the Young Intellectuals
proposed to build.

Bourgeois society and its ideology of bourgeois liberty joined together
in the unwanted procreation of socialist political movements, their ideology of socialist democracy and, short of abortion, miscarriage, or prior

parental mortality, socialist society. The bourgeois image of the free man, exercising self-mastery and independence with respect to the means of production and with respect to the disposal of his life-time and the ownership of his own labor-power and its fruits, dissolved in the historical unfolding of bourgeois society – in the continuous dispossession and proletarianization of growing numbers of people, in the cleavage between capital and labor, necessarily consequent upon the free play of bourgeois liberty. Bourgeois liberty initially embodied, ultimately negated, the principle of self-mastery. But bourgeois society made the belief in the principle the ideological property of countless numbers of its members, and hence made it into an irrevocable driving force of historical reality. Locke gave the principle its paradigmatic articulation; Rousseau reasserted, against the contrary social reality, the universal claim to the principle by all persons as an indefeasible right by virtue simply of their human birth, a claim already implicit in the natural rights doctrine lying in Locke's formulations. Marx transcended the contradiction between the image of the free individual contained in bourgeois liberty and the principle of self-mastery: He preserved the principle, the transhistorical human kernel wrapped in bourgeois liberty, by bringing to systematic consciousness the negation of abstract individualized self-mastery in the realm of economic activity and its restitution initially through socialist democracy, and enduringly through socialized self-mastery. Recalling classical antiquity's concept of freedom as residing in the realm of leisure (*scholé*), Marx completed the negation by positing the ultimate extrication of the principle of self-mastery from the realm of immediate production, on the basis of the development of the productive forces begun with, but fettered by, capitalism, and brought to higher development and relegated to the periphery of social life under socialism. Locke and Rousseau and Newtonian mechanics produced their negation in Marx, bourgeois democracy and the steam-powered factory system their antithesis in socialist consciousness and socialist politics, as inexorably as the dyspeptic oyster produces the pearl, more of kin, less of kind – to draw on Shakespeare and amortize Hegel. As for the Old World, so for the New World, only more completely so, in words Marx liked to quote: *De te fabula narratur est.*[57]

The rise and growth of the socialist political movement in the United States in the late nineteenth century and first two decades of the twentieth century represented the emergence to social consciousness and historical substantiality of bourgeois liberty's negating progeny responding to the accumulationist phase of capitalist industrialization. It represented the growing recognition by Americans of the obsolescence of the prin-

57. "The story is about you."

ciple of self-mastery in its Jeffersonian image, as well as its incompatibility with capitalism. As such the socialist political movement expressed the passage by some Americans beyond the vain attempts to restore bourgeois liberty in response to proletarianization, to the demand for the social reunification of productive means and labor, and the right of people to exercise social control over the disposal of their life-time in the production process. The appearance, on the other hand, of the outlook expressed by the Young Intellectuals in the period of about 1915 to 1930, represented the somewhat later but partially concomitant, and wholly interrelated, emergence to social consciousness of the theoretical negation of bourgeois liberty and bourgeois society, in the early phase of capitalist disaccumulation.

Although sharing a common source and a common antagonist in bourgeois society, and although sharing a common general objective in the self-disposal of life-time along lines of endeavor constituting ends in themselves, the people caught up respectively in these two phases, historically, more often than not, have appeared in distinct, if not wholly estranged, spheres of social life and consciousness: the first in the realm of political-economy, as the predominant element in socialist political thought, the second in the realm of art and intellect, as a major current of aesthetic and philosophical avant-gardeism. This division has been central to the separation, in antibourgeois circles, of history and politics on the one side from art and aesthetics on the other. It helps to explain why from the point of view of avant-garde artists and intellectuals, the political socialists have often appeared as "primitives," as only another variant of the bourgeois, immersed as the socialist movements and their constituencies still were in the realm of production and necessity-compelled labor; and why from the standpoint of political socialists, the avant-garde artists and intellectuals have often appeared as abstract idealists, utopians, and only another variant of the bourgeois individualist, unconcerned as they were, in a serious systematic way, with the ways and means of achieving the collective reunification of labor and the means of production, as the material and social basis for realizing the commonly held grand objectives repressed by bourgeois society. This division has been central, accordingly, to the failure, in the Western industrial nations, of the socialist political movements and the avant-garde artists and intellectuals to unite their resources and efforts in their shared desire for a revolutionary transformation of bourgeois society, and bring to realization a consciousness appropriate to a society passing beyond relations of production. The inability to overcome this division was decisive to the ultimate failure of the Young Intellectuals, in their own terms, to overcome the dualism of ideas and reality in American life, to actualize their consciousness in the predominant social relations of America, to achieve their stated objectives and dreams, and permanently to lay to rest the American Adamic mythos.

But if only temporarily, rudimentarily, and gropingly, yet nevertheless certainly, the outlook the Young Intellectuals expressed in the period of about 1915 to 1930, represented an elemental though unstable synthesis of the two phases of consciousness otherwise associated with and most systematically developed by Marx. In this further important sense, it represented the emergence to a significant and relatively widespread social consciousness in America, of a world-view comprising a break with, and a transcending negation of, the American Ideology and its Jeffersonian and Adamic image of America and the American.

Accordingly, and more specifically, the outlook of the Young Intellectuals expressed their response, on the immediate plane, to the extension of bourgeois liberty with its values and social relations from the sphere of production and exchange into spheres related to their own life-activity; their response as well, therefore, to proletarianization of their own working conditions and social status. Less immediately, and by corollary, their outlook also expressed their response, in broad philosophical and ethical principles, to bourgeois society and proletarianization in general. In terms of this outlook, the Young Intellectuals were conscious of themselves as a distinct group arrayed against the bourgeoisie, its ideology, its values, and its society, which they viewed as depriving them of self-mastery in access to the means of life and ease, and more important in the disposal of their life-time. They experienced and comprehended that deprivation in three basic and interrelated ways: (1) the reduction of themselves and other artists and intellectuals to the position of, in effect, employees whatever the formal or ostensible status; (2) their being forced to place their art and intellect at the service of antipathetic purposes represented by their employers, publishers, universities, patrons, alias the market; (3) their conception of those purposes as essentially bourgeois in character, that is, oriented to the exploitation of the American people's deprived needs and starved desires, and serving to sustain the existence of externalized people and their exploitative social system rather than upsetting, perturbing, challenging, and changing them. In responding against their own proletarianization, and against proletarianization in general, they also rejected any aspiration to become property-owning entrepreneurs or employers of labor themselves, as well as regarding such aspiration in others as immoral, psychologically regressive, and socially deleterious.

Abstractly at first, and increasingly in more specific political terminology, the Young Intellectuals identified with the industrial proletariat and with the dispossessed generally. They presented themselves as partisan, in varying degrees, to socialism; partisan, that is, to a democratically governed social system that would extricate production and distribution of goods from private or corporate ownership and control, which would reduce the production technique to means of general welfare for society collectively and for each individual personally, which would thereby release society from the all-pervasive domination by the production sphere, and which would therefore require depriving the bourgeoisie of social, economic, and political leadership by installing in such leadership workers, intellectuals, artists, and professionals, seeking these objectives. The Young Intellectuals' outlook assumed that working men and women, and especially the young among them, given the opportunity, would recognize and assert the same objectives as their own, a fuller, richer, deeper personal and social life where work might increasingly become a self-expressive activity, and where the techniques of production and the corresponding social and political relations might serve people as a means to their self-determined ends, rather than operating as ends whose requirements and perpetuation people must serve as means: in short, where the condition for the development of each is the condition for the development of all.

The young intellectuals could therefore preoccupy their writings to a large extent with their own immediate situation and their own role as intellectuals and artists in their society, and could write about their society from the perspective of their own situation and role, as the manner of criticizing the existing society and projecting the outlines of the new society. They could criticize society with reference to their self-image, an image that embraced both their current condition denying what they thought they ought to be as artists, intellectuals, and whole men and women, and their anticipated condition in a society transformed to honor and actualize it. In this way, they could view themselves as seeking to create the new society in their own image, which for them meant the negation of bourgeois values, or the transvaluation of values, and a society shaped by and expressing the transvaluation. Their outlook, accordingly, projected their own needs, interests, aspirations and values, as those of the entire society and, since they represented, inchoate, individual and society passed beyond production-inhibited social relations, a passage made possible by the development of productive technique in the bourgeois epoch, they did so with a compelling substantiality and historical realizability approaching that of the outlook of revolutionary bourgeois movements of the seventeenth, eighteenth, and nineteenth centuries, and the revolutionary proletarian movements of the nineteenth and twentieth centuries.

The Young Intellectuals' outlook of the 1920s *approached,* but had not yet reached historical realizability. They had yet to unite their transhistorical consciousness with a social-theoretical consciousness concretely comprehending their own specific historical reality. This was due decisively to their emergence at an early phase of the disaccumulation process, from within which they were still unable clearly to grasp U.S. social relations and their own position within them.

As mental workers, their number was still relatively small and their class position still ambiguous. It was only later in the United States, to a degree by the latter 1950s, but more forcefully by the latter 1960s, that the proletarian class character of mental workers had become firmly established in real social relations – in the media, educational systems, professions and technical pursuits, government bureaucracies, advertising, etc. – and increasingly clarified in consciousness. That is, it was only later as the disaccumulation phase and its consequences matured that mental workers, as a sufficiently numerous sector of the proletariat, divorced from control over the conditions and purposes of their work and forced to sell their labor, no less than manual workers, for wages or salaries, could begin viewing themselves and their own historical needs and potentialities in terms of the broader class of the proletariat, of which they now comprised an integral and substantially large component.

In the 1920s, and until more recently, mental workers, including "intellectuals," still characteristically viewed themselves from the standpoint of special function, or quasi-interest group, rather than from that of class – as a "middle-class" stratum or "intellectual class," dangling or floating in the interstices of the larger and socially, politically, and economically more powerful class formations of society. Even for those intellectuals who *identified with* the proletariat, therefore, their transhistorical outlook still remained parochial, limited, and insufficiently world-historical – still insufficiently historically class-conscious, and so disabling them for class-directed sociopolitical action effective for realizing their own revolutionary aspirations. They were unable, in short, fully to comprehend their society and themselves from the standpoint of their own immediate situation and their own role as intellectuals and artists, so long as that comprehension remained at the level of functionalism (however self-exalted the function), rather than of class. Their consciousness, that is, still remained substantially alienated from their own broader, and historically concrete, humanity. They were caught in an historical situation where they could not make the passage from apparently declassed radicals to class-conscious revolutionaries. In the immediate outcome, accordingly, the Young Intellectuals by and large in the later 1920s and afterward either reverted to embracing the Adamic mythos and the American ideology to one degree or another, or they surrendered their transhistorical consciousness to a narrow functional chauvinism, or kept it stowed away and compartmentalized in the special sphere of aesthetics, literature, and philosophy, apart from effective participation in politics.

On the other hand, the proletarian class in the United States, given the phase of capitalist development reached in U.S. society, could not come to a full consciousness of its historical significance and transforming potential, until it had more completely absorbed to itself, side by side and intermingling with manual labor, its mental-labor component; so that within itself the proletarian class could overcome the previously enforced class-division between mental and manual labor, and comprehend itself as self-sufficiently representative of the entire society moving into its next world-historical epoch. By the late 1960s, this comprehension, expressing the maturing social class reality, has emerged in growing force, manifesting itself in the swelling movement for revolutionary socialism of the variegated proletariat against the oligarchic, parasitic, and increasingly devitalized corporate bourgeoisie – a movement of the modern universal class to transmute that universality from its constricted class, to its more fully human, form.

The modern proletariat can not realize its historical significance on the plane of its individual members' particular aims, "interests," " needs," but only on the plane of a universal world-outlook. This is because the proletariat can not socially satisfy its individuals' needs through the use of a particular external property form, the immediate use of which (as with the bourgeois owner) establishes a universal order to which each member adjusts himself. The mode of bourgeois existence is rational calculation in submission to irrational "laws" and circumstances set in motion by the bourgeois individuals' use of their privately owned property. It is different with the proletariat: It must from the outset, in order to free itself from the domination of bourgeois rule, in order to reappropriate its own humanity, establish a new universality consciously – rooted in the only "property" proletarians have, namely their human capacities, talents, and potentials as social beings. The proletariat does not assume to power, therefore, by asserting its established existence – as did the bourgeoisie – but by negating it. Or put a different way, the only essence waiting to be realized in the proletariat, beneath its existent servile position, is its existence as freely developing humanity, freely developing, self-determining associated human beings. The modern proletariat is the first class in history with the capability of reshaping society, whose universal principle is not latent in, and does not unfold from, the particularized aims of its individual members as proletarians – as against the bourgeoisie whose universal principle is latent in and unfolds from the particularized aims of its individual members as bourgeoisie – but for whom the individual aims of its members lie latent in and depends upon the realization of its universal human principle – that is, for whom the transhistorical must be brought into unity with the historical. Upon the actualization of the proletariat's self-negating universal principle, the individual particularizes and actualizes the universal in a concrete diversified personality, rather than merely as before with both bourgeois and proletarian existing as a mutilated, fragmented, and particular function, an "external" universality.

The outlook and action of class struggle are the only viable grounds upon which proletarians may realize their humanity as self-determining, self-mastering men and women at home in their own world. The psychological barrier to recognizing, affirming, and acting upon proletarian historical class-consciousness may, for some, reside in a gnawing idea that it is unworthy of us: Given the material wealth and advanced technology of the industrial nations, some of us may feel in our bones that we should have long ago passed well beyond class-conflict theory to the "truly human" or "truly revolutionary" mentality of people shaping and changing and controlling their own social and personal lives; that we are still in need of an "old" theory seems to stand as a devastating self-reproach: we should have brought the capitalist system to an end long ago. It reminds us of our failure; it is something like facing an ordeal, a labor of agony, we thought or wished or dreamed we were finished with, only to find that in fact we have not so much as begun. Some of us may prefer the "ideology of the future" – it is incomparably more "human" and intelligent. True, but it does not come cheaply – we have not yet earned the right to it: It has no real political force because it is the consciousness of a postpolitical era; our thoughts and dreams may lie in the future, but we live in a political society dominated by the economic past, whose accounts can be settled only by a consciousness still rooted in that past. For it is only by this settlement that present society can be released from the grip of the dominating moribund past and transformed into the theater of the future – and then, but not before, the "ideology of the future" may become the expression of practical affairs. We cannot get to the future conceptions of progress by bypassing the old ideologies and concepts of progress, but by transforming them; for this is only another way of saying that we cannot bypass the old society to get the new, but must transform the old into the new; that we can not bypass our present selves to get to our new selves, but must confront ourselves as we are, express ourselves as we are, and in so doing transform ourselves into what we will become.

VI

Disaffected with development: Henry Adams and the 1960s "New Left"

1. Strange times

We live in strange times: peasants rally to proletarian standards; proletarians vote for liberal slogans; liberals glorify authoritarian nationalism; communists are evolutionary reformists; constitutional republicans are expropriating revolutionaries; conservative aristocrats are patrons of social revolution; multilateral internationalists are the worldwide bastions of parochial reaction and counterrevolution; orthodox Marxists are sober analysts of on-the-one-hand-on-the-other; ultra-rightists are Jeffersonian Democrats; urbane "Marxist-Leninists" are men-of-the-deed Bakuninists; big business men are welfare-state humanitarians; American-Firsters are NATO-enthusiasts; racial equalitarians are political separatists; existentialists are Marxists; new Bolsheviks are old Mensheviks; free-marketeers are revolutionary anti-imperialists; New Leftists are old instrumentalists; "Stalinists" are "Trotskyists" and vice-versa; Protestant theologians are catholic atheists; impious libertines are

This essay was originally published as "The Corporate Ascendancy and the Socialist Acquiescence: An Inquiry into Strange Times," in *The Maryland Historian*, XII:2 (Fall 1981). It is republished here with *The Maryland Historian's* consent.

Much in the introductory remarks to Chapter V of this book concerning U.S. leftists' estrangement from their own times, applies also to this essay, which I wrote in the summer of 1966 for presentation at a panel of the Socialist Scholars Conference convened in the fall of 1966 in New York City. If the essay in Chapter V drew parallels between the 1960s and the 1920s, the essay here drew parallels between the 1960s and the Progressive Era, that is, intellectual disaffection with the course of U.S. development in both periods, each of which was marked by "prosperity," reform, imperialism, and war.

When the editor of *The Maryland Historian*, in late 1980 or early 1981, invited an essay on the "New Left" of the 1960s, I offered this as a "document." In my cover letter, I wrote that I did not regard myself as a "New Leftist," that I was not sure what the term meant, and that, if anything along these lines, I would consider myself an "extremely old left thinker, a socialist, and an historian." The words *"extremely* old left" was meant to convey a rootedness in the Enlightenment and nineteenth-century rationalism, humanism, and evolutionism. The essay is published here exactly as it appeared in *The Maryland Historian*, except for the correction of typographical errors. Quaint though it may seem, I still consider myself an "extremely old left thinker, a socialist, and an historian," but of course, among other things.

reverential believers; direct-actionists are transcendental idealists; Christian gentlemen are economic determinists; partisan assembling socialists are careful scholars; careful scholars are dissembling political partisans. Everyone calls himself by one name, bespeaks another, and acts a third. No one looks in the mirror without seeing an unfamiliar face. Everyone has learned to expect the unexpected. Only surprises no longer surprise. Time-honored words and phrases, leaders and movements, parties and nations, seem to assume incredible juxtapositions. Whatever its career in the world of art (which tends to anticipate life by a few decades or more in any case), surrealism appears to have invaded the world of intellect and politics. It is now for the political intellectuals, the students and professors of social reality, the deft dividers of fact from value, the impartial rationalists and objective theorists, and not only for the impassioned theorists of the socialist persuasions, to experience what they would have imagined only in their most fanciful dreams or terrifying nightmares – what a handful of intellectuals, writers, and artists pled with them to perceive and understand (from a different perspective indeed and often in an esoteric way) well over thirty years ago.

The old certainties are gone because they are here in fact and decaying before our eyes; the new certainties are yet to be made. This is what "strange times" means.

So it may be put at the level of immediate perception. To approach the level of comprehension, to proceed from the plane of description to that of understanding our times and making them not "strange," but our own, we should say, rather, not that this is what "strange times" means, but that this is how they *appear*.

The meaning lies in understanding these apparent "brute-inversions," in the reasons for the decay of the old certainties and the delayed genesis of the new. In the search for this meaning, and in its continuing elusive concealment, lie our present political paralysis, our narcotic escapes, our mind-shattering vagaries – that anguish which we will transform, if we are to survive as self-determining people, into a prelude of recreating and rediscovering ourselves through discovering and creating another social existence.

Heroic words – yes. But unless we find our way of doing this with an appropriate historical consciousness, finding thereby that it can be done, it will be accurately said of us, as we may say of others in times past, that there is an error in what we have just asserted, an error of ahistorical wish-projection, of delineating our times in terms appropriate to epoch-making periods of the past and in terms of a utopian, anachronistic, or mystical future upon which, variously, we on the left in the United States have placed our most cherished expectations for the past fifty years. The error at this point is obvious from the simple reality that after perhaps stirring us, such words still ring hollow and sink us deeper into the melancholy mill of thoughtless duress and contrite despair.

The work before us, then, is to convert an apparently obvious error into an emerging historical reality.

2. Adams *redivivus*

American society in the United States at the turn of the twentieth century, the dawn of its present crepuscular era, produced just one Henry Adams (and perhaps a few others like him). Today it produces thousands in miniature: too intelligent to affirm what is, too sensitive and indignant to say yes to the Here and Now, but too much *in* and *of* their own history to penetrate, comprehend, and change it. American "radicals" by the thousands today are the miniature Henry Adamses. If we can understand the meaning of this metaphor; if we can look at ourselves in the face by seeing something of ourselves in something of a bygone despairer, we may then say good-bye to the old man in us and wish him well, and we may then take ourselves from fussy, feckless radicalism to revolutionary intelligence.

The mature Henry Adams was born *of* one age that was gone, the age of the yeoman farmer and incipient manufacture, of the republic of small producers and civic virtue, of the humanistic transcendental outcome of the New England Enlightenment. He lived *in* another age that he abhorred, the age of industrializing capitalism. He longed *for* a third that never existed and never would, what might be called an age of Medieval humanism symbolized by the mythical Virgin Mary. That was in his mind's eye. But he also apprehended that historically he and his generation in Western Europe and the United States stood between two ages – between imperialist industrial capitalism and, as he perceived it, state socialism, the one at the height of its development, predatory, avaricious, dehumanizing and degenerative, the other forming beneath the surface in the productive forces, the working class movements, the intellectual currents of the day, but either powerless to emerge and develop, or if it did so, equally as abhorrent to him as industrializing capitalism. For he saw in the Tendency of History the conquest of the Dynamo, human submission to mechanical force, even should the passage from capitalism to socialism be inevitable; and he called himself "wholly a stranger" in his own country, indeed in the western world.

He knew that the world of pre–Civil War America was gone beyond recall, and in return for the trick history had played on him, in return for feeling so disinherited by his own country, his own home, he determined by silent penmanship (not by anything Yankee-practical) to play a trick on history, to disinherit his bourgeois-Protestant country by leaving it no

patrimony of good works, and by committing against it the ultimate irreverent outrage of glorifying Catholic Medieval Europe. By an historical
regression and intangible evocation, he sought to "transcend" the nation
that glorified progress and tangible vocation. He carried his expatriation
further and deeper than those who physically removed themselves to
other shores. But not entirely, because he always felt, and never stopped
mourning, his loss – and that of all Americans – the squandering not
merely of a continent, but of the great chance America had always been
thought to represent for humanity. It was, as it were, a stupendous cry of
anguish, – "America, what did you do with your chance?" – at watching
helplessly as "history" seemed inexorably to overwhelm and demolish
the hope for the redemption of the ancient dream of a promised land, a
promised age, where humanity would find fulfillment.

But Adams was neither religious mystic nor myopic romantic; it is not
by such careless characterization that he, his significance, his historical
comprehension, or his relevance to us, may be understood. He saw better
and further than most of his contemporaries, and than most of those
who came after him, only he balked at presuming too much. He never
did leave behind completely his pristine Protestantism – he never did embrace that degenerate bourgeois Protestantism which obliterated its
source by making the worse seem the better world and glorifying rather
than detesting and mortifying "fallen man." He thereby kept his faith
with the dialectical visionaries and social theorists ranging from Blake
and Hegel to Melville and Marx.

What did he see that requires that we so distinguish him? He looked
with the eyes of a true son of the Enlightenment – the source of the hope
he had held for America and which he shared widely with others, especially other Americans, and thus also the source of his despair, because
he did not balk at using those son's eyes to see unblinkingly what he
most feared to see. His Enlightenment-historian's eye had taught him to
see that "to historians the single interest is the law of reaction between
force and force – between mind and nature – the law of progress" (*Education,* 493). In other words, history, as a record of progress, comprised
the interaction of two great forces, one of which was mind, that is, intelligent, purposeful, willful human beings. History, or progress, was the
function of human comprehension and transformation of nature expressed in successive and higher, that is, more consciously controlled,
societal formations expressing increasing human wholeness and facilitating the elaboration and fulfillment of that wholeness. But this law of
progress itself appeared to him to have delivered the crushing blow, by
eliminating human will, human mind. With the onset of industrialization, the law of progress seemed to dictate the triumph of inanimate

force, unliving energy, the Dynamo, the triumph of humanity's own creation over mind and will, over that which is distinctively human; and since the law of progress was indefeasible so was, in this crucial sense, human defeat. The triumph of mind over nature appeared to proceed only to the obliteration of mind and the reconquest by nature – the turning of mind into nature – not the nature of instinct and feeling, but the Newtonian nature of abstract, quantified, inanimate force.

Adams recorded that he now saw "lines of force all about him, where he had always seen lines of will." Modern politics was "at bottom, a struggle not of men but of forces." The ultimate reality behind all appearance seemed to be the force of coal-power, steam-power, electrical power, insensate energy, and no longer the force of conscious humanity grappling with nature and with itself; a reality involving historical development "represented not by souls, but by coal and iron and steam" (*Education*, 421–422, 426, 493; *Letters*, II, 279). History now not only proceeded independently of human will, but was proceeding to abolish it, to reabsorb it to nature – an irony on pantheism and all holistic mysticisms.

Adams responded in two ways that were at once thoroughly bourgeois American and thoroughly un-American: First, he eloped with a Mary who "concentrated in herself the whole rebellion of man against fate; the whole protest against divine law; . . . the whole unutterable fury of human nature beating itself against the walls of its prison house," a Mary who "delighted in trampling on every social distinction in this world and the next." He did so "seized by a hope that in the Virgin man had found a door of escape" (*Mont-Saint-Michel and Chartres*, 213). The American Adams found a symbolic frontier, a symbolic escape from history – a frontier not in virgin lands or virgin markets, but in the mythical Virgin Mary. Second, he fought science and technology with science, by invoking the law of entropy. If the machine age meant the running down of the mind, the enervation of mental energy, the laws of science governing the machine meant the eventual expiration of the machine itself and all inanimate energy, the self-demolition of this humiliating progress, and the march of a future with no future but in the nebular, amorphous, prescientific past. His twofold response, therefore, was truly American in manner (escape and science), but, perversely inverted, in neither purpose nor effect.

But this is only a part of the reason that requires distinguishing Adams. The other part resides in his particular attitude toward socialism. His distaste for socialism stood on the ground, not that it was illusory, utopian, or revolutionary, but on the contrary, that socialism was inevitable, that it represented the necessary next stage of history, but that it too had become bourgeois; not that socialism would destroy capitalism and the world it built, but that it would only extend the sway of their leading characteristics under a different political form. His aversion to socialism flowed not from a love, but from a detestation, of capitalism. That the historical alternative to capitalism was socialism, that the replacement of capitalism by socialism was near at hand, he was convinced, but this left him neither delighted nor elated, but dejected, because of his no less firm conviction that socialism, as then developing politically and intellectually, only promised to sustain and administer all the more efficiently, the victory of the machine over humanity. The inevitable, and the only historically possible alternative to capitalism he perceived as no alternative in essence; the agency of social change – the working class and the socialist movements – he perceived as promising to effect a change that would keep things essentially the same.

Adams's perception was not arbitrarily fickle; he followed closely and observed incisively the development of the socialist movements in the Western industrial nations, and he viewed them as increasingly absorbed in the bourgeois mentality.

When in 1899, his brother, Brooks Adams, sent him Eduard Bernstein's *Die Voraussetzungen des Sozialismus und die Aufgaben der Sozialdemokratie* (1899; known in English as *Evolutionary Socialism*), and urged him to read it, Henry Adams did so immediately and found no support whatever for any glimmer of hope that he might still have harbored for something different, but only confirmation of his assessment of the socialist movement and of his own pessimism and despair.

Five days after receiving the book, he wrote to Brooks and observed with remarkable acuity, "Absolutely nothing is left of Karl Marx except his economic theory of history in its crudest form. . . . Bernstein not only argues, but proves, that the Marxian theory of a social cataclysm has been abandoned, [note: not, is wrong, but abandoned] and that the Socialist has no choice but to make himself a *petit bourgeois,* with all the capitalistic machinery and methods. He preaches [note: not, proves, or demonstrates, but preaches] the bankruptcy of the only idea that our time has produced" (5 November 1899, *Letters,* II, 248). He added soon after, that "The Socialists have sold themselves, like the rest of us, and are now simply *petit bourgeois* with capitalist methods." Referring to the Dreyfus affair, Adams wrote, with a significance going far beyond that particular event, "Juares and his Socialist organization sold out to the *bourgeoisie,* expecting to swallow the government in the end, and without calculating the chance that the government might swallow them" (to Charles Milnes Gaskell, 22 November 1899, *Letters,* II, 249).

But what is of particular significance for us today was Adams's wry comment to his brother that Bernstein "is very much in my intellectual-condition. He throws up the sponge in the whole socialist fight" (5 November 1899, *Letters*, II, 248). Adams may not have studied Marx's works deeply, nor for long, but his disaffected Yankee mind understood Marx in his essence, and shared a deep kinship with the outlook of the German transplant in the British Museum.

Adams came to believe that evolutionary positivism was a pedagogic alias of submission to the prevalent social, political, and economic currents; that whether one visualized, or hoped for, something nice like socialism and its brightest humanistic ideals fully realized at the end of the evolutionary road, or whether one saw something else, the intellectual position was essentially the same. In principle, the difference might be that the one contemplated the hereafter as heaven, the other as this world somewhat more developed, or as hell. But either way it left the prevailing directing consciousness in society – in the social, economic, and political spheres – to the bourgeoisie, by apprehending consciousness as the secondary effect of ongoing "objective conditions," rather than as an active component in the shaping and reshaping of society.

Adams knew that intellectually and politically you either stayed with the assertion of historically conscious human will as against the drift of things as they seemed to be dictated by "economics" and technology, you either held to Marx's formulation such as expressed in his *Theses on Feuerbach* that the point is to change the world, and understood that this is the essence of science, or you threw in your lot with evolutionary positivism and the insistence upon human adjustment to, accepting or suffering, that which was. As Adams in irony said of himself (*Education*, 225), precisely defining the alternatives offered to serious thinkers, "By rights, he should have been also a Marxist, but some narrow trait of the New England nature seemed to blight socialism and he tried in vain to make himself a convert. He did the next best thing; he became a Comteist. . . . Unbroken Evolution under uniform conditions pleased everyone – except curates and bishops; it was the very best substitute for religion; a safe, conservative, practical, thoroughly Common-Law deity. . . ." Needless to say, since Adams implicitly says as much here, the "next best" is always the worst.

This, then, is what particularly distinguishes Adams with respect to the questions raised here: He knew that his own outlook remained within the limits of the society extant and that in this respect the socialists were no different. In this sense, the socialists he critically assessed could not properly be considered "revisionists" of Marx, but since they adopted the evolutionary positivism of technicoeconomic determinism, their revisionism was in essence, if anything at all, a mild and tepid revision of Comte – or Spencer.

The difference between Henry Adams and ourselves, as it was between Adams and the evolutionary socialists of his own times, is that unlike us, he understood the significance and historical role of his own thought, caught within the limits of, and subsumed by, the predominant bourgeois thought and conditions of the time. *Like* him, we see history proceeding independently of, and against, our hopes, ideals, and aspirations, that is, against our will, against our ability to influence, let alone determine, its course; *like* him, we talk about the overwhelming determining impact of technology; *like* him, we cast imprecations, against capitalism, capitalists, and bourgeois politicians; *like* him, we see socialism as sustaining the subordination of people to technique and the machine; *like* him, we look to "objective conditions" as the *personae dramatis* of history, perhaps expecting them to evolve toward something different or their own self-destruction and bring this hated historical reality to an end; *like* him, we feel ourselves strangers in our own country and to our own times, for whom the old formulas are dead and whatever new ones we choose make us only caustic spectators of the passing scene; *like* him, we cannot bring ourselves to be socialists; *like* him, we have submitted to the onward rush of the status quo; *like* him, we seek escapes from the present in bygone abstractions and ideals and mythic heroes and heroines. But *unlike* Adams, we seek escape in roundtrip flights from thoughtless action to unactionable thought, and we try to convince ourselves that all of this amounts to a revolutionary consciousness and revolutionary will, instead of realizing that it amounts only to a consciousness of disaffected acquiescence caught within the limits of bourgeois society and bourgeois ideology.

To see and comprehend this something of Adams in something of ourselves may help us to see that which is fundamentally characteristic of ourselves, the crucial thing we have concealed from ourselves in our present state of mind. If we cannot see ourselves as we are and as we might be, let alone will be, neither can we see our history as an expression of our will. Which is precisely what Henry Adams had concluded: that history had no correspondence with his or any other's will, from which apprehension the great American high-society steppenwolf descended into an epic despair, and decided that the only professional, responsible, and honorable course to take was to remain silent and suffer the mutilation of humanity in its fallen state, in the face of which his flirtation with the Virgin was his one desperate act of romantic defiance in the throes of a monumental submission.

As with Adams, our biography appears to us sundered from history; he referred to the condition in terms of the concept of "entropy," we with other concepts that amount to the same thing – "malaise," "anomie," "alienation." We have trouble seeing ourselves "inside" history; we feel estranged, powerless, dangling, and sometimes we soothe ourselves with a dessicated thought of "transcendence." But this is only the inverted perception of an entirely contrary condition: not that our biography is sundered from history, but that we are unable to comprehend our age and ourselves historically, because our biography, our lives, are so entirely determined and defined by a history over which we have no control and over which we are not actively seeking to exercise control. If anything, some of our disparate *ideals* may be sundered from history, because our *lives* and consciousness are so completely "inside" it.

3. "Between ages"

This inverted consciousness has found frequent, recurrent expression in literature and social thought throughout the bourgeois epoch in the Western world since the late eighteenth century – to the effect that we live *between* ages, in a limbo of neither here nor there. On the eve of the French Revolution, in 1788, Goethe wrote to Herder in words that might have been written today: "Now the generations are confused, the individual is a wretched thing no matter what party he declares himself for, the whole is never a whole, the human race tosses to and fro upon trivialities, none of which would be so important did it not exert great influence upon points which are so essential to man!" Almost four decades later, observing the disillusionment in France with the bourgeois revolution, Goethe wrote to Zelter (7 June 1825) that everything now was "ultra" and "transcendent" in thought and action. "No one knows himself any more, no one understands the element in which he lives and moves, no one understands the material which he shapes. There can be no talk of pure simplicity, but of simple nonsense there is plenty" (Karl Löwith, *From Hegel to Nietzsche*, 21, 26). About the same time, addressing himself to accusations of his servility to Church and State, and in anything but words that might be expected from him, Hegel referred to his times in terms of "a crisis in which everything previously dependable seems to become problematic," where "the enormous interest of politics has swallowed up all others," and where "So little can philosophy stand up to the uncertainty, violence and evil passions of this great unrest . . . that – even for the purpose of bringing calm – it is only for the few" (to Goeschel, 13 December 1830, Löwith, 27).

This, too, is Adams's refrain, it is Lincoln's, it is Matthew Arnold's, it is Rilke's, and each of us may add others to the almost endless list. It seems to have reached its most poignant expression by Germans, as for example, in Hermann Hesse's *Steppenwolf* (1929). There he writes of a "sickness of the soul" that "is not the eccentricity of a single individual, but the sickness of the times themselves, . . . a sickness . . . that by no means attacks the weak and worthless only but, rather, precisely those who are strongest in spirit and richest in gifts"; a sickness that comes in those times "when a whole generation is caught in this way between two ages, two modes of life, with the consequence that it loses all power to understand itself and has no standard, no security, no simple acquiescence" (*Steppenwolf*, 26–28). Or, as Hermann Broch put it, an age that is "no longer and not yet," "for which everything comes too late and too early" (*The Death of Virgil*, 335–36). An age and a sickness that produce in Musil's conception *Der Mensch öhne Eigenheit*, the man without qualities, or Dostoevski's superfluous man. Thomas Mann's Tonio Kröger cries, "I stand between two worlds. I am at home in neither, and I suffer in consequence" (1903). Rilke compressed the agony of this "living-between-ages" sickness into two lines of his *Seventh Elegy*:

> Every brute inversion of the world knows the
> disinherited
> to whom the past no longer belongs, and not yet
> the future

To be aware of living sometime after a past era and sometime before an anticipated future era, to think in terms of living *between* ages, rather than *in* one, is not to be taken as historical consciousness. Otherwise, the mere perception of time and space common to every brain we regard as normal would suffice. Indeed, it is symptomatic of quite the reverse. It is in effect to give expression to an outlook devoid of an historical consciousness pertaining to the present. It is no more possible to live *between* ages, *in* no age, or, what is the same thing, *outside* history, than it is possible for there to be a location on a line between points that is not at a point itself. To view ourselves as living in a limbo between ages – or in an undefinable "time of transition" as it is more familiarly expressed – is in essence an incapacity to comprehend our own times historically, as within the historical continuum.

The "between ages" view of social conditions corresponds with an outlook that comprehends the present not in its determinate, and conditional, qualities, but in terms of its indefeasibility, subject to intercession only by some suprahuman or suprarational force: an outlook, then, that in effect grudgingly or willingly affirms the present as the natural and inevitable product of the past – a finished product, as it were, rather than as an ongoing process of social relations involving development and change fashioned by living, thinking, creating mortals – a finished product extending itself here and now and into the future. A decisive ideological inversion is the necessary consequence: By thereby placing the present outside of history, it squeezes history within the contours of the immediately perceived present.

The result is that the past is seen from the vantage point of the present, as having been so designed as to prescribe the present, which then proceeds on its own, *and* as having been so perverse as to require a total break, or escape, from it – in the American ideology, the perversity having occurred somewhat earlier than the design (and in the "Old World"). The comprehension of the present in terms of the genesis and development of social relations ever undergoing changes and transformations at the hands of conscious human beings, finds no more than formal expression in this outlook and otherwise falls into subversive disrepute.

So stated, a paradox is immediately apparent: How can people, who after all live in the present, have any outlook other than that determined by their present conditions and thought, and therefore have any outlook other than one that makes it impossible for them to view their present historically, or to view the past from any other standpoint than that of the ahistorically perceived present?

The dialectical historical theory, which Hegel first systematically formulated, and which Marx subsequently developed, represents the attempt to resolve this question, because it also represents the emergence of historical consciousness that presumes to humanity making its history in accordance with human will, rather than being entirely made by a predetermined past; it presumes to people shaping their society more and more to accord with their desires, rather than continually accommodating, repressing, and sublimating their desires to accord with existing social relations. The resolution of the question offered by dialectical historical theory amounted to finding the method of overcoming present-determinism – or, what is the same thing, since the present is only the furthest point of the past, the tyranny of the past, without the illusion of escaping from history.

The method was essentially that of physical science, but properly understood: In order to comprehend something it is necessary to try to change or sustain it in a predictable way; or, to put it another way, the meaning of "comprehending something" is that knowledge adduced from and in the process of attempting to change or sustain it in an intended way; in order for people to comprehend their nature and the nature of their society, it is necessary for them to seek to determine themselves and their societies in accordance with their conscious intent, their desires, their will. To know thyself is to determine thyself: Self-knowledge is self-determination. In seeking to determine themselves, people might achieve a social understanding, by its nature an historical understanding, of themselves and their society, such that they could begin increasingly to understand where they have been, where they are, and where they can *take themselves*, – and where they will in all probability go if they don't. The attempt to determine social existence to actualize intent is the condition of understanding the present historically, that is, scientifically. Accordingly, social consciousness so oriented embraces an outlook that not only views the present as temporary, transitory, determinate, and conditional, but also it seeks to understand the present in terms of its genesis from, and negation of, the past, forges a view of the future as a choice among alternatives made possible by the past in its present state, and expresses the engagement in the effort to actualize the choice. It means knowing what choices are historically realizable, what choice is yours, and what your choice is. It means having a realizable sociopolitical objective, or in broader terms, a political theory and a social ethic.

That we are unable to identify our own age, that we continue to view ourselves as living *between* ages, as estranged from our history, that we are unable to define our epoch in terms of its characteristic social, political, and economic conditions, actual and potential – subject to our practical efforts at change in accordance with our intent – this is the measure of our submission to the present social system and its predominant mode of thought and activity. The lament that our present society is, as it were, "one-dimensional," in the sense that it does not produce a consciousness and social movement suited to negating or transforming the present age, is only a further measure of the extent to which our consciousness is caught within that of the prevailing positivism, which sees *society* as "producing" ideas, rather than seeing people as producing their ideas in the course of affirming and submitting to the existing social conditions, *or* in the course of understanding their society in historical perspective by trying to change it in accordance with their willful intent. In other words, in this respect, our consciousness is a rather faithful expression of our real life acquiescence in the prevailing social order.

Henry Adams had the intelligence and the courage to acknowledge his acquiescence. We masquerade our acquiescence in radical rhetoric, revolutionary bombast, and bromo-socialism. We *appear* revolutionary while *remaining* circumspect. Our mothers always told us, Honesty is the best policy. It would at least free us to acknowledge our acquiescence without pretense, and either to choose it or cast it off. Then perhaps, we might begin to make history instead of having it made.

VII

The corporate reconstruction of American capitalism: A note on the capitalism–socialism mix in U.S. and world development

The triumph of capitalism and the failure of socialism is a commonplace theme today in both scholarly and publicist circles. In particular, it seems to be taken as irrefutable in widening spheres of the highest intelligence, including many of those on the political left, and in all parts of the world, that in modern – and more especially "postmodern" – circumstances, capitalism most proficiently induces, and socialism most dolefully obstructs, development.

The question of development, however, including its conditions and prospects, is as relevant, urgent, and problematic for societies like the United States, Britain, West Germany, France, Italy, Canada, and Japan, as it is for societies like the Soviet Union, Poland, Hungary, East Germany, Czechoslovakia, and Yugoslavia, as it is for societies like China, the Philippines, Argentina, Cuba, Chile, Pakistan, Egypt, Nigeria, and Iran, as it is for societies like Angola, Mozambique, Ethiopia, Zimbabwe, Bolivia, Peru, and Nicaragua, as it is for societies like Mexico, India, Brazil, South Korea, Taiwan, and South Africa. In other words, development is not a problem simply for "Less Developed Countries" (LDCs), or for Communist-ruled countries, or for clerical-ruled countries, but for all countries of every degree and kind of development.

As this implies, societies of various types, and most of those in the world today, currently embrace, in principle or in effect, a commitment to or an affirmation of, something we call development. In this sense, we

This is a slightly revised and edited version of a paper, "A Note on the Corporate Reconstruction of American Capitalism, 1890–1916: The United States as a Developing Country," delivered, on invitation, at a session of the Center for Social Theory and Comparative History, at the University of California, Los Angeles, 27 February 1989. The Center had asked me to comment on aspects of my book, *The Corporate Reconstruction of American Capitalism, 1890–1916* (Cambridge University Press, 1988), and I took the occasion to draw out some of the implications of matters dealt with there.

have come to understand that all countries of the world are in some ways "less developed": That is, each is not so much less developed than others (however plausible or useful it might be to say, on the basis of some objective or selected standard, that it is), but less developed than each may want to be, or may be, or will come to be.

We are *all* "LDCs."

As it is for countries throughout the world, therefore, development is a "problem" for the United States. For example, it was confidently assumed, not too long ago, that the United States was "Number One," and that this was the "American Century"; today, experts and lay leaders of opinion alike observe that in many respects, if not on the whole, the United States is Number Two or Three, or lower on the scale, and some other country is Number One. Similarly, development was a problem for the United States in the 1880s and 1890s and early twentieth century. The further continuing development of the United States in the ensuing years was not foreordained. Indeed, the central debates in American politics at the time were about development: How should the United States develop? What kind of development should it have? Should it continue to develop along the lines of large-scale industrial capitalism, or perhaps stand in place, or return to some golden age? What were the necessary or desirable conditions and characteristics of development? And so on.

In the American vernacular, Progress has been the word for Development (also, Growth and Prosperity). That we call the period under discussion the Progressive Era is indicative of the centrality of the development problem in American national politics at the time.

The corporate reconstruction of American capitalism may be understood historically as a road of further development of the United States in that period: economic development, and also social, political, and cultural development. It can not be taken for granted as a road that had to be taken, or as something that had to happen, but needs to be studied as an historical situation of conflict, alignments, thought, movements, and politics, in which people were both taking and resisting the taking of this developmental road, all the while, in the process, designing and building the road, or resisting the designing and the building.

The period of the 1890s to 1916 may be understood as involving a conflict between a declining and an ascending stage of capitalism. But that may not be an altogether satisfactory way of seeing it. Rather, the corporate reconstruction refers to the movement or set of movements taking capitalism beyond the extant competitive stage to a corporate stage, as the condition of further development: as the alternative to stagnation or retrogression. There is, therefore, the implication of something "progressive" about moving from one stage to the other.

This brings us to a pause, to ask what we might mean by "development." The word presupposes some unfolding *from* something *toward* something else. It carries the implication of a cumulative, or progressive, evolution. It also implies human intent and volition, and to that extent, surprising as it may seem, a normative, even a teleological, dimension. Modernization theory has been largely concerned with identifying the essential constituent components of such evolution and with, it seems to me, no little success.

In the case of the United States in the late nineteenth and early twentieth century, and in the modern – and "postmodern" – case in general, I believe, a society's development has involved a growing human knowledge (Hegel's Reason), and along with that knowledge an instrumental shaping, of the natural world and of social relations, nurturing an enlargement of individuals' engagement in governing and self-governing functions and authority, both individually and associationally, and generating a growing diversification of choices available to individuals in vocational and avocational pursuits, as well as, therefore, in thought and culture. On a transnational scale, development may be taken to involve social diversity and complexity as the substance of a globally spreading societal uniformity, embodying a broader and deeper knowledge of the natural and social realms, although not necessarily a broader and deeper wisdom.

Although not usually taken in this sense, Karl Marx expressed this idea in his formulation that communism, or human development as he anticipated it, meant that increasingly "we shall have an association, in which the free development of each is the condition of the free development of all." Note, not the other way around (not that the development of all was the condition of the development of each), and note, the developmental outcome was an association (*Gesellschaft*), not a communality (*Gemeinschaft*). Marx stood squarely in the classical liberal tradition.

The various difficulties or "crises" afflicting, for example, the United States and the Soviet Union alike arise in part from special historical circumstances, but in larger part and in a more general way, they register the driving forces of development, at different stages and under different historical conditions, pressing against institutions, social relations, and modes of consciousness that generated, facilitated, channeled, or contained those forces, but are no longer sufficient or viable for those purposes. Remember the worried questions raised in the United States in the 1970s about malaise and about whether democracies are governable, and the questions today about United States' "decline" or "competitiveness." The events currently transpiring in the Soviet Union, on the other hand, may not be simply a matter of "failure of Communism" (or of state command), but also of its "success." Further development instead of chaos, stagnation, or retrogression, will depend upon whether and how Soviet society will deal with the "success." The more modernized or developed a society is, the more easily it can deal with the crises of success. The United States, for example, could in the past, since the Civil War, and can in more recent times, take them in relative stride; the Soviet Union, for example, will be taking them in relatively more dislocation, stress, and strife, short of rather massive involvement and assistance by more modern foreign societies or agencies.

One might say that the more modern a society becomes, the less likely, and the less necessary, it is that profound – even revolutionary (transformative) – change take an explosive or cataclysmic form, or, the more capable it is of transacting such changes in and through its existing institutions, however much the latter may themselves change in the process. A symptom of this is, for example, American "radicals' " perennial agonizing over whether they should act "within the system" or " outside the system," and their equally recurrent complaints about being "coopted" when their proposals are adopted, implemented, and absorbed by society, not to mention their own employment in the work. A similar symptom of this, on the other side of the political spectrum, is the disillusionment "right-wingers" or "true conservatives" repeatedly suffer with conservatives whom they have worked to elect to office and who prove to be less "truly" conservative than expected. Developmental variability is the soul of modern society.

The passage from state-directed mercantilism to competitive, or liberal, capitalism in the Western world of past history, may be taken to have represented the "success" of mercantilism that brought on its "failure"; societies transacted the handling of the "success" and the passage to competitive, or liberal, capitalism with varying degrees of completion, effectiveness, and felicitous results. In the same vein, the Soviet Union, for one, seems to be passing from a mercantilist, or state-directed, to a liberal, or society-driven, stage of development. Similarly, the passage of the United States from the proprietary-competitive, to the corporate-administered, stage of capitalism registered the success of competitive capitalism, culminating in *its* "failure" in the great crisis of the 1890s – the last great crisis of the competitive regime in the United States – and the passage to a new stage of development represented by corporate capitalism.

Development means continuous change. Change means the new replacing the old, hence, conflict and turning points, or crises. Continuous change means recurrent crises. Crises are normal to development. To a prodevelopment outlook, the absence of crises is an alarm bell signaling that something is amiss. It is no accident, therefore, that in the thought of Karl Marx, the first great theorist of capitalism as a dynamic developmental process or system, the concept of crisis plays a central role. Similarly, in the thought of procorporate-capitalism thinkers like Charles A. Conant, and increasingly in the mainstream of economic and social science thought in industrial societies by the end of the nineteenth and the early twentieth century, crises and their analysis became of central importance – business cycle theory and disequilibrium studies moved to the center of economic thought. It became more and more commonly understood among policy-oriented thinkers that modern society evolved in and through economic crises, that recurrent crises were the sign of a modern progressive society, and that the more developed a modernizing society was becoming, the larger and broader the recurrent crises. Not to have such crises would be a bad sign. In this regard, procorporate-capitalist thought and Marxian prosocialist thought shared common ground. Remember, too, that the worst fear about capitalism's long-term prospects gnawing at the hearts and minds of modern economists – from Ricardo and Mill to Schumpeter and Hansen – was that of an onset of a crisisless stationary state, or stagnation. In Marx, the same idea came in the form, not of fear, but of millenarian (or revolutionary) anticipation: The falling-rate-of-profit-tendency manifested the fetter on the forces of production posed by capitalist relations of production, a fettering that would ultimately prove fatal to capitalist relations.

Crises, however, presented an unevadible challenge to procapitalist leaders, as to others. Not successfully transacted, crises could become socially and politically explosive, as both procapitalist and prosocialist thinkers and leaders believed. Left to themselves, the crises of capitalist development – social and political along with the economic crises – could set in train such wrenching class warfare and other degenerative forces as to renounce or wreck or pervert or grotesquely channel further development – as indeed happened in some societies and in world politics (including two world wars) in the twentieth century. Just as, for socialists a publicly planned economy promised a developmental alternative to the chaos or "anarchy" of the market and its crises, so the question for procapitalism theory and statecraft became how to have crises without jeopardizing or perverting development; or, to find some way of managing and attenuating crises; or, without eliminating necessary cyclical business rhythms, to find some equivalent of crises. In other words, crises elicited further development of human knowledge about social relations, indeed, applied human knowledge brought to bear upon shaping and reshaping social relations, however slowly, partially, or imperfectly. The irony of communism, in this respect, among many others, is that it succeeded in preempting or eliminating cyclical market crises, but not in finding an effective equivalent for them aside from terror and authoritarian command. It "oversucceeded." Or, it might be said, it replaced market crises and their developmental economic, political, social, and cultural consequences, with political, social, and cultural crises along with their long-term antidevelopmental consequences, flowing from but obscured by short-term developmental gains. Instead of forced sales, unemployment, and bankruptcies – purges, labor camps, and mass liquidations. The Great Revolutionary party of the twentieth century thereby became, among those great parties of sustained duration, the quintessential Conservative party, and then, Reactionary party, of the twentieth century. However much in the name of Marx, it became, in the words of Marx, "a fetter on the forces of production," and what is the same thing more broadly, an authoritarian and ideological obstruction to the development of human knowledge about social relations and its applicability to their shaping and reshaping.

As in William James's lovable phrase, modern society needed to find a moral equivalent of war, so it needed to find a developmental, and moral, equivalent of crisis, or to put it more precisely, a developmental management of crisis, to prevent its degenerating into cataclysmic catastrophe, and to steer it instead into constructive channels and reconstructive results. This the movements constructing corporate capitalism in its liberal mode sought, in effect, to find – in the United States with relatively greater success than elsewhere, but even in the United States not without periodic crises of relatively short duration and another long and deep crisis of *corporate* capitalism in the 1930s, the first and as yet the only Great Crisis of corporate capitalism, a crisis of global, or at least transatlantic, dimensions, out of which came the general catastrophe of World War II, and the developmental postwar world order that has been evolving since.

The developmental equivalent discovered, or largely stumbled upon, bit by bit, piece by piece, in the United States (and elsewhere), but with much impressive broad-ranging vision and theoretical conceptualization from the Progressive Era onward, consisted of an outlook that we may call The Mix – that is, the mix of the public and private sectors as seats of authority and initiative in shaping, planning, regulating, and containing development, or, to put it in baldly ideological terms, the mix of socialism and capitalism. The corporate reconstruction of American capitalism in the period 1890–1916 represented an early phase of the mix. Those societies that have made the mix, in an adequately evolving balance, have developed better and further than those that from doctrine or circumstance have not. What has succeeded and failed in recent times is not, respectively, capitalism and socialism; rather, the mix has succeeded. What has failed is an insufficient or ineffective mix or a stout resistance to it.

Why was the mix relatively more successful in the United States in the first half of the twentieth century than in many other of the larger industrializing countries, so that by the 1960s the United States had become the most stable, and yet also the most dynamic, progressively developmental nation in the world? Aside from insulation from direct physical devastations of war, here are *some* of the reasons I would begin with in studying and searching for answers to this question:

1. The prevalent labor and socialist tendencies in the United States were antistatist; that is, they were modern-oriented, not backward (communitarian) looking. They were constitutional-republican in outlook, rather than doctrinal-statist, as historian Richard Schneirov has well put it. The same is to be said of the farmers and agrarian tendencies: Richard Hofstadter's, Louis Hartz's, William A. Williams's, and Barrington Moore's insights here are quite pertinent: That is, for the most part, or prevalently, American farmers, especially after the Civil War, were neither peasant nor junker, but market-driven agribusiness people with a constitutional-republican outlook (or with a warped and restricted one in the case of Southern whites). A Louis Napoleon could not happen in the United States. Neither could a Bismarck, a Kaiser, or a Duce, a Führer, or a General Secretary. A Polk, but not a Louis Napoleon; a Lincoln and a Grant, but not a Bismarck; a Theodore Roosevelt and a Wilson, but not a Kaiser; a Franklin D. Roosevelt, but not a Duce, a Führer, or a General Secretary.

Elsewhere, working class, small business, peasant, and traditionalist movements aggrieved by conditions of commerce and capitalism involved strong antimodernizing, prostatist, protectionist tendencies. Think of Germany, Italy, Austria, Russia, Japan, and Mexico, for example. That is why one may speak of left- and right-socialism, not in the way Lenin and Leninists defined it, but precisely opposite to it. In other words, for another example, Eduard Bernstein is more validly to be understood as a left-wing socialist, not the right-wing socialist some of his Marxian adversaries accused him of being. Similarly, in the United States: Victor Berger, Morris Hillquit, John Spargo, and such others. To identify left-socialism with authoritarianism, doctrinalism, statism, and political despotism is to embrace a terminology that came from the perspective of populistic "mercantilist" elites or activists of preindustrial societies, or of semi- or antimodernizing elites in industrializing societies. They may have been on the "left" in preindustrial societies (although in his own time, Marx regarded such elites as utopian radicals or reactionaries), but it is not only ahistorical to fix such an identity with respect to the modern political history of the Western industrializing world, but entirely inconsistent with the thought we associate with John Stuart Mill and Karl Marx alike, that is, the two major trends of promodernizing sociopolitical thought in the Western world in the later nineteenth and much of the twentieth century.

2. Prevalent thinking among U.S. intellectuals and professionals, both prosocialist and procapitalist, or something lying in between, and ranging from social scientists and economists to clergy and politicians, has been antistatist, experimental, instrumental, pragmatic, nondoctrinal – that is, in general, "modern" – in spirit and substance, or at least resistant to, or sensitive to avoiding, doctrinalism. The belief among them was widespread that both socialism and capitalism had many good things to offer, to be retained or adopted, but also some bad things, to be superseded, discarded, or rejected. There was, in other words, a large receptiveness to a mix of capitalist and socialist attributes and ideas, rather than some ingrained belief that they were mutually exclusive.

3. The republican tradition of the sovereignty of the people, the sovereignty of society, and limited government under law, remained dominant among all classes of the American people.

4. Capitalists were largely antistatist, and there was no significant prostatist agricultural or landowning upper class. At the same time, the capitalists' building of a global system as the condition of a viable national system of corporate capitalism proceeded as an extension of the public–private mix, and as an aid to its development at home, not as an alternative to it or as a weapon against it.

5. The military was (and always has been in the United States, at least since George Washington scotched the Newburgh flurry of impecunious officers) entirely apolitical, in the sense of party politics, and completely subordinate to, and separate from, civilian authority, and fully contented to remain so.

6. Corporate capitalists oriented themselves increasingly to the "cooperative-associational" principle and outlook, including administered markets involving a public–private mix of authority and responsibility, with primary initiative and decision-making lodged with the private sector. Although they generally accepted in principle ultimate state supremacy in the realm of public utilities, they nevertheless moved pragmatically toward a public–private mix in the general economy, which allowed for government regulation, modification, or repair of

market practices and results, but without government command. Even in the public utility field, where outright government ownership as well as government command were to be found, the public–private mix prevailed in practice and administrative law. Farmers, for their part, combined individual and associational methods in a public–private mix of subsidies, banking and financing facilities, production controls, and marketing agreements, that in general rewarded efficiency and economies of scale, and eliminated less efficient and marginal producers. The public–private mix may be perceived to have come to permeate every other sector: housing, social security and health care, urban development, education and research, military security, and so on.

7. The political system of constitutional government, checks and balances, federal division of powers, due process, and individual rights remained basically intact and strongly adhered to by citizens and officials alike, and in the course of the twentieth century those people previously excluded from the system have been increasingly included.

Finally, what may we identify, again preliminarily, as some of the basic principles of the mix as it emerged and developed in the United States? The following are offered, from my study of the formative period – the Progressive Era – to begin with:

1. The supremacy of society over the state (the sovereignty of the people): By corollary, the distinction between positive government and state command; the insistence upon positive government *as against* state command, and on that basis, as much positive government and as large a public sector as the times and circumstances permit or demand. In the economic realm, the distinction at law and in policy between "public utilities," which may be subjected to state command, and the general economy, which may not, however much it may be regulated.

2. A global, or international, system of development (investment and trade) as an essential condition of national development, and ultimately as the successor to discrete national development.

3. Honoring and extension of human rights as a function of further development of property relations and property rights, and if necessary, as a modifying or limiting restraint of property rights.

4. Government responsibility – ultimately, paramount among its responsibilities, and its paramount responsibility – for assuring continuing development ("Progress and Prosperity," "Growth"), within the framework of reconciling economic activity with social goals and human rights.

5. A political consensus that debate over government's developmental responsibility is to be the principal content of party politics, and that

providing for that responsibility is to be the principal content of legislative work and governmental function.

6. Hence, party politics and government as concerned above all with defining and redefining, shaping and reshaping, the public–private mix.

7. Federalism – which permits an interplay of local, state, and regional initiative and authority, with national (interstate and international) initiative and authority; or, an interplay of decentralized *and* centralized initiative, coordination, and control.

These are some of the reasons and principles preliminarily offered. There are more, and the reasons and principles themselves suggest countless other important questions leading to large fields of fresh study and research. For example: What, more precisely, is the nature of The Mix – and at different stages of history in each society? Why and how does it vary from society to society? Why and how is it in essential ways similar? How is the mix to be understood in international relations and institutions? Is it not necessary to develop new economic theory premised on the mix, and on a transnational scale, rather than theory based on "markets" or the "private sector" in one compartment, and theory of "public administration" or "planning" in another, each set off and apart from the other, and usually cast on a national scale? Does not all the perplexed concern about governmental and trade deficits and imbalances, and their impact on the national and international economies, point to the need for theory based on the mix in its transnational stage of development? Would it not be good for university political science and economics departments and business schools to train their students in the mix? And so on.

The questions are endless, but addressing them, and also identifying the right questions, might well begin as soon as possible. Indeed, it already has, as in one notable example, Herbert Stein's recent book, *Governing the $5 Trillion Dollar Economy*. Is it too much to say that addressing and identifying such questions is the next great task of human knowledge in the realm of social science and politics?

Index

abundance, 157, 158, 160, 166, 169, 186–7
academic community, 170, 171
accumulation: in bourgeois ethic, 187–8; in corporate capitalism, 153–60; passage from, to disaccumulation, 35, 154–60
Acheson, Dean, 140n87
Adamic myth, American, 177, 178, 180, 182, 185, 192, 194–5
Adams, Brooks, 48, 116, 202–3
Adams, John, 47, 70
Adams, Henry, 199–208; rejection of American society by, 199–205, 208
Adams, Henry Carter, 1
administered markets, 22–3, 24–5, 26, 27, 34, 39, 76, 216; effects of, 25
administration, 43, 72
advertising, 166, 167, 170
aesthetic consciousness, 148, 149
aesthetic ethic: of Young Intellectuals, 188, 189
aesthetics, 147; and politics, 188, 191
affirmative action, 15n8, 18
African-American movements, 18, 39, 43, 44, 64, 67, 69
African-Americans: exclusion of, 75n37
age of innocence, 178, 182
Age of Jackson, 152
Age of Normalcy, 40, 160
"Age of Reform," 42
Age of Reform, The (Hofstadter), 46
agrarian areas: development of, 115, 123, 125; development of, as exploitation, 137, 139–40; U.S. economic expansion into, 82, 85, 86, 95, 96, 98
Agricultural Adjustment Administration (AAA), 28
agricultural cartel arrangements, 168
agricultural cooperatives, 28, 39, 70
agriculture, 22, 28, 72, 155, 166, 167; adaptation of, to administered markets, 39; interests in, 130, 131; labor requirement in, 164–5, 168; productivity in, 163–4; subsidized, 18
agrocommercial stage, 20

agropeonage market society, 14, 18, 21
ahistorical (idea), 30, 30n13, 31
alienation, 149, 150, 205; glorification of, 145
America: rediscovery and reconstruction of, by Young Intellectuals, 179
America and the Young Intellectual (Stearns), 177n40
American Asiatic Association (AAA), 79n2, 83, 97n41, 98–9, 115, 118, 119, 123; Journal, 86
American Banking Group, 79n2, 89, 93, 97n41, 119n45
American development: and world development, 78–101
American exceptionalism, 36, 45
American history: acknowledgement and transformation of, 144n; turning points in, 38
American Ideology, 178, 192, 207; critique of, 180–2, 193–6; Young Intellectuals and, 176–96
American Manufacturers Export Association (AMEA), 79n2, 115, 117, 118
American political development: in Progressive Era, 37–77
American Political Tradition, The (Hofstadter), 47n7
American Revolution, 19
American society; codevelopment of capitalism and socialism in, 34–6; critique of, 178, 208, as political society, 9–10, 13–16; rejection of, by H. Adams, 199–205
American Tobacco (co.), 112
Americans: as self-made people, 9n6
America's Coming of Age (Brooks), 177n40
anarchosyndicalists, 69
angelicization, 65
anomie, 144, 205
anti-Americanism, 139
anticapitalist theory, 52
antidiscrimination measures, 14–15n8
anti-imperialism, 35

219

226 *Index*

government role in economy, 14, 18, 22,
74, 159, 168–9; in
capitalism–socialism mix, 217; in
corporate capitalism, 24, 29–30, 32; in
Wilson administration, 111–12,
115–16, 125–6, 134–5, 137
government role in economic expansion,
85, 88–9, 90–8
graduate schools, 172
Grant, Ulysses S., 215
Great Britain, 104, 156, 209
Great Evasion, The (Williams), 53n15
Great Society programs, 18
Green, William, 162n6
group: as basic unit of economy, 75
Grundrisse (Marx), 153
Guam, 85
Gutman, Herbert, xi, 46n7, 64n28

Hamilton, Alexander, 47
Hamilton, Alice, 164n15
Hansen, Alvin H., 213
Harding, Warren G., 162, 169n27
Harding administration, 168
Harrington, Fred Harvey, xi, 46n7
Harrison, Shelby M., 164n15
Hartz, Louis, 42, 47n7, 151, 215
Hawaii, 85
Hawley, Ellis W., xi, 73n35, 75n36
Hay, John, 82, 115
Hayes–Tilden arrangements, 18
Hays, Samuel P., 38n1, 46
Hegel, Georg W. F., 7, 56, 77, 183, 189,
200, 205, 211; dialectical historical
theory of, 207
Heisenberg, Werner, 31n14
Hepburn amendments, 126
Herder, Johann Gottfried von, 205
Hesse, Hermann, 205–6
high school enrollment, 173
Hillquit, Morris, 215
historians, 5–6, 38, 42, 54–5, 78, 200;
American, 151–3; and capitalism, 141;
on emergence of corporate capitalism,
71n33; free-market, 65;
interdisciplinary trend among, 45; left,
44; and modernization theory, 54–5;
and periodization in terms of
capitalism, 63–4; radical, Marxian,
63–5; revisionist, 47n7, 55
historical (the), 6–8, 9, 20; market society
in, 20–30; and the transhistorical, 150,
158, 196
historical consciousness, 143–9, 198–9,
206; divorced from archetypal
consciousness, 148; humanity making

its history in, 207–8; unifying
transhistorical with the
social-theoretical, 151–2; of Young
Intellectuals, 181–3, 186–7, 188,
194–6
historical context, 55, 65
historical continuity, 161–2, 163
historical continuum, 7, 206; desire
among Young Intellectuals for
disruption of, 179, 180
historical evolution: of capitalism, 67;
linear, 69
historical period(s): passages from one to
another, 20; *see also* periodization
historical process: life and society
liberated from, 177–8
historical reality: American, 184–5
historical research: in primary sources,
5, 6
historicism, evolutionary, 132–3, 135
historiography, 149; periodization and,
1–36
history: acknowledgement and
transformation of, 144n; art and, 185,
186, 188, 189, 191; being outside of,
206–7, 208; as composed of diverse
components, 7–8; conscious, intentional
shaping of, 9–10, 69, 151–2, 207–8; as
continuum, 7, 179, 180, 206; critical
trends in, 38–40; in critique of
American life, 178–9, 186–7, 193–6;
and human will, 200–1, 204–5, 207;
lost in bourgeois social theory, 148;
man as shaper of, 150; materialist
conception of, 55, 58; mind and nature
in, 200–1; modern, 21; periodization as
theory of, 2–4; and reason, 150;
reexamination of, 181–2; renunciation
of, 144; as science of laws of social
development, 144; U.S./world, 151–3
Hoffman, Frederick J., 174
Hofstadter, Richard, 46, 47n7, 215
Holmes, John Haynes, 180
Holmes, Oliver Wendell, 112
Honduras, 96
Honduras Convention, 94–5
Hoover, Herbert, 35, 86, 117, 160,
169–70; conferences and reports,
162–70
Hoover administration, 168
Hoselitz, Bert F., 53n13
Howe, Frederick C., 180
Hubbard, Thomas A., 80n5, 84n13
human (the): intended conception of,
150–1;
human agency: in evolution, 12

228 *Index*

intelligentsia, nonacademic, 170–6; characteristics of, 175–6
intention/intentionality, 10; in administered markets, 22–3; in development, 211; in history, 9–10, 69, 151–2, 207–8; in shaping social existence, 28–9, 150–1
intercity associations, 39
interest-group theory, 70
interest groups, 20, 51, 59, 60, 61
Interests (the), 40
international associations, 39
international economy, 90, 139; U.S. government role in, 40
international relations, 24, 72; *see also* foreign relations
investment, 25, 68, 89–90; globalization of, 26, 29; and foreign trade, 85–6, 87–8, 90–8 (*see also* foreign investment)
investment capital, 26–7, 131, 161
investment cycle, 169
investment system: production capacity and, 167–9
Iran, 42, 209
Italy, 30, 209, 215

Jacksonian Democracy, 19
Jacksonian laissez-faire, 18
James, William, 214
Japan, 11, 30, 74, 156, 209, 215
Jefferson, Thomas, 47n8, 133n80, 147
Jeffersonianism, 111, 112, 177
Jenks, Jeremiah W., 71n33
Jerome, Harry, 162n6
Johns Hopkins University, 105
Johnson, Alba B., 118–19, 120, 126, 129n72
joint-stock companies, 31–2
Journal of Commerce, 82
journalism schools, 173
judicial process/review, 74
judiciary (the), 73, 76

Kaplan, Abraham, 5n3
Keynesianism, Keynesians, 27, 160
Kidd, Benjamin, 84
Kierkegaard, Soren, 183
King, Willford I., 162n6
Klein, Julius, 162n6
know-how, 12
knowledge, 211; evolutionary principle of cumulative, 57n18; in shaping social relations, 213–14
Knox, Philander C., 79, 80, 91, 93, 94–5, 96, 100, 106, 121n50

Kolko, Gabriel, 46n7
Kuhn, Thomas S., 38n1
Kuznets, Simon, 162n6

labor, 56, 72, 74, 147, 161; antistatist, 215; class-division between mental and manual, 195; as commodity, 14n8, 158; in corporate capitalism, 23–4, 32; domination of, by capitalist class, 159, 169; as factor of goods production, 155, 157, 163; relation with capital, 28, 59n22, 68; released from production process, 187; reunification with productive means, 191; shift from goods production to services, 163, 164, 165–6; *see also* division of labor
labor exploitation, 149, 154, 158
labor movement, 39
labor-power: as commodity, 14n8; declining requirements of, 162; ownership of, 190; release of, from goods-production, 155, 157; salable, mobile, 48
labor requirement: and education, 170; in goods production, 155, 157, 187; net investment in, 168
labor-time: in capitalist industrialization, 154–5; in productivity, 35
LaFeber, Walter, 47n7
LaFollette, Robert M., 94, 95
Laidler, Harry W., 162n6
laissez-faire, 18, 20, 74, 111, 112, 137, 142
Lamont, Thomas W., 162n6
land grant state colleges, 18
Lansing, Robert, 94n36
Lasch, Christopher, 175n39
Latin America, 74, 122; U.S. trade/investment in, 95–6, 97
law, 12, 28, 56; in capitalist society, 59, 60, 61; and corporate capitalism, 67, 71; and economy, in Wilson, 108–9, 110, 111, 112, 116, 132, 140; and government, 76; in market society, 15, 16; regulatory, 29; uniform codes of, 48–9
Lawrence, D. H., 177
Lawrence, John S., 162n6
Left (the), 143n, 209
left-socialism, 215–16
legal order, 15, 67
legitimacy, 59, 68
leisure, 190
Lenin, Vladimir I., 30, 34n18, 58, 215
Less Developed Countries (LDCs), 209–10

purposiveness, 146
purposelessness, 144–5

quality of life, 158, 161
quantum physics, 7–8, 31n14

race relations, racism, 18, 35, 68
radical movements, 41, 42, 64–5, 67
radicals, 44, 171, 199, 212; Left, 143n
Raskob, John J., 162n6
rationalism, 47, 183; ahistorical, 148
realism: of Young Intellectuals, 179
reality: consciousness and, 180; ideals
  and, 185; ideas and, 191–2;
  intentional creation of new, 183–4; *see
  also* social reality
reason, 7, 185; and history, 150
Redfield, William, C., 117, 118, 120,
  124, 127
reflective generalization, 2, 3
reform: conservatism of, 41–2; and
  corporate capitalism, 76–7; "good,"
  64–5; legislation, 70
reform-liberalism, 41–2
reform movements: Progressive, 132
reformers, 43, 67, 150; liberal, 180–1
regional development, 17
regulation: commission, 110–11, 112–13;
  market, 69–70; public/private, 22; *see
  also* government regulation
Reinsch, Paul S., 94, 95, 116
religion, 35, 56, 61
"Religion of Man," 148
Religious Man, 143
*Report on Cooperation in American
  Export Trade*, 127–8
republican tradition, 70, 73, 199, 216
Republicanism, 18
research technique, 5
resource allocation, 26, 28, 29
"Response to Industrialism," 42, 43
Response to Industrialism, The (Hays), 46
restraint of trade, 127n65; Wilson and,
  112, 113
revisionists, 55
revolution: as condition of evolution, 19;
  in modern society, 212; of Young
  Intellectuals, 179–80, 188–9
revolutionaries, 150–1, 171
revolutionary bourgeois liberty,
  145–6, 148
revolutionary consciousness, 152n3
revolutionary movements, 64–5, 193;
  conservatism of, 42, 214
Rhett, R. G., 127
Ricardo, David, 147, 213

rights: in corporate liberalism, 75;
  developmental, 19; individual, 76
Rilke, Rainer Maria, 205, 206
"Rise of Finance Capital," 40
Rockhill, William W., 80
role assignment/definition, 51
romantics, romanticism, 144, 176
Roosevelt, Franklin D., 35, 169n27, 215
Roosevelt, Theodore, 35, 106, 109,
  110n23, 112, 132, 133, 136, 215;
  "New Nationalism," 137
Root, Elihu, 79n1, 80
Rosenwald, Julius, 168
Rousseau, Jean-Jacques, 189, 190
Rublee, George L., 113, 116, 127
rule of reason doctrine, 112, 113, 125
ruling class, 61
Russia, 181, 215; *see also* Soviet Union
Ryan, John D., 126

St.-Simon, Claude Henri, 48
Samoa, 85
Saunders, William L., 127
savings, 26, 27
scarcity, 157, 158, 160, 166, 186, 187;
  artificial, 159; release from, 163
Schiff-Harriman interests, 79n2
Schneirov, Richard, 74n35, 215
Schumpeter, Joseph A., 30n13, 213
science, 201, 203; fallibilist view of, 3n1;
  theory in, 3n1
science of complexity, 77
scientific method, 5n3
Seager, Henry R., 127
"search for order," 42, 43, 75–6
Search for Order, The (Wiebe), 46
sectional conflict, 46n6
sectional theory, 70
Secular Man, 143
self-determination, 12, 148, 198,
  207–8
self-employed market society (mode
  of production), 13–14, 21
self-governance, 29
self-interest, 49, 161
self-knowledge, 207–8
self-mastery: principle of, 153–4, 157,
  190–1, 192; and republic, 146
separatism, 39
service sector, 161; shift of labor to, 163,
  166; *see also* goods and services
Seventh Elegy (Rilke), 206
Seward, William H., 85n14
Shaw, Arch W., 162n6
Sherman Act, 126, 127
Simmel, Georg, 183

Index